To Leonie

Hope you enjoy this

Love Cherilyn

JUNE 1998

The Paull family of Vaughan, Central Victoria.
Photograph: Verey, Castlemaine. *Collection:* Ashley Tracey.

The FEDERATION CATALOGUE

Household Life in Australia
1890-1915

PETER CUFFLEY

The Five Mile Press

The Five Mile Press

The Five Mile Press Pty Ltd
20 Summit Road
Noble Park Victoria 3174
Australia

First published 1997

Copyright © text Peter Cuffley
Copyright © design Peter Cuffley & The Five Mile Press
All rights reserved.

Design: Peter Cuffley, Emma Borghesi
Editor: Maggie Pinkney

Printed in Australia by Southbank

National Library of Australia Cataloguing-in-Publication data
Cuffley, Peter
ISBN 1 86463 099 X.
1. Australia - Social life and customs - 1851-1901 - Catalogs.
2. Australia- social life and customs - 1901-1922 - Catalogs.
3. Australia - History - 1891-1901.
4. Australia - History - 1901-1922.
5. Australia - Social conditions - 1851-1901 - Catalogs.
6. Australia - Social conditions - 1901-1922- Catalogs.
994.032

FEDERATION CATALOGUE
Contents

Introduction	....	7
1.	The Federation Era 1890-1915	9
2.	A Catalogue Cornucopia	16
3.	Federation House Styles	22
4.	The Nesting Instinct	28
5.	Furniture for Everyone	36
6.	Leisure and Entertainment	54
7.	Clothing — Plain or Fancy	62
8.	Jewellery and Toiletries	74
9.	Children and Childhood	86
10.	Pictures, Cards and Keepsakes	96
11.	Practical Considerations	102
12.	Federation Memorabilia	114
Acknowledgements, Catalogue's Key	....	119
Bibliography	....	120

The wonderful horse and cart seen in this photograph was probably a studio prop, and the boys are obviously in their best clothes. *Collection:* the author.

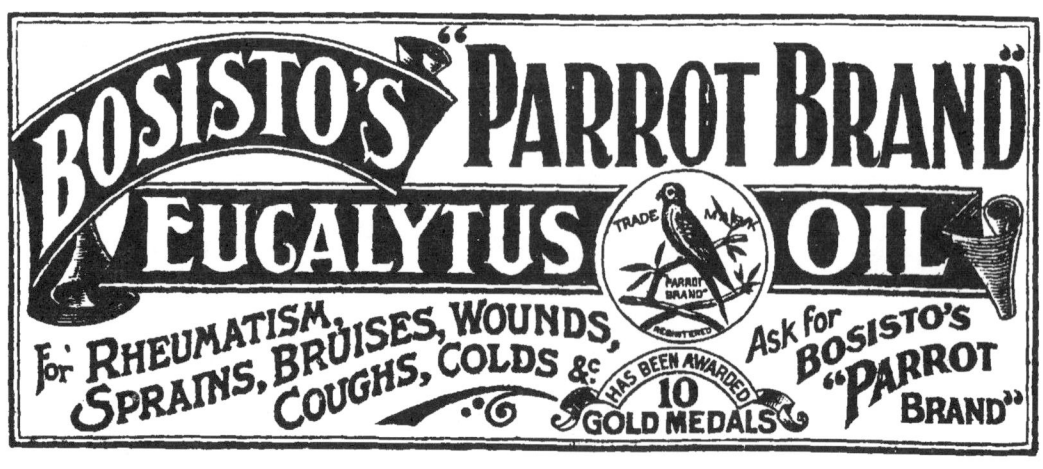

FEDERATION CATALOGUE
Introduction

Here is a collection of words and images which, for some people, will stir up old memories. Younger folk will probably be intrigued with things that now seem strange, but which were once familiar to the whole community. For the purposes of this book, the Federation Era has been stretched in two different directions to encompass the important years from around 1890 right up to World War 1 and that momentous year, 1915, when the Anzacs landed at Gallipoli. The years closest to the turn of the century and that pivotal date, 1 January 1901, are naturally given emphasis, but the decade from 1890 is essential to the story because it encompasses the era of public and private debate and the eventual majority acceptance of the idea of Federation. In the years following 1901 Australia went through the process of establishing a national approach to many concerns that had once been regional, and even competitive. Some interstate rivalry did survive, however, with parochialism likely to be found in various guises.

The companies who issued the catalogues, which have provided most of the material for this book, were in some cases single-state enterprises, while others were looking to a national market. My 1985 book *Chandeliers and Billy Tea* looked at a broader span of Australian history: the years from 1880 to 1940. *The Federation Catalogue* takes a closer look at household life and offers a fresh crop of images to tell the story. Items seen on these pages tell us of everyday demands, practical needs and the hopes and aspirations of dreamers. Some of the pages reproduced here are direct facsimiles, others are composites from within a single catalogue, while others again are a gathering of items from several catalogues.

For those who wish to know the year of availability of certain items, there is a key to the catalogues on page 119. I hope you will find as much pleasure in this book as was found in the creation of it.

Peter Cuffley, 1997

Upper: The first Ministry of the Commonwealth of Australia, 1901. *Collection*: the author.
Lower: Miners from the eastern states provided the decisive swing to provide a majority YES vote for Federation in Western Australia. *Collection*: the author.

FEDERATION CATALOGUE
1. The Federation Era 1890-1915

Celebration of the centenary of Federation offers a fresh appraisal of a momentous period in Australian history. Many of the concerns of that era seem remote or difficult to comprehend today, but others remain as vital issues. Importantly, national identity continues to stir hearts and minds. Debate still includes many different views on the Constitution and the possibility of a republic. In the broad picture of Australian society it can be noted that household life is still the central focus for a large percentage of people. Magazines, newspapers, radio and television all devote space or time to satisfy a demand for homemaking topics. We can learn a great deal about everyday life in the twenty-five years between 1890 and 1915 from the catalogues and advertisements of the period. By the Federation Era, mass consumption of manufactured goods had gathered powerful impetus. Traditional crafts were important, but the products of the machine were affecting family and household life in an increasing number of ways.

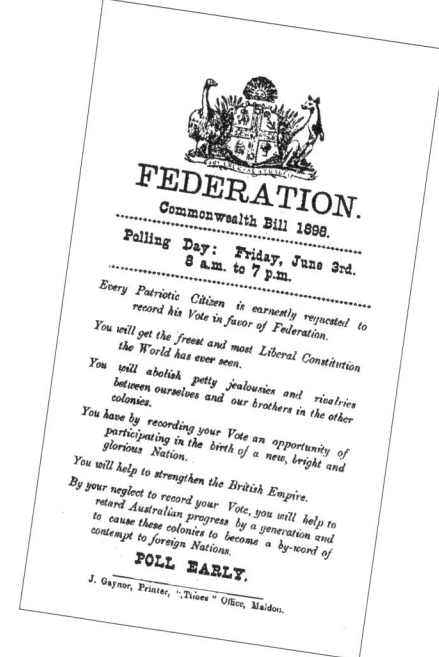

Concern is often expressed that the majority of our citizens have little or no knowledge of the Australian Constitution and are generally vague about how Federation was achieved. There are many detailed accounts available to all, so we need offer only a brief summary in this work. From the first European settlement of this land in 1788 to the official celebration of Australian nationhood in 1901, there had been all kinds of forces working for increasing self-determination for the diverse group of people who soon became the dominant population. Disease, dispossession and genocide had brought the Aboriginal population to extinction or near-extinction in many places. In remote areas the conflict continued into the Federation Era and beyond.

On 24 October 1889, Sir Henry Parkes, Premier of New South Wales, gave his famed 'Tenterfield Oration'. It was a powerful call to the colonies to join in a Federation with a two-house parliament. This historic speech gave impetus to the movement for a unified Australia, and a national conference was called in Melbourne in February 1890. In March 1891, a second convention was held in Sydney, with each state sending seven delegates. Various resolutions were debated, including the notion of a parliament made up of a House of Representatives and a Senate. It was also suggested that a Supreme Court should be established as a High Court of Appeal. Committees were appointed and it is believed that Sir Henry Parkes suggested the term 'Commonwealth of Australia' at one of the meetings.[1]

Australian nationalism found popular expression in the journal, *The Bulletin* but, ironically, this publication was a late supporter of Federation. The Labor Party was concerned at the imperialist overtones of Federation, while conservatives were worried about the rights of individual colonies. So it was

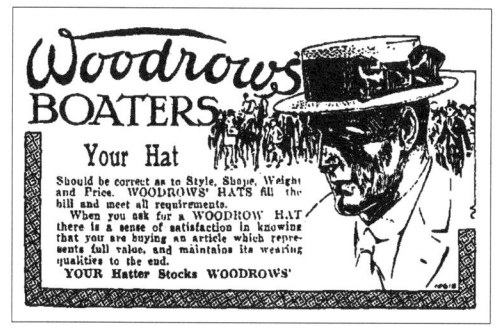

from the middle ground that the most effective support for Federation was drawn. As might be expected, the path toward a majority agreement on a constitution was not a smooth one. Finally passed by the constitutional convention in March 1898, the Bill gave the Australian people a working constitution which then needed a referendum for its implementation. Support for a Federated Nation of Australia achieved a majority of votes at the first referendum on 3 June 1898, but not enough to see the *Constitution Bill* passed. A majority vote in all colonies was gained at the second referendum held on 21 February 1899, with a YES vote of 107 420 and a NO vote of 82 741.[2] With royal assent, the Commonwealth of Australia was officially born on 1 January 1901, the first day of the new century. Parliament was opened by His Royal Highness the Duke of Cornwall and York on 9 May 1901. Melbourne's grand Exhibition Building, constructed in 1879/80, provided a suitable venue for such an occasion of pomp and circumstance. Civic gatherings and celebrations were held throughout Australia, including large-scale street parades. Souvenirs of every kind were produced to satisfy people's desire to commemorate this pivotal event in Australian history. Favourite patriotic symbols were the British flag and the so-called Federation flag or Australian ensign. This was a white flag with the Union Jack in one corner and a blue cross with white stars to represent the Southern Cross. The latter detail was a close echo of the 1854 Eureka flag which had reappeared as a popular symbol during the Queensland shearers' strike of 1891.

Historians have observed that the overall standard of living in Australia in the period from 1890 to World War I was comparatively high. Economic depression in the early nineties, widespread drought from 1895 to 1902, falling wool prices, crop failure and rabbits in plague proportions were the negative factors. On the positive side, the gold rush in Western Australia, other mining developments, the expansion of sugar-growing and increasing exports of meat and wheat were all important. Industrialisation and urban development was also changing the balance so that more Australians dwelt in cities and suburbs. There was a new breath of idealism about suburban development. Town planners were inspired by the Garden City movement in Britain and dreamed of leafy streets with idyllic cottages. If the perfect plan was achieved in only a few enlightened subdivisions, there were at least new suburbs around Australian cities which offered a sense of space and improved living conditions.

Home-ownership and comfortable family life in the suburbs gathered momentum as a core ideal for middle-class Australians in the Federation Era, and took a further leap forward after World War I. An individual house on its own lot has continued to be one of the powerful icons in Australian life. Improved public transport played a vital role in

The opening of the first Parliament of the Commonwealth of Australia, 1901.
Courtesy: La Trobe Picture Collection, State Library of Victoria

This Melbourne street is suitably decked out for The Duke of Cornwall and York's visit to the city to officially open Parliament at the Exhibition Building on 9May 1901.
Courtesy: La Trobe Picture Collection, State Library of Victoria.

suburban development in the period 1890 to 1915. As yet, the motorcar was mostly a novelty and motor buses did not proliferate until the 1920s. Railways and tramways were the prime movers, while horses still provided the motive power for a whole range of activities in both the city and the country. Beyond the railways and the riverboats, the horse-drawn coaches of Cobb & Co. continued to offer a relatively efficient service. Ordinary households might have stables for a horse and a place for a two- or four-wheeled vehicle, but walking was still an accepted means of getting about, even over considerable distances. With the introduction of the safety bicycle in 1885, cycling was taken up as an ideal personal transport for both work and recreation.

Activities centred around the church, lodges, clubs, societies and unions were the most likely reasons for being away from hearth and home during leisure hours. Dances, concerts, theatre performances and the early moving pictures were also a possible drawcard, but people made a lot of their own entertainment at home. Widely differing expectations and degrees of affluence meant a great variation in the way people used any spare time. Holidays and travel were possible for some families or individuals, while others only managed to find a few precious hours to relax at night.

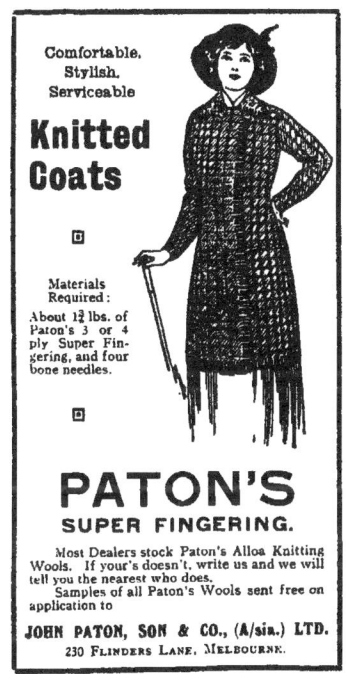

In 1885, Australians had their first experience of official involvement in overseas conflict. Troops were sent to the Sudan and it was noted that Australia was becoming a nation rather than just a name on the map.[3] A larger commitment to fight for British interests was manifested in the Boer War of 1899 to 1902. More than 16 000 young Australians went off to fight, and 588 were killed or died from fever.[4] Sadly this was all leading up to World War 1, in which Australia lost so many of its young men.

At any time in history, there can be found stark contrasts between the lives of the rich and the poor. In Australia in the Federation Era, a large middle ground was evolving where life's expectations were by earlier standards quite reasonable. For a large proportion of the population, day-to-day existence was at least bearable, and for many, relatively comfortable. The shops, stores and mail-order catalogues were filled with all the goods seen as essential for survival, as well as lots of things which would express prosperity and material well-being.

Notes
[1] Leslie Horsphol, *The Story of Australian Federation*, View Productions, Sydney, 1985, p. 18.
[2] Horsphol, p. 47.
[3] Manning Clark, *Manning Clark's History of Australia*, abridged Michael Cathcart, MUP, Melbourne, 1993, p. 372.
[4] Humphrey McQueen, *Social Sketches of Australia* 1888-1975, Penguin Books, Victoria, 1978, p. 36.

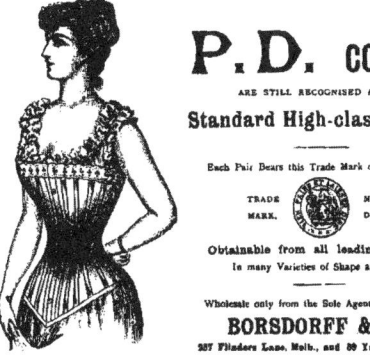

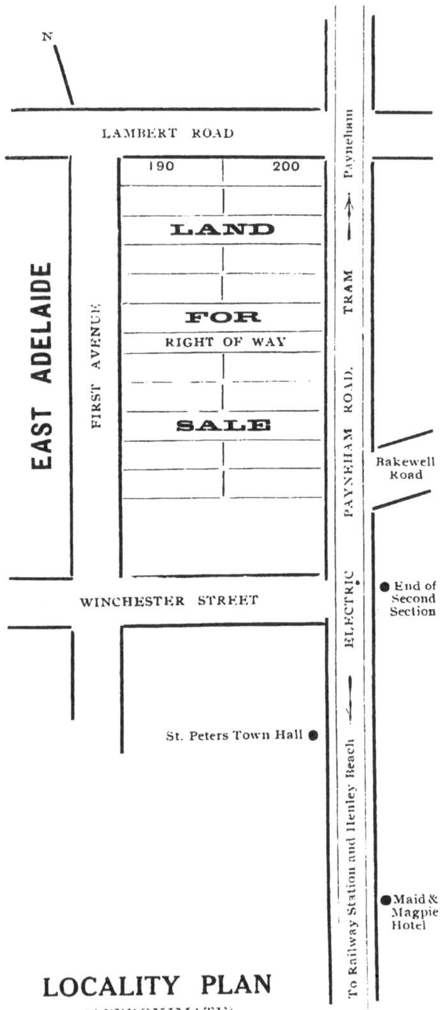

LOCALITY PLAN
(APPROXIMATE)

NOW
IS THE TIME TO
BUY LAND
ON AND NEAR THE
PAYNEHAM ROAD

FINE RESIDENTIAL SITES
With southerly aspect, just east of
WINCHESTER STREET,
EAST ADELAIDE (Second Section).
A Double Line of Electric Cars pass direct to the
Railway Station and **Henley Beach.**
Home to Lunch in Five Minutes!
Electric Light, Gas, Deep Drainage, and all other Up-to-date Conveniences and Comforts of Civilization.

Allotments, 60 x 200 (about), High, Dry and Level, can be secured on payment of 10 per cent. Deposit, 10 per cent. in three months, and the Balance payable at any time during three years at 5 per cent.

Payneham Road Frontages, £3 a foot.
First Avenue Frontages, £1 15s. to £2 10s. per foot.

Plans and Specifications prepared, estimates submitted, buildings supervised during erection, and progressive loans arranged for those desiring to build homes.

Jackman & Treloar,
AUCTIONEERS & VALUATORS,
LICENSED LAND BROKERS,
73, KING WILLIAM ST

TELEPHONE 1224.

For Your Holiday Tours.

A 2¼ H.P. BABY TRIUMPH.

WEIGHS ONLY 125 lb.   **£65.**   STRONG and RELIABLE.

This splendid Triumph Model has been built in response to the demand for a light, runabout Motorcycle.

It is strong and efficient—fitted with two-stroke engine—strong front forks and spring—two-speed countershaft gear, with chain-cum-belt drive.

Though light in weight, this machine is a good hill climber, and will stand the strain under all conditions.

Your holiday riding will prove enjoyable if you select this model, as there are no valves to get out of order, and only three wearing parts in the engine.

If you want the maximum of pleasure from your summer touring—get a Baby Triumph.

Call and see this model in our showrooms.
If you can't call write for full particulars.

BENNETT & BARKELL Ltd.
"THE HOUSE FOR BRITISH GOODS,"

Agents for New Hudson, Triumph, Rudge-Whitworth and Bat Motor Cycles, J.A.P. Engines, and Manufacturers of B. & B. Cycles & Motor Cycles.

124-132 CASTLEREAGH STREET, SYDNEY.

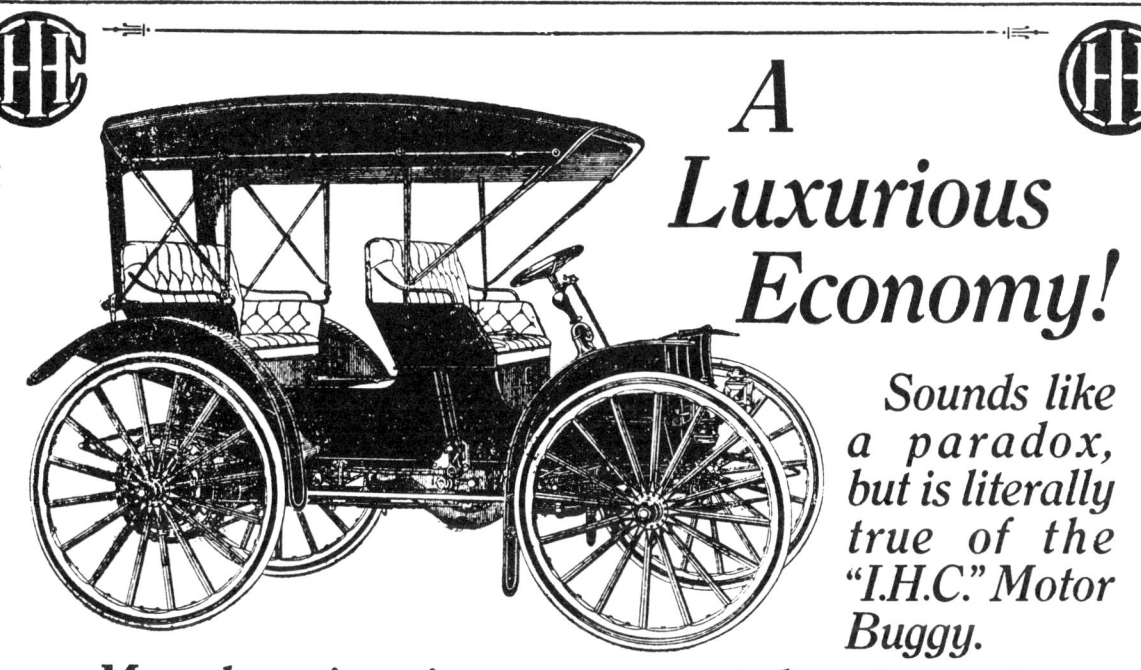

A Luxurious Economy!

Sounds like a paradox, but is literally true of the "I.H.C." Motor Buggy.

More luxurious in every respect than horse-drawn vehicles.

Economises considerably on cost per mile travelled.

Enables one now using a horse conveyance <u>to do a year's work in six months.</u>

Will get you there and back over any road that a £1,000 motor car will travel, and over some that the latter would be useless on.

Don't be afraid that you can't operate one of these buggies—a couple of days' instruction and you'll be quite prepared to take it anywhere.

Remember there are more than 7,000 of them in satisfactory use, and that our warranty protects you from all risks but carelessness.

If you order <u>before</u> May 3rd, price will be £183—if you delay thereafter price will positively be higher.

We are giving you ample notice of the increase—don't blame us if you have to pay more.

Ask our nearest branch for free trial run—see the fuel measured, and figure out the cost per mile for yourself.

Address Dept. 33

INTERNATIONAL HARVESTER COMPANY OF AMERICA
(Incorporated)
200 Roma Street, Brisbane   37 Broadway, Sydney.   545 Bourke Street, Melbourne.
17 Bank Street, Adelaide.   75 York Street, Launceston.

FEDERATION CATALOGUE

2. A Catalogue Cornucopia

Life in the cities and larger towns was improving in many ways in the period from 1890 to 1915. Gas for cooking, heating, lighting and the supply of hot water found much wider usage after the introduction of penny-in-the-slot gas meters. In Melbourne, these were introduced in 1902 and, while electricity was connected to some households, it would only begin to rival gas in the 1920s and '30s. Reticulated water had generally been available in cities for some decades, but the real advance of the Federation Era was the dramatic improvement in sanitation due to the introduction of sewerage systems. Prior to such changes the death rate was much higher for city-born children than for their country cousins.[1] Cities had more noxious industries, high-density housing and often inadequate food-handling and transportation. Modern technology helped make built-up areas better places to live; public health was now a widespread concern and new standards were applied to foods, household drugs and medicines as well as to medical care.

Householders in the cities, suburbs and larger towns were generally well placed as consumers of all the goods offered by a great variety of businesses. To capture a wider market, the larger firms not only advertised locally but also spread their catalogues far and wide. Mail order was the ideal means of trading with people who could not readily visit large general merchants or specialist stores. It was also available to country or interstate merchants who were buying wholesale stock. Local stores and travelling hawkers could supply many needs, but could not always compete with the larger firms who had the economies of scale. Many were also manufacturers who could claim cheaper prices even when freight and handling were added. The well-known department store of Dimelow & Gaylard at Richmond, Victoria, called their 1906 autumn and winter catalogue 'Our Drummer' and began with the following: 'Our object in issuing this "Drummer" is to assist residents in the country to do their buying through the post. It will be found a simple, money-saving, and time-saving medium, giving prices and showing illustrations from all the different departments of our Stores.' Sydney merchants and manufacturers A. Hall & Company claimed to offer 'The Grandest Display of Household Furniture in the Colony, Reliable and artistic at Economical Prices.'[2] Halls invited readers of country newspapers to send for a free catalogue, and offered free packing and free transport of the goods to the railway or the wharf.

Catalogues from the period 1890 to 1915 vary in size, quality and content. All of them are interesting social documents, but everyday household catalogues are of particular interest to collectors, restorers, homemakers and social historians. Some of these catalogues have just a few pages, while others are extensive works filled with an extraordinary array of items covering every possible household need. These items ranged from ribbons and laces to cast-iron stoves or washing mangles, from a packet of pins to a full-size billiard table. Goods were listed under headings such as manchester, drapery, mercery, millinery, haberdashery, costumery, corsetry, hosiery, perfumery, jewellery, cutlery, furnishings, crockery and glassware, kitchenware, hardware, travel goods, musical instruments, stationery, toiletries, patent medicines, fancygoods, leather goods, smokers' requisites, games and toys, laundry equipment and household provisions (foodstuffs).

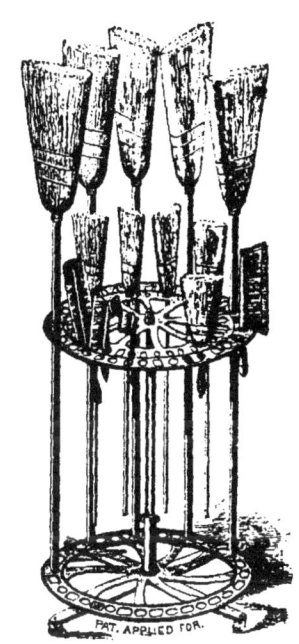

Household life was in some ways quieter before the introduction of radio and television. While the urban world was filled with advertising when people ventured out, inside the home the only commercial assault was likely to be found in newspapers or magazines. In some houses, company calendars or advertising posters might find a place in the kitchen or utility area, and Pears prints were a subtle reminder of that brand of soap. The arrival of a catalogue was an opportunity for a careful perusal of all the possibilities. Here were things within the range of most pockets; then there were items which might require a stretch of the budget. Beyond these were the luxuries which many people on ordinary incomes could only dream of owning. A grand double-bed with 'half tester' canopy, polished posts, heavy brass mountings and inlaid mother-of-pearl trimmings was a vision splendid worth three weeks' average wages. In 1897, the 'Princess Ada Bedroom Suite' with wardrobe, dressing-table, washstand, towel rail, bedside table and two cane-seated chairs (see page 37) was equal to around six weeks' average wages. Way beyond all of this was the cost of a good-quality metal-framed piano. Around 1910 they could be £40 to £45 ($80 to $90) when the basic weekly wage was 42 shillings ($4.20) for six days.

Making a house a practical and comfortable place to live was a task well served by catalogues. Here could be found locks and door handles, towel rails and toilet seats as well as a host of useful gadgets. As part of the culture of that era, many proud householders went way beyond simple needs and did all they could to make their home a showpiece. Again, catalogues could offer fashionable furniture, decorative wallpapers and fabrics, impressive rugs and carpets, ornamented lamps and light-fittings, along with enough knick-knacks to ensure that both occupants and visitors would have a sense of prosperity and respectability.

For a large proportion of people in Australia, the detached house in a garden setting has long been a source of pride, making an important first impression on visitors. In the Federation Era, catalogues offered all sorts of decorative

elements for both house and garden, some of which also had practical value. Fancy window hoods and ornamental woven wire fencing are two examples of the latter. Roof gargoyles, wooden finials and rose arches are examples of the former. For gardeners there were wonderfully illustrated seed and plant catalogues, as well as extensive offerings of edging and paving tiles, birdbaths, sundials, statues, seats, fountains and various sorts of structures such as arbours and aviaries.

With the arrival of the push mower for use around average gardens, allied to the increasing availability of reticulated water, the area given over to lawn became a dominant feature. Catalogues offered a range of cast-iron mowers as well as garden taps, hoses, sprinklers and anything else likely to be needed in growing and maintaining areas of lawn. A new emphasis on outdoor life was part of the Federation Era. Lawns allowed children to run and tumble, and both children and adults could play games such as tennis or shuttlecock. For much of Australia, good times meant material prosperity and the catalogues symbolised the cornucopia of products now available for general consumption.

Notes

[1] Tony Dingle, *The Victorians: settling*, Fairfax, Syme & Weldon Associates, Melbourne, 1984, p. 177.

[2] *The Grandest Display of Household Furniture in the Colony*, A. Hall & Company, Sydney, 1897; reprinted with introduction and comments by Garry Smith, Wongoolah Publishing, NSW, 1994.

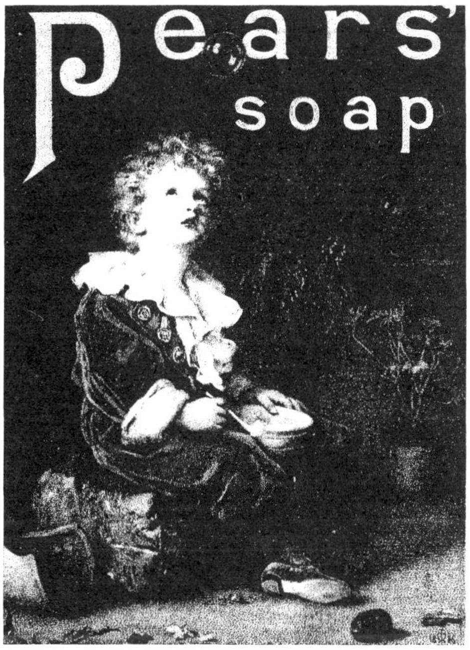
Pears' soap

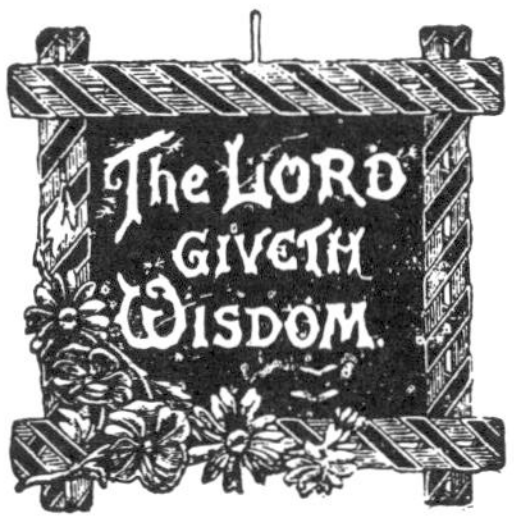
The LORD GIVETH WISDOM.

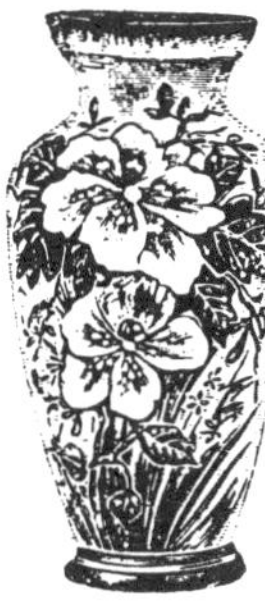

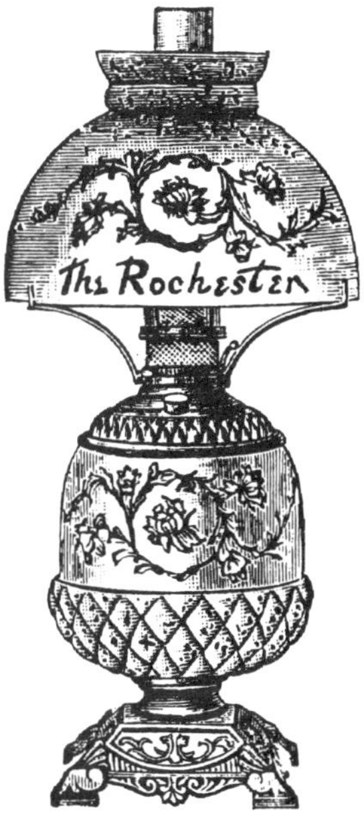
The Rochester

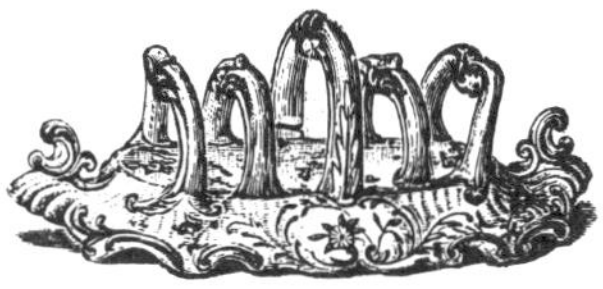

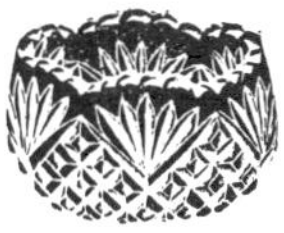

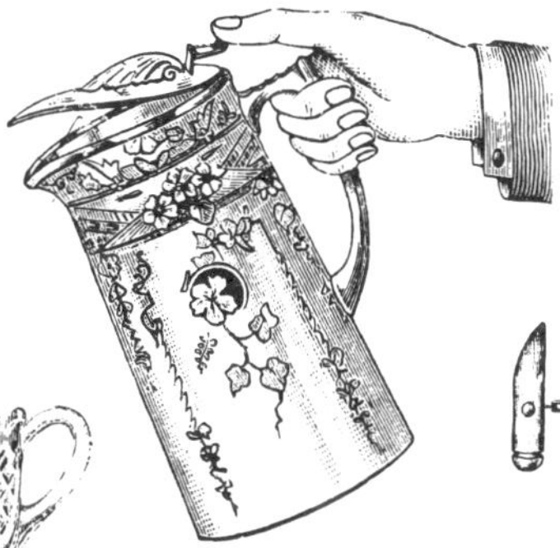

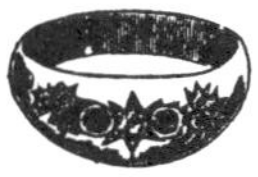

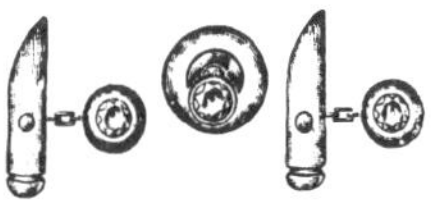

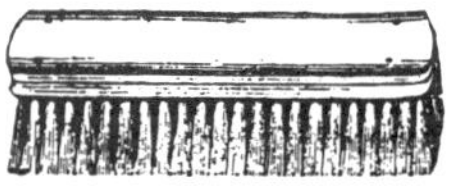

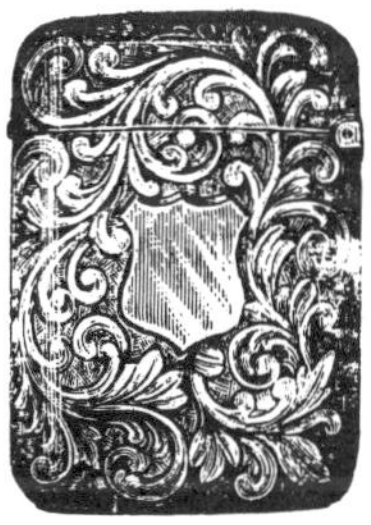

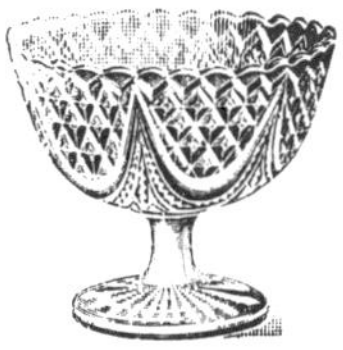

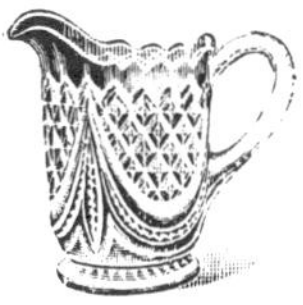

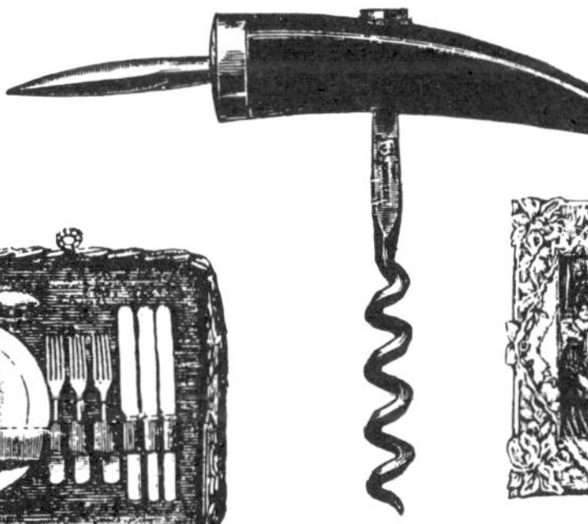

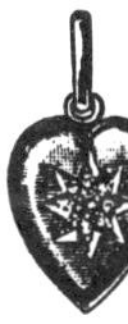

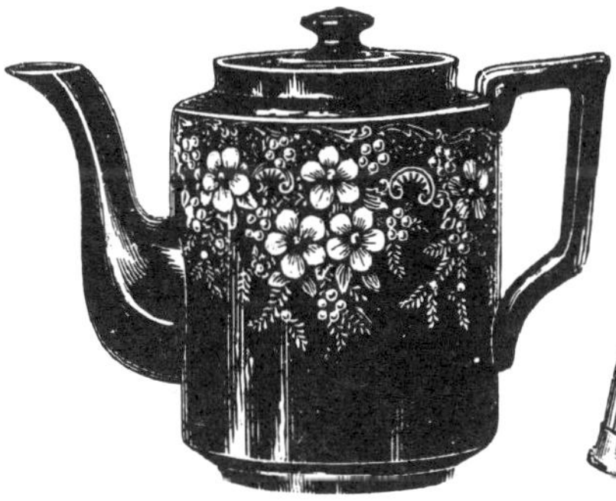

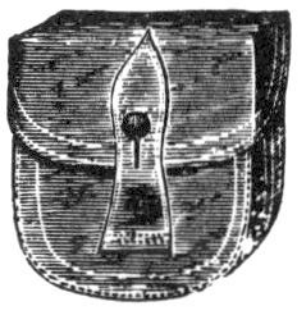

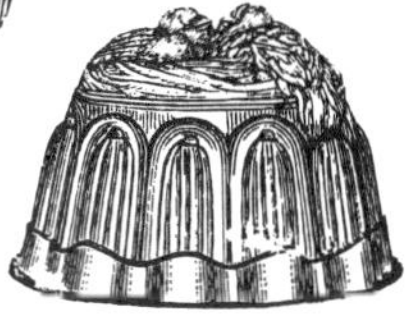

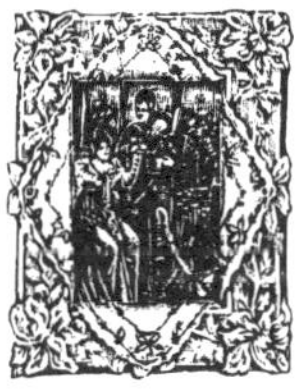

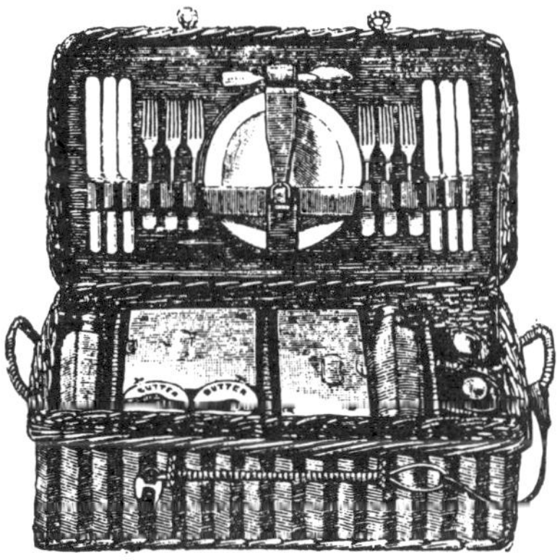

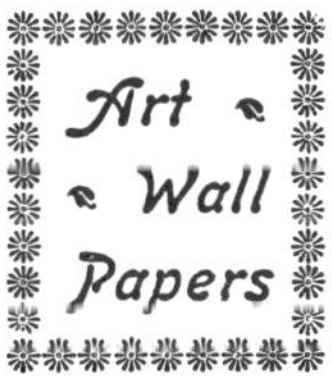
Art
Wall
Papers

The Farmer & Grazier
"TO UPLIFT AGRICULTURE FROM A WEARY DRUDGERY TO A HEALTHFUL SCIENCE!"
Melbourne, JUNE
THE FARMERS' FRIEND.
ALWAYS SMOKE THE BEST TOBACCO

CRINKLED AND CRÊPE PAPER
IN 36 COLOURS
for
making
LAMP SHADES.
CANDLE SHADES.
FANS, HANDSCREENS
DOLL'S DRESSES.
FANCY BALL COSTUMES
AND AN ENDLESS VARIETY
OF FANCY ARTICLES.
Also for Decorations of all Kinds
SOLD IN ROLLS 20 INCHES WIDE AND ABOUT 7 FEET LONG

FATHER TUCK'S
CRAYON PICTURES AND PAINTING BOOK

A MERRY CHRISTMAS

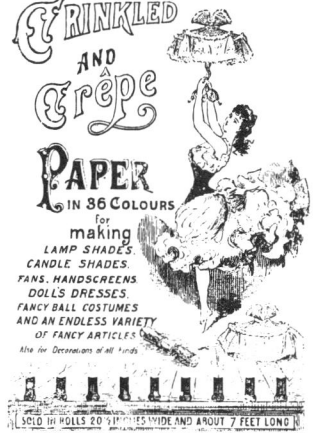

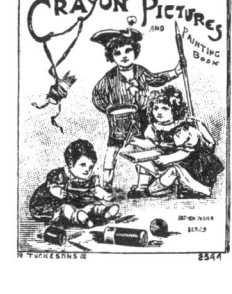

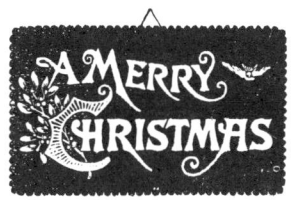

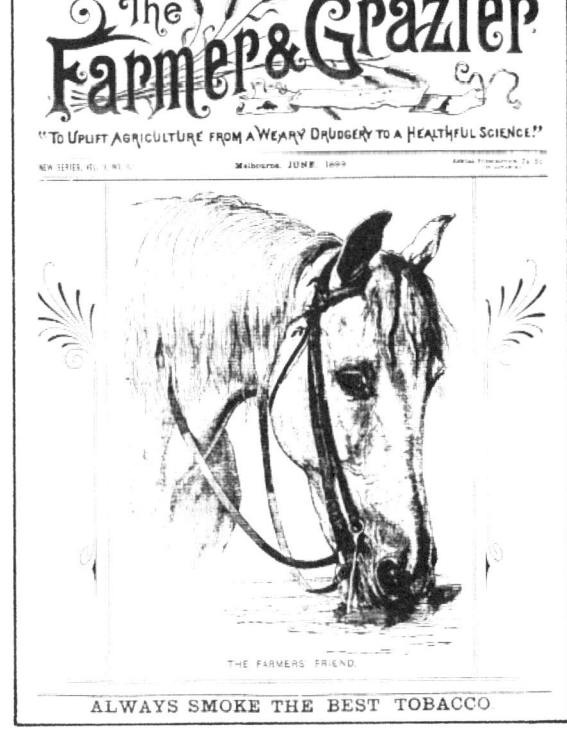

DIMELOW & GAYLARD, Drapers and Importers,
"The Beehive," Railway Station, Richmond.

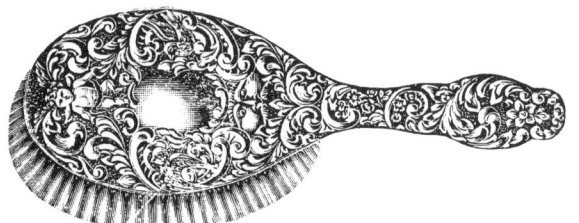

G751—Hair Brushes, mounted with solid silver, beautifully ornamented, 8/6, 11/6, 15/6

G753—New and Pretty Design Serviette Ring, heavily plated on Britannia metal, 13/6

G752—Very Pretty Design Sugar Scuttle, good electroplate, beautifully chased, 15/6

G754—Handsome Egg Stand, with salt cellar, pepper box, and 4 egg cups, heavily plated on white metal, 18/6

G755—"Australia" Silver Hat Pins, 1/6 each

DO NOT CUT the Book. Quote Numbers only.

G756—Handsome Teapot, electroplate on Britannia metal, 18/6, 21/-, 25/-, 30/-

G757—Biscuit Barrel, in oak, with silver-plate bands, as illustrated 12/6; or without centre bands, 9/6

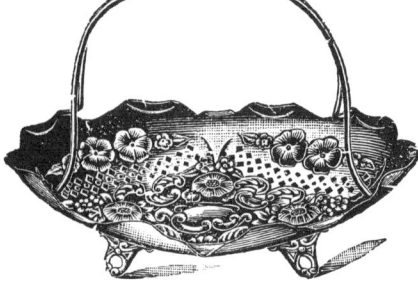

G758—Very Handsome Cake or Fruit Stand, heavily plated, beautifully chased, 22/6

G759—American Revolving Dinner Cruet, fine plate, handsomely engraved—4 bottles, 12/6; 5 bottles, 15/-

G7510—Exquisite Biscuit Barrel, good silver-plated mountings, 17/6

G7511—Hot Water Kettle, pretty design, with stand, good silver-plate, 37/6 and £2/2/10/-

G7512—Butter Dish, electroplate on nickel silver, with cut glass bowl, splendid value, 7/6

G7513—Afternoon Tea Set, 3 pieces, best electroplate on nickel silver, 57/6

OUR SPECIAL LINE.
No. C 116. Twenty-one Pieces.
Light Semi-Porcelain Tea Sets. Lacquered Pink "Kenwood" Pattern. Victor shape.
No. C 117, as above, but in Lacquered Green.

No. C 149.
Printed. Various patterns, shapes and colours.

No. C 533. Electro-plated Afternoon Tea Spoons and Sugar Spoon, on Cards.
No. C 533/1. " " " " " " Tongs, on Cards.
Various patterns.

OUR SPECIAL LINE.
No. C 115. Twenty-one Pieces.
Light Semi-Porcelain Tea Sets, Victor Shape. Flow Blue "Melbourne" Pattern, with Gilt Edges and Handles. See page 286 for Dinner Ware to match the above.

Spiral Tea Ware, Printed "Alexandra" Pattern, in Blue, Green, Red, or Heliotrope.
No. C 119/21. Twenty-one Piece Tea Sets.
" 119/40. Forty Piece Tea Sets.

Metal-covered Stone Teapots.
Various patterns.
No. C 177/1. Small.
No. C 177/2. Medium.
No. C 177/3. Large.

Fancy Decorated China Teapots, with Sliding Lids. A large variety.
No. C 178/1. Small.
No. C 178/2. Medium.
No. C 178/3. Large.

No. C 179.
Fancy-shape China Teapots, with Floral Decorations.
A large variety of shapes and sizes.

No. C 180.
Fancy-shape White China Teapots, with Gilt Edges and Handles.
Various shapes and sizes.

No. C 129.

No. C 130.

No. C 131.

No. C 133.

Fancy China Afternoon Tea Cups and Saucers. Assorted patterns.

No. C 17.   No. C 18.
English-make Afternoon Tea Sets. Electro-plated on Britannia Metal. Assorted patterns.

No. C 32. Bent Plate Brushes. Several sizes.

No. C 30. Crumb Brushes. Various qualities.

No. C 31. Straight Plate Brushes. Several sizes.

No. C 107.
Carved Oak Biscuit Barrels.
Electro-plated on Nickel Silver Mounts.

No. C 108.
Plain Oak Biscuit Barrels.
Electro-plated on Nickel Silver Shields and Mounts.

Crumb Trays and Brushes.
No. C 186. Silvered, cheap quality.
No. C 187. Nickel.
No. C 188. Copper.
Various shapes and qualities.

No. C 112.
Moulded Glass Biscuit Barrels, with Electro-plated Mounts.

No. C 113.
Plain Oak Biscuit Barrels, with Electro-plated on Nickel Silver Shields and Mounts.

FEDERATION CATALOGUE

3. Federation House Styles

There are many readily recognised elements in what is now described as Federation-style architecture. As at any time, there were houses of high fashion, slightly modified traditional vernacular and all sorts of variations in between. The overall trend was toward a less formal, and, in some ways, more romantic house design. Rooflines were often picturesque, with decorative elements such as 'candle-snuffer' turrets. Bay windows, sheltering window hoods, deep verandahs, attic rooms and boldly designed details all added to the impact. Catalogues offered the builders fancy ridge tiles, finials, fretted or turned ready-made woodwork and a wide assortment of fittings. Houses of the period from 1890 to 1915 could be in brick, stone, or even concrete, while in many places wooden construction predominated. A large proportion included some form of pressed or rolled sheet iron in their construction. Roofs of corrugated, galvanised iron were widely favoured. However, in the more substantial suburbs of cities such as Sydney and Melbourne, terracotta tiles were the height of fashion. Gable-ends and sometimes walls might be clad with Wunderlich pressed-metal panels. Also available were pressed panels which imitated cement roughcast or even blocks of stone. For interiors there were pressed panels and trimmings for rooms of every description.

Free-standing suburban houses on spacious allotments offered the greatest scope for a relaxed arrangement of rooms with picturesque roof shapes. The narrow cottage and the semi-detached pair were also given elements in keeping with the romantic ideal. The preference for single-storey houses is a central theme in the story of Australia's domestic architecture. This has meant, in most cases, a more immediate awareness of the roof. Popular styles in the Federation Era celebrated the dominant roof as both a symbol of shelter and a chance to display ornamental effects. Chimneys were similarly given emphasis, being tall with interesting details. Much of this character can be related to the interest in old English country houses and the influence of the Arts and Crafts movement. 'Federation style' has become a term used to describe houses with readily identified elements, mostly from the style traditionally called Queen Anne. There are, in fact, a number of stylistic types within the Australian use of the term 'Federation'. Historians use four main subdivisions for domestic architecture in the period 1890 to 1915: Federation Queen Anne, Federation Arts and Crafts, Federation Bungalow and Federation Filigree. While the fashionable styles can be traced to a greater or lesser degree to Britain and Europe, the contribution from America is also very important. In the United States, English 'Queen Anne' was transformed into a wildly picturesque style with complicated roof forms, verandahs, balconies and lots of busy details. Timber was readily available in North America and was used lavishly, especially in the decoration of verandahs and gable-ends. Much of the turned, fretted and moulded woodwork was produced by machines and a lot was exported to Australia. Having verandahs as an element in our tradition, we were happy to take on some further elaboration. Woodwork painted white or cream to contrast with brickwork, stonework or darker-painted weatherboard became the general fashion.

The so-called Queen Anne style in England had used red brick with white-painted timber window sashes. It was a style for urban houses while 'Old English' was favoured for places in the country. In Australia, Old English elements such as 'half-timbering' in gable-ends became popular as too did the bay window with sets of casements. Roughcast or pebbledash was another means of suggesting English vernacular buildings with walls of rough plaster rendering. From America we borrowed the use of the wooden shingle as a wall or gable-end cladding, and these were usually stained or in dark colours. Leadlight windows in both plain and 'stained' glass added to the Old World character, although they were often given designs of Australian motifs. Native flowers, gumleaves and kookaburras were favourite subjects and sometimes appeared in the plasterwork or woodwork. After the turn of the century, the influence of Art Nouveau made a belated appearance and soon spread to features such as verandah valances, or brackets, interior grilles or arches and mantelpiece designs.

House names were often reminders of the 'Homeland'; Kirkleatham is in Yorkshire (now Cleveland). This house was photographed in Rochester, Victoria. *Collection:* the author.

Front Elevation

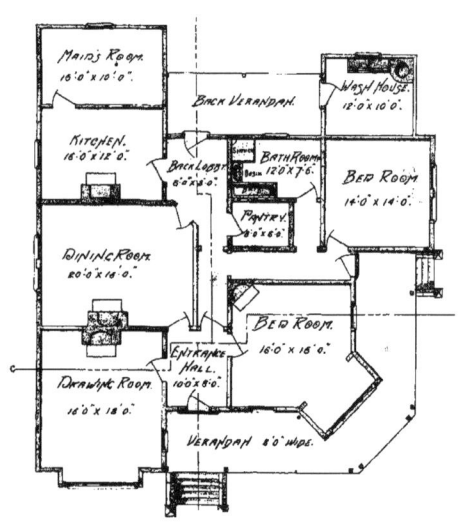

Design for a Queen Anne-style house by Castlemaine artist Stanley Ellis. *Courtesy*: Don and Zara Latimer.

Federation Arts and Crafts style in its notable examples was generally the work of architects, although there were houses created by builders following 'Craftsmen' designs from America. The important difference between this style and Queen Anne was that it was very low-key, with little ornamentation. Gable roofs, tall, tapering chimneys and roughcast walls were typical elements. Of similar character and from the same Craft-oriented ideals, the Federation Bungalow style has been described as a transition between Queen Anne and the Californian bungalows so popular in the 1920s.[1] There was still a strong emphasis on the roof, which usually had wide eaves with exposed rafters. These houses were meant to have a natural 'homely' feel and were influenced by the American 'bungalow' fashions. By contrast, Federation Filigree style could have a simple basic form but would have lots of decorative details. There are many examples in Queensland which have all sorts of fancywork in both wood and metal.

Interiors of ordinary houses, from small and compact to large and rambling, were often a mixture of the fashions which influenced the exterior. Some had bright and airy rooms with light-coloured paints or wallpapers, while others went for the shadowy Old English or Craftsman effect. This meant dark ceiling beams and dark woodwork generally. Often the walls were panelled, with a 'specimen shelf' running around the room, usually at door height. Before Art Nouveau and Arts and Crafts arrived in the early Federation years, interiors were still under the spell of the Aesthetic movement. 'Artistic' decoration had become high fashion in Australia in the 1880s, however, its original ideals were generally lost and rooms were crowded with 'artistic' objects and effects. High ceilings were still to be found in most houses, although Old English and Bungalow fashions set a trend toward cosier interiors. Apart from the drawing room or parlour which could be given a larger area, most rooms were of a similar size. The bathroom, if there was one, would be more compact, as would a maid's room if the family could afford or even find such a person. Young women were now finding other jobs, and most housewives did the cooking, washing and housework and counted themselves lucky if they could have some help for a day or even a few hours.

Most ordinary rooms and a large proportion of best rooms were still box-like throughout the Federation Era. However, there were many pleasant examples of a break from this rigidity. Parlours or drawing rooms boasted window nooks and possibly a fireplace set in an inglenook. Small, cosy areas opening off larger spaces were artistically framed by fretted wooden screens or grilles. One wall might be at an angle, as might a fireplace or even a doorway. Bay windows, often with window seats, had a romantic feel with their casement windows and 'artistic' curtains. Here was a place to relax and look out over the garden, or if the day was warm, the cane and wicker chairs on the spacious verandah or piazza were a perfect retreat. A well-made and well-stocked fernery with room for comfortable seating was another cool option. Modern insulation materials have made many houses and cottages from the Federation Era far more liveable, as have modern appliances and services. It must be said, however, that many had and continue to have, great charm. This is why originals are much sought after and new versions have proliferated.

Notes
[1] Richard Apperly, Robert Irving & Peter A. Reynolds, *Pictorial Guide to Identifying Australian Architecture*, Angus & Robertson Publishers, North Ryde, NSW, 1989, p. 144.

A weatherboard vernacular cottage photographed in the Federation Era.
Collection: the author.

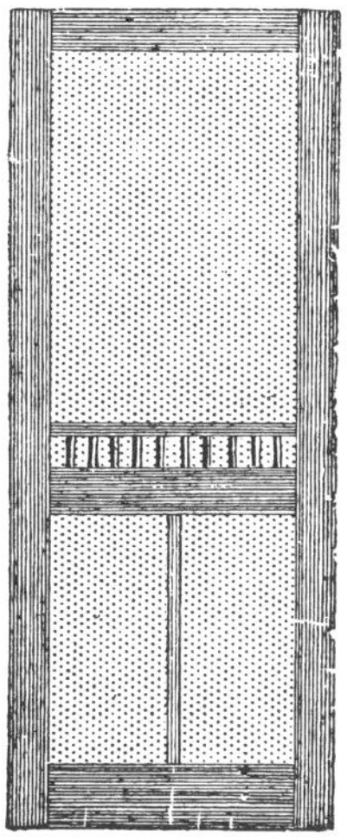

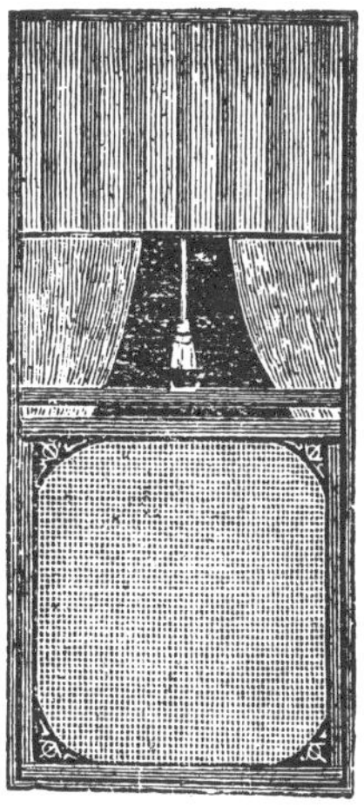

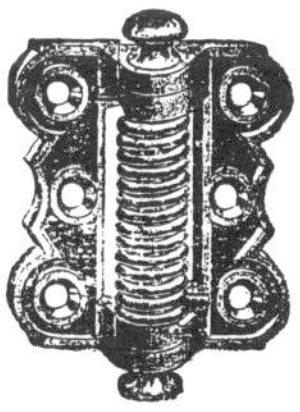

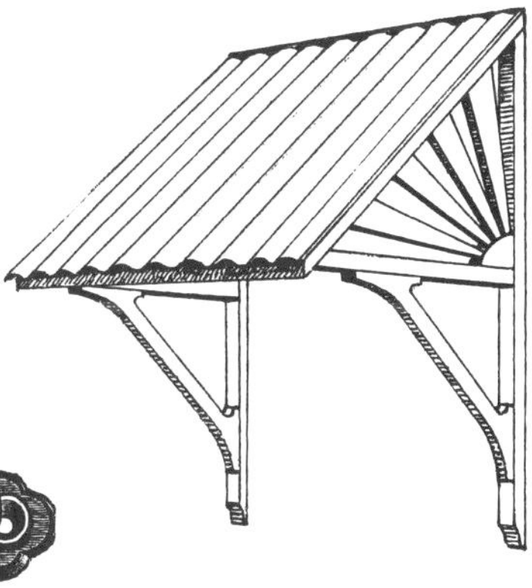

FEDERATION CATALOGUE

4. The Nesting Instinct

Creating a pleasant place to live is a fundamental drive for most people. Once possessed of the basic structure, and with time, money or just plain determination, householders set about the task of making a house into a home. In the era covered by this book, some people were happy with basic comforts and few, if any, decorative elements. Many could just manage to survive. Those who did have the opportunity and desire to decorate were encouraged along a number of paths by the fashions of the day. Most chose one of the approved artistic directions seen first-hand in other houses or promoted in furniture stores, home decoration books, magazines or newspaper columns. Up-to-the-minute decorators and architects were leading the charge toward simple, well-lit interiors with fresh colours or delicate tints, rather than the ponderous stodge of the heavier Victorian interiors. Light-painted walls or bright wallpapers combined with painted woodwork were a great help, as were large areas of window glass with muslin or lace curtains and not so much heavy fabric. White or cream ceilings had been long favoured in Australian houses when plaster was given coats of distemper or whitewash. Fancy plasterwork was used in the best rooms of substantial houses, although Wunderlich pressed-metal panels and trimmings were so easily handled they became synonymous with early twentieth-century domestic interiors. Soft shades of blue, pink, sage green or buff were applied to pressed-metal ceilings which were often given contrasting tones to highlight the embossed pattern. In some examples, elements such as flowers and foliage were painted in softly naturalistic colours.

Patterned wallpapers, or stencilling applied to painted surfaces, provided a generally accessible means of creating the desired decorative effects. These ranged from subtle harmonies of colour and design to bold combinations which, to modern eyes, are either wonderful or overwhelming. A fine sitting room could have single colour walls with an 'artistic' frieze encircling the room just below the ceiling. The dado had lost favour with the fashionable elite, but it was still seen in many houses, not only in the hallway but in the parlour, sitting room and dining room. The dado would be achieved by either special dado paper with a 'filling' above or by a section of darker paint with a stencilled band along the top. Many wooden houses and cottages were still given a dado of lining boards around 1.2 metres high with a moulding along the top. The area above was often hessian and paper on backing boards. This would typically be wallpapered with a frieze at ceiling height.

Many bedrooms were given plain colour walls or a light, fresh wallpaper but a lot were entirely lined in board. This was sometimes relieved by a coat of colour wash but was often left to go darker as it aged, creating a rich molasses hue. In spite of the movement toward lighter and simpler interiors, many people were still keen to fill their walls with pictures, mirrors, framed homilies, specimen shelves and craft works.

Woodwork such as doors, window frames, architraves and skirtings could be varnished, woodgrained or painted. To add further character to these elements, the mouldings and panels were often painted in a combination of subtle colours. For instance, the main body of a door might be pale olive with the mouldings in a dark stone colour. Some were given softer schemes such as pale blue-grey, with pale cream mouldings and rose-pink panels. The rich or sombre colours of the mid-Victorian period retained their hold where a dignified but conservative interior was required. A newer generation was in raptures over dusty-pink, buttercup, slate-blue, china-blue, old rose, *eau-de-Nil*, old gold, ivory and various shades of cream. White and off-white also found their way into interior schemes, having been banished for many decades.

Arts and Crafts brought an emphasis on such colours as deep cream, buff, tan, terracotta and Morris green. The British Arts and Crafts movement led by William Morris had championed the 'pre-industrial' crafts as a response to a world swamped by machine-made products. Fabrics, wallpapers, metalwork and furniture were just some of the items in Australian households which were, in time, influenced by designers following Arts and Crafts ideals. Wood was valued for its own character; metals such as copper and iron were hand-worked; and 'honest' fabrics such as hessian and 'art serge' were used for simple drapery. Many other threads were drawn into the fashionable Federation interior; there were 'Moorish' screens and occasional tables, Japanese sideboards

A pioneer family in their Sunday best. *Collection:* the author.

The doll-like baby is real; the dog is not. *Collection:* Ashley Tracey.

and potplant stands, Dutch dressers, Jacobean chairs and even reproduction Sheraton and Chippendale. As the Georgian and Colonial Revival was just beginning to take hold, some of the newest schemes had 'old-fashioned' chintz chair covers and curtains, combined with wallpapers in eighteenth-century patterns.

Aesthetic drapery was almost in danger of engulfing some of the 'best rooms' of the Federation Era. Window curtains were only part of the story; doors, arches, fireplaces, screens and mantelpieces could all be given artistically arranged swathes of fabric. Valances for windows, shelves and mantelpieces were made up of fabric arranged in festoons. Fringes, tassels, pendants, tails and cords were all added to enrich the effect, and magazines offered novel and artistic ideas in draping. To add further to the exotic effect, palm fronds, ostrich or peacock feathers and Japanese-style fans were applied at strategic points. The wide doorway was considered the ideal place for the decorated *portière*, the *pièce de rèsistance* in aesthetic drapery. Some designs were so heavily interlaced they made it difficult to pass through.[1] Because much of the furniture was set at various angles in the room, even the piano back might be exposed and was therefore in need of artistic drapery. Asymmetry was the central ideal, even in rectangular, box-like rooms. In fact many earlier rooms succumbed to the new fashion with the addition of cosy corners, inglenooks and fretted timber screens known as grilles. Decorated folding screens were another high fashion item used for breaking up large spaces. Palms in tubs on various sorts of stands were similarly employed.

Carpets and rugs either quietly complemented the exotic cosiness of fashionable rooms, or were an integral part of its bold impression. There were large carpets in squares with traditional floral patterns or rugs with borders as part of the design. Where floor showed round the edges of the room it was usually stained to a dark brown colour or given a coat of japan. Persian rugs, long used in better-quality interiors, possessed the required exotic character. The East was a clear influence, even in rugs made in Europe. Eastern rugs were also a source of patterns for linoleum, that hard-wearing, easy-care floor covering which was widely used in the Federation Era, particularly in utility areas. Catalogues offered linoleums, carpets, rugs and a long list of soft furnishings, decorating materials, household fittings and bric-à-brac. Here was all the nest-building material any householder might need.

Notes
[1] Elizabeth Wright, *Soft Furnishings 1830-1930*, Historic Houses Trust of New South Wales, Sydney, 1995, p. 8.

Stencil Designs

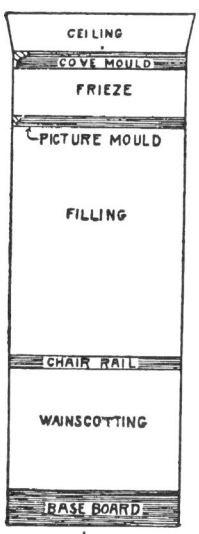  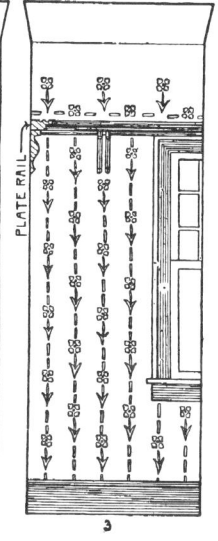 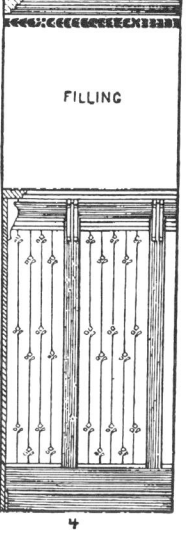  

Plate 105.—Common Names Used to Designate Various Wall Areas for the Purpose of Decoration.

 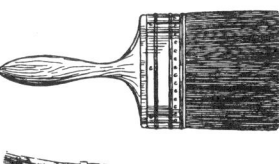

Wall Papers.

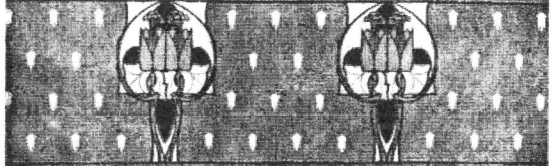

THE "BURCOT" DESIGNED BY C. K. LENNOX
WALL-PAPER EXECUTED BY C. KNOWLES & CO., LTD.

THE "KYNASTON" DESIGNED BY WILLIAM TURNER
WALL-PAPER EXECUTED BY C. KNOWLES & CO., LTD.

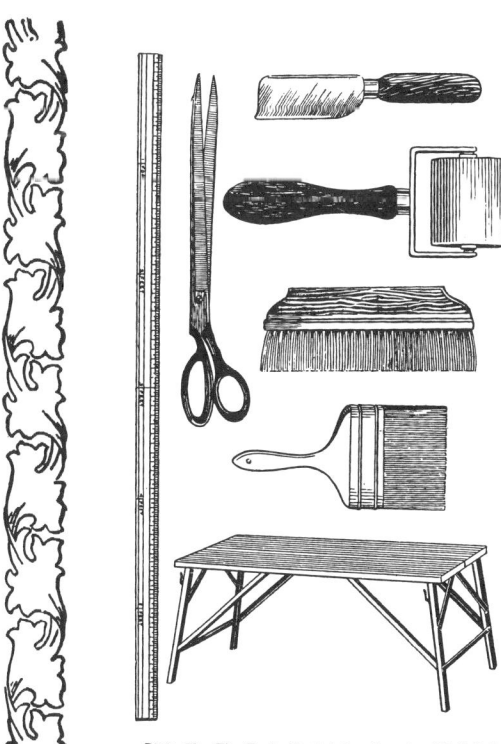

THE "EVERLEY" DESIGNED BY THOMAS TURNER
WALL-PAPER EXECUTED BY C. KNOWLES & CO., LTD.

THE "CELTIC ROSE" WALL-PAPER DESIGNED BY ARTHUR WILCOCK
EXECUTED BY C. KNOWLES & CO., LTD.

Plate 78.—The Tools Needed for Hanging Wall Fabrics.

No. C 737.
Japanese Bamboo Corner Whatnots, with Lacquered Panel Trays. Various Sizes.
No. C 738. As above, but with Matting Trays. Various Sizes.

No. C 746.
Japanese Bamboo Flower-pot Stands. Various Sizes.

No. C 532.
Japanese Paper Fans. Various patterns and prices.

No. C 744.
Japanese Bamboo Music Cabinets, with Shelf and Bevelled Mirror at Back, Lacquered Panels. Various Shapes and Sizes.

No. C 543. Feather Fans. Assorted colours and sizes.
No. C 544. Ostrich Feather Fans. Cream, White or Black.

No. C 526.
Strongly Bound Palm Fans, with Bone-tipped Bamboo Handles. Two sizes.

79—£9/10/-. A handsome, solid, new design; it is 5ft. wide, and most substantially built from thoroughly seasoned, specially selected timbers; one of the very highest grade. Sale price, £9/10/-.

G441—Pretty Lace Curtains, 3½ yds. by 53 in., bold design, white or ecru, 6/6 pair

G442—Splendid Nottingham Lace Curtains, 53 in. wide—3 yds., 4/6 ; 3½ yds., 5/6

G443 — A Very Effective Lace Curtain, new design, overlock corded edge, 60 in. wide—3½ yds., 11/6; 4 yds., 13/6

CURTAINS, 1.

White Lace Curtains, 2½ yds., 1/6, 1/11 pair
White Lace Curtains, 2¾ yds., 1/11, 2/3, 2/11 pair
Lace Curtains, 3 yds., taped or corded edge, 3/6, 3/11, 4/6 pair
3 yds. Nottingham Lace Curtains, 4/6, 4/11, 5/11 pair
3½ yds. Lace Curtains, taped edge, 4/11, 5/11, 7/6, 10/6, 13/6 pair
4 yds. Lace Curtains, taped edge, 8/11, 10/6, 12/6, 15/- pair
3½ yds. Creme Curtains, 4/11, 5/6, 7/11, 8/6, 12/6 pair
4 yds. Creme Curtains, 8/11, 12/6, 15/6, 18/6, 21/- pair
Creme or White Applique Curtains, 3½ yds., 15/6, 17/6, 21/- pair
Creme or White Applique Curtains, 4 yds., 17/6, 21/-, 25/,. to 45/- pair
40 in. Creme or White Floral Muslin, for Bed Drapings, &c., 9d., 10½d., 1/- yd.
48 in. White Frilled Muslin, for Curtains, &c., 12½d., 1/3 yd.
Creme Madras Muslin, 10½d., 1/-, 1/3 yd.
54-in. Creme Tasselled Madras Muslin, 1/6, 1/9, 1/11, 2/3 yd.

G444—Nottingham Lace Curtain, overstitched edge, white or ecru, 60 in. wide, 3½ yds., 8/6

G445—Beautiful Lace Curtains, creme or white, very fine net, 62 in. wide—3½ yds., 15/6; 4 yds., 17/6

G446—New design, 3½ yds. by 60 in., corded edge, 13/6

G447—Handsome Lace Curtains, patent Ariston Unbreakable Net, 60 in. wide—3½ yds., 12/6; 4 yds., 14/6

G448—Special Pattern Fine Net Curtain, white or ecru, handsome design, 60 in. wide—3½ yds., 7/6; 4 yds., 8/11

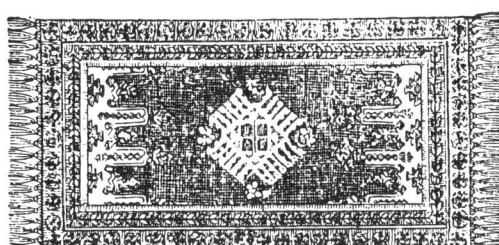

G417   G416

G416—Axminster Pile Hearth Rugs, handsome designs, all colors, 10/6, 12/6, 15/6

G417—Heavy Brussels Hearth Rug, all colors, 5/11, 6/11, 8/6, 10/6; jute Brussels, 2/11, 3/11, 4/6

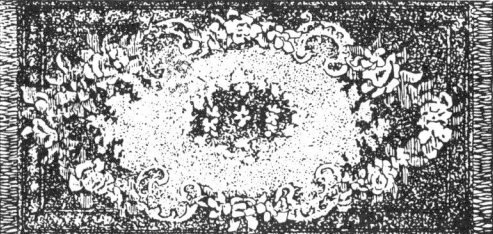

G431—Pretty Floral Design, in 6 ft. Linoleums. Brown ground, red, fawn, or blue flowering. 2/11 per running yard

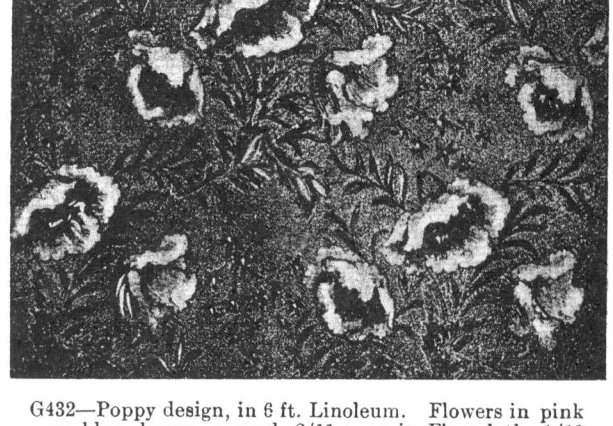

G432—Poppy design, in 6 ft. Linoleum. Flowers in pink or blue, brown ground, 2/11; or in Floorcloth, 1/11 per running yard

G433—A favorite design in Tiled Linoleum. Brown ground, green or red tiling; also in fawn ground. 2/11 per running yard

G434—6 ft. wide, extra heavy, Linoleum. Brown ground, red or green tiles. 3/6 running yard

G435—Heavy 6 ft. wide Linoleum, in superior quality. Brown or fawn ground, tiled designs. 3/11 running yard

G436—6 ft. wide, newest design, in fawn or brown ground, light or dark tiling. 3/11 running yard

G422—Three feet wide Floral Passage Oilcloth, in tile or floral patterns, light or dark ground, 1/2 yard; also in two qualities of Linoleum, 1/9, 2/3

G421—Three feet wide Tile Pattern Oilcloth, light or brown ground, 1/2; also in Linoleum, 1/11, 2/3

No. C 582.
Hand-painted Opals
in White Enamelled
Reed Frames.
Various sizes.

No. C 789.
Dried Palms for
Decorating.
Various sizes.

No. C 787.
Artificial Flowers.

No. C 786.
Coloured Paper Flower
Pot Covers.
Assorted colours.

  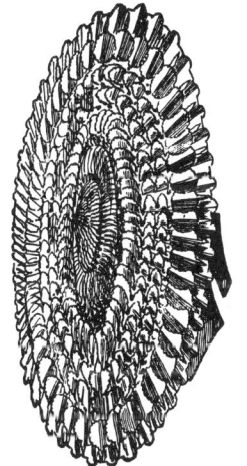 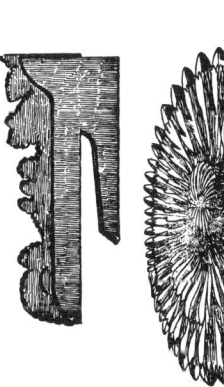

No. C 790.   No. C 791.   No. C 792.   No. C 793.
Grass Bouquets.   Various sizes and colours.   Coloured Tissue Paper Folding Fire Screens.   Assorted sizes.

   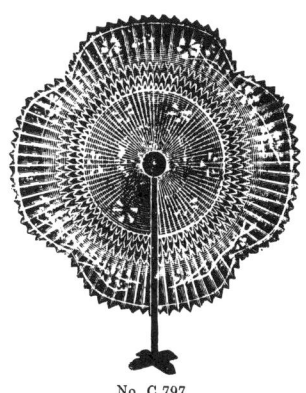

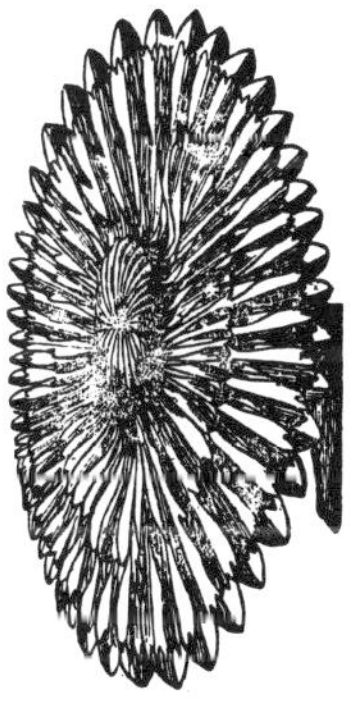

No. C 794.   No. C 795.   No. C 796.   No. C 797.
Folding Millboard Fire Screens.   A large assortment of sizes and patterns.   Round Shape Japanese Folding Fans, on Wood Stands. Various sizes and patterns.   Fancy Shape Japanese Folding Fans on Wood Stands. Various sizes and patterns.

FEDERATION CATALOGUE
5. Furniture for Everyone

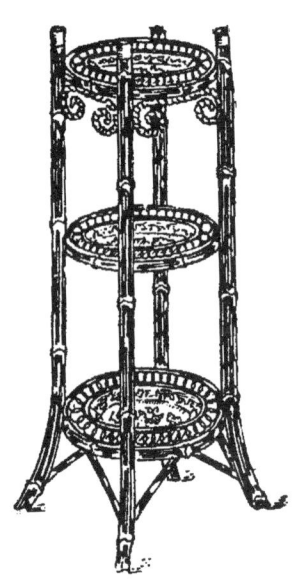

Furniture factories proliferated in Australia in the late nineteenth and early twentieth centuries, bringing a wide range of household items within reach of most people. Better-quality pieces were still imported, but with the protection of new Commonwealth tariffs, local industry could compete with the cheap, mass-production items from Europe and America. Some furniture was beautifully crafted, most of it was sturdy by today's standards and some was just plain shoddy by any comparison. The mass production of functional, low-cost, everyday items such as chairs, tables, cupboards and beds ensured that average households could be adequately furnished.

Pictures of the best rooms in houses of the Federation Era show that for many people prosperity and respectability were best expressed through the quantity of decorative elements able to be crammed into a room. As previously discussed, the kinds of furniture seen in mansions, homesteads, houses and cottages reflected an eclectic gathering of influences. 'Early English', 'Renaissance', 'Queen Anne', 'Sheraton' and 'Chippendale' were all applied to styles claiming some sort of historical legitimacy. Other important ingredients were Japanese and Moorish traditions and both British and American versions of Arts and Crafts. Much of the furniture seen in Australian houses in the period from 1890 to 1915 was a mixture of 'Early English', 'Renaissance' and 'Queen Anne' elements. The square lines of fashionable furniture came from the 'design reform' which inspired British furniture-makers in the second half of the nineteenth century. Medieval, Renaissance and Japanese influences were all important in the drive to break with the curvaceous lines of the popular 'French Antique' look favoured earlier in the century. Some of the newer designs were refined and even delicate, but most were robust and 'honest'. Timber was not generally veneered, being valued for its solid character. A typical Federation-era dining table with 'massive' legs harks back to 'Neo-Renaissance' designs of the 1870s and '80s. That sideboard in oak with 'carved' panels in the doors and a mirrored back surmounted by a 'broken' classical pediment is a mixture of historical references. The door panels came from notions of medieval and Renaissance designs; the turned wooden pillars holding the shelf or shelves could be Renaissance. Classical influences such as the 'broken' pediments were associated with Queen Anne. Because turning and carving could now be done by machine, it was often lavishly applied to fashionable designs. Rows of turned spindles were often used in the backs of chairs and settees, in the tops of overmantels and as 'galleries' along the back of chest or sideboard tops. Timbers favoured were English oak, Australian silky oak, walnut, blackwood, kauri, Australian cedar, rosewood or 'polished pine'. Customers would need to be careful to read the fine print because furniture was often pine given a 'walnut' or 'cedar' stain. A 'Morris green' stain, a popular Arts and Crafts finish, was also available. Catalogues offered drawing-room suites 'luxuriously upholstered' in Genoa velvet with silk plush borders. 'French tapestry' was similarly used with plush borders. These borders were usually in rich red, blue, green or brown, while the panels of tapestry or Genoa velvet were boldly patterned.

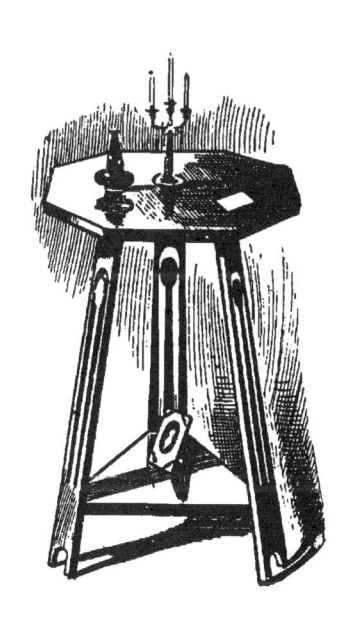

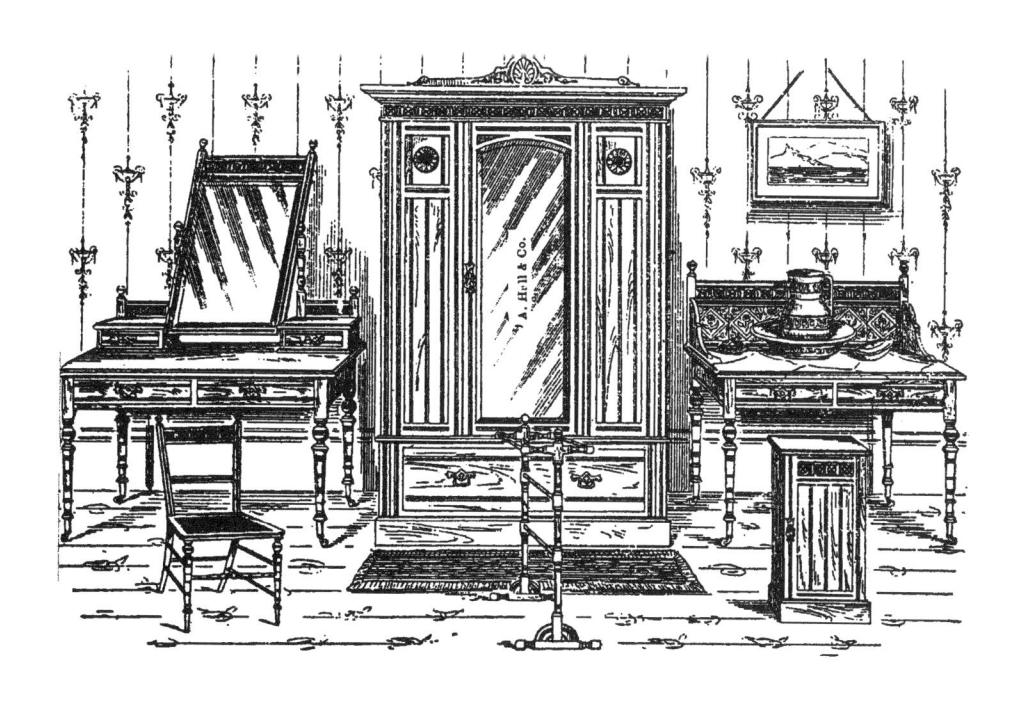

Bamboo and rattan cane drawing-room chairs offered a moderately-priced alternative to the more formal suites. They were used in all kinds of homes, but were considered ideal for houses in the tropical zones. All sorts of bamboo fancy tables are seen in old catalogues, along with settees, lounges, chairs, tables, shelves and even overmantels. Much of this furniture is patterned Japanese bamboo, with the tops of tables and shelves given lacquered designs. Contrasting with these 'oriental' pieces, the 'old-fashioned' cedar chiffonier was still on offer for conservative folk, as were traditional whatnots in solid walnut or walnut stain on pine. Bentwood furniture from Europe was available in a wide range of designs which, apart from all sorts of chairs, included hat-racks, hallstands, tables and wonderful cradles. Standard cottage or utility chairs were imported from the United States in huge quantities, although Australian versions did find a market after tariffs were raised against imports in the early 1900s. Around 1906 the famed 'kangaroo', 'emu' and 'lyrebird' designs came into production in Melbourne and were widely advertised. Australian motifs were, at this time, seen on many products and house-fittings. Eucalyptus leaves, nuts and blossoms, waratahs, flannel flowers, Sturt's desert pea, fern fronds and wattle all found their way into the decoration of houses.

Bedsteads could be large and highly ornamented or very plain, following Arts and Crafts ideals. Some of the iron or brass models were finely proportioned, contrasting with the ponderous designs proudly advertised as 'massive', as if quantity equalled value for money. Still, even the latter continue to appeal, being such a statement of their era; they look striking when fully restored with all the trimmings. Iron or brass single beds for children or for second and third bedrooms were generally less ornate and could even be very plain. This hierarchy of furniture designs from the best rooms to the lesser ones applied to all the essential items of furniture. Washstands are a typical example. The best were given marble tops, ceramic tiles, towel rails and chamber-pot cupboards. Others were simple designs, having a wooden top with a hole for the jug and basin. For really humble rooms the wrought-iron stand to hold a dish was a reasonable option.

In the Federation Era, people could be living in houses ranging from newly built back to early colonial survivors. It was possible also for households to have furniture of varying ages, including very old items brought from overseas. Collecting antiques and curios was increasing in popularity in the latter decades of the nineteenth century, and it became fashionable for them to be included as part of the decor of the best rooms. The interest in Old English furniture took time to reach the wider community. At the end of the Federation Era 'Jacobean' and other reproductions or derivatives were beginning to appear in Australian middle-class houses. Fumed oak was considered very stylish in that it suggested age-darkened timber.

Utilitarian furniture, such as tables, chairs and dressers for use in kitchens, were mostly plain and functional. These designs remained much the same over many decades. Meat-safes and chiffonier safes varied from perfectly plain to more decorative pieces such as the one on page 51 which has a fancy top, recalling designs of the 1850s and '60s. Storage safes for meat and other foodstuffs were essential items in both town and country, although the increasing availability of ice-chests was a boon to people in the cities, suburbs and country towns. Food bins, storage cupboards and fully-fitted pantries were also important in an age when most provisions came in bulk. Canned and packaged foods were gaining on the latter but took a long time to become almost universal.

One of the important items in any household was a reliable clock. This was particularly important for workers in cities and towns who needed to be on time for work, which was often reached by public transport. The number and quality of clocks in a house would depend mostly on the socio-economic level of the occupants. For ordinary people, and even those on very low incomes, the availability of the cheap American clock from the mid-nineteenth century was a significant development. By the 1890s, stores and catalogues offered a wide range of mantel and wall clocks as well as bedroom clocks, including the ubiquitous cheap alarm clock. Less vital to townsfolk were barometers for weather prediction. However, these were an important item for farmers and anyone else watching for changing conditions. Watching the sky and the air pressure variations was a natural habit for all those who counted on rain. The Federation Era began with a terrible drought and in 1914 many areas suffered another one, with World War I close at hand.

Kitchen at 'Stourpaine', South Australia, c. 1911.
Collection: Mortlock Library, State Library of South Australia (B39483).

Height 3'11"
Width 3'2"

Height 3'10"
Width 3'2"

Height 4'2"
Width 3'2"

DINING ROOM SUITES.

VARIOUS PATTERNS.

No. C 94. Nine Pieces, comprising Couch, Two Gents' Easy Chairs, and Six Small Chairs, Solid Blackwood Frames. Handsomely Carved, Well Upholstered in Best Roan Skins.

No. C 95. As above, but Upholstered in Morocco.

No. C 96. Nine Pieces, comprising Couch, Ladies' and Gents' Easy Chairs, and Six Small Chairs, Stained Walnut, or Solid Blackwood Frames, well Upholstered in Good Quality Duck or Roan Skins.

No. C 97. Superior quality, Nine Pieces, comprising Couch, Ladies' and Gents' Easy Chairs and Six Small Chairs, Solid Blackwood or Walnut Frames, Upholstered in Extra Fine French Roans, or Morocco Leather, Seats and Backs, all buttoned.

No. C 98. Comprising Couch, Ladies' and Gents' Easy Chairs and Six Small Chairs, Spindle Back, Kauri Frames, Stained Walnut, and Upholstered in American Cloth.

No. C 99. As above, but with Upholstered Back Small Chairs.

No. C 100. Nine Pieces, comprising Couch, Ladies' and Gents' Easy Chairs, and Six Upholstered Back Small Chairs, Stained Walnut Frames, Well Carved, and covered in Heavy Duck. A reliable Suite.

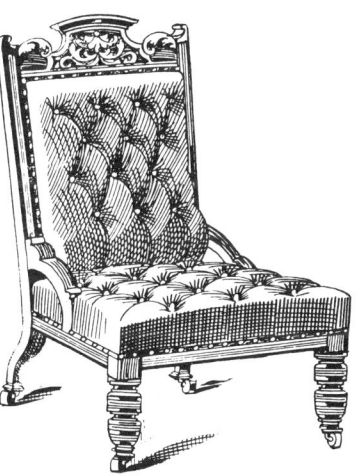

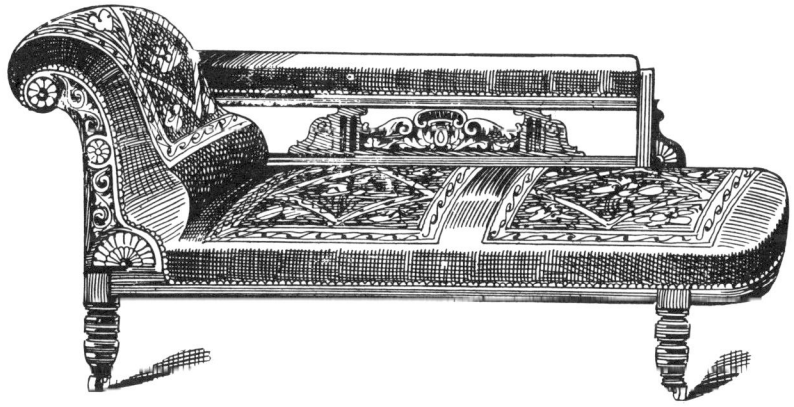

DINING ROOM SUITES.

No. C 101.

Nine Pieces, comprising Couch, Ladies and Gents' Chairs, and Six Small Chairs, Solid Blackwood or Stained Walnut Frames, well Upholstered in Saddle Bags and Utrecht Velvet of any Shade.

No. C 102.

Superior Finish, Nine Pieces, comprising Couch, Two Gents' Easy Chairs, and Six Small Chairs, Solid Blackwood or Walnut Frames, Upholstered in best manner with Choice Saddle Bags and Utrecht Velvet.

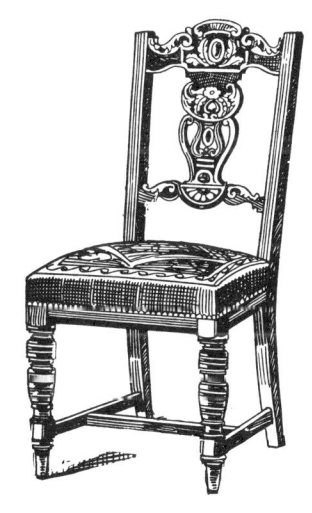

THE FEDERATION CATALOGUE   42   FURNITURE FOR EVERYONE

No. C. 734.

No. C. 747.
Japanese Bamboo Cabinets, with Lacquered Panels and Bevelled Mirrors. A Large Variety of Shapes and Sizes.

No. C. 745.
Japanese Bamboo Hall Stands, with Bevelled Mirrors and Lacquered Panels. Matting Trays. Various Shapes and Sizes.

No. C 739.
Japanese Bamboo Music Stands. Various Shapes.

No. C 743.
Japanese Bamboo Flower-pot Stands. Various Sizes.

JAPANESE BAMBOO

With Lacquered Panels and Bevelled Mirrors.

Occasional Tables.
Polished Octagon Tops, on Castors.
No. C 222. 24 in. Stained Walnut.
No. C 223. ,, Solid ,,
No. C 224. 30 in Stained ,,
No. C 225. ,, Solid ,,

Occasional Tables.
Polished Octagon Tops, on Castors.
No. C 226. 24 in. Stained Walnut.
No. C 227. ,, Solid ,,
No. C 228. 30 in. Stained ,,
Fo. C 229. ,, Solid ,,

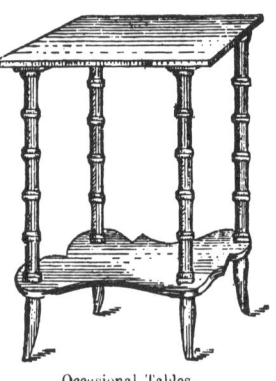

Occasional Tables.
Stained Walnut Legs and Tray.
Top, 18 in. by 18 in.
Various designs.
No. C 230. Plain Top.
No. C 231. Polished Top.

Occasional Tables.
Stained Walnut Legs and Tray.
Top, 24 in. by 18 in.
Various designs.
No. C 232. Plain Top.
No. C 233. Polished Top.

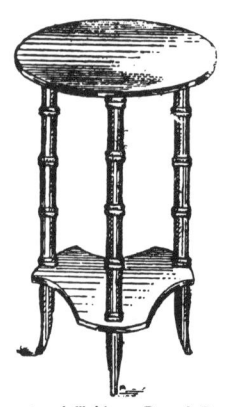

Occasional Tables. Round Top.
18 in. by 18 in.
Stained Walnut Legs and Tray.
Various designs.
No. C 234. Plain Top.
No. C 235. Polished Top.

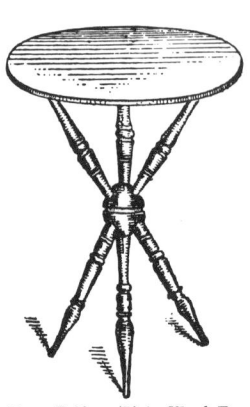

Gipsy Tables. Plain Wood Top.
Stained Walnut and Gold or Black and Gold. Top, 18 in.
No. C 236. Square.
No. C 237. Octagon.
No. C 238. Round.

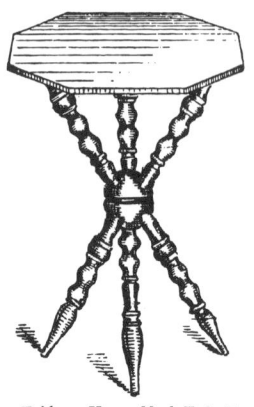

Gipsy Tables. Heavy Mock Twist Legs.
Plain Wood Top. Stained Walnut and Gold or Black and Gold. Top, 18 in.
No. C 239. Square.
No. C 240. Octagon.
No. C 241. Round.

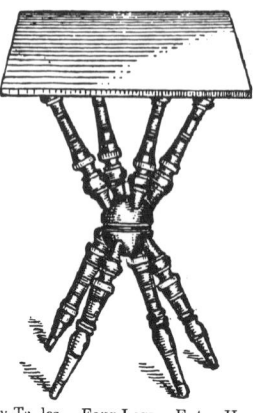

Gipsy Tables. Four Legs. Extra Heavy, Plain Top. Stained Walnut and Gold or Black and Gold. Top, 20 in.
No. C 242. Square.
No. C 243. Octagon.
No. C 244. Round.

256

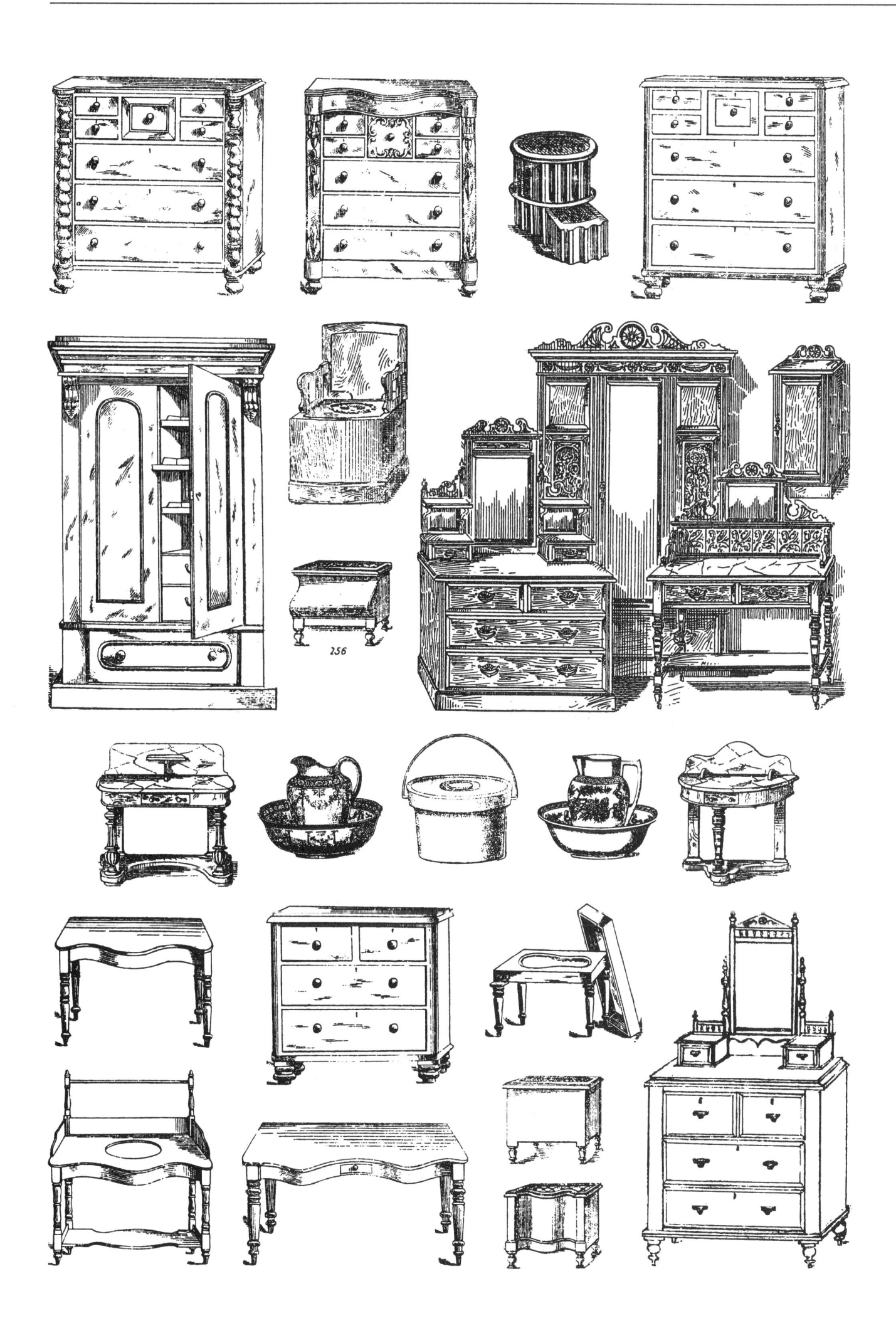

BEDSTEADS.

We can supply more elaborate designs than those shown here, and shall be glad to submit designs and prices if desired. We give Exceptional Value, and PACK FREE, but DO NOT pay carriage on Bedsteads or Bedding.

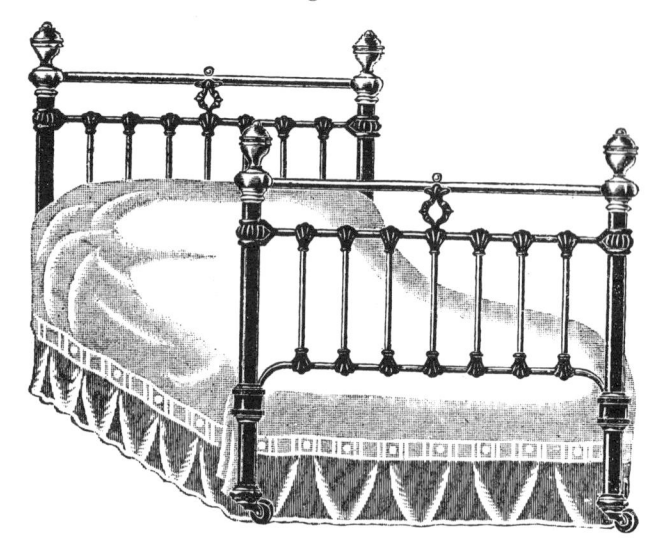

D761—The newest design in French Bedsteads, mounted in Nickel or Brass, 1in. Pillars, Extended Foot-rail, full size, 4ft. 6in.; special price, 30/-.

We ask you to Compare Our Prices— then your Order is Ours.

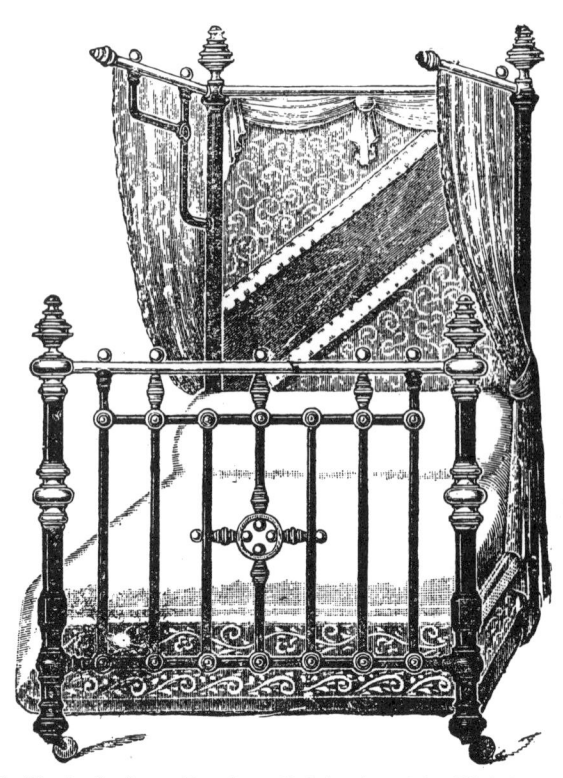

D762—Neat design, Persian Bedstead, with Nickel or Brass Mounts, 1¼in. Pillars, full size, 4ft. 6in., £2/17/6. French Bedstead, same design, £2/9/6.

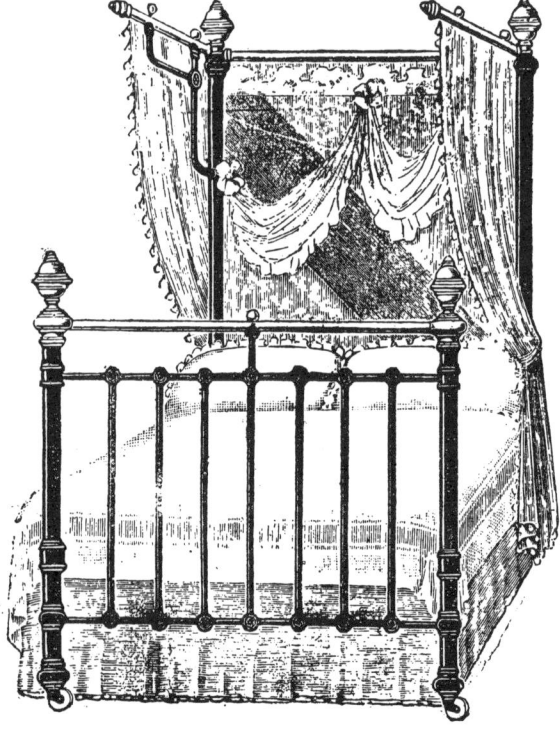

D763.—A good, serviceable Bedstead, Persian style, Nickel or Brass Mountings, Extended Foot-rail, 1in. Pillars, full size, 4ft. 6in., £2. French Bedstead, same design, 33/6.

DO NOT Cut this "Drummer," Number and Price is sufficient.

Stretcher Bars, if required, 2/3 extra.

D764—Elaborate design Persian Bedstead, in Nickel or Brass Mountings, Extended Foot-rail, 1¼in. hand-polished Pillars, full size, 4ft. 6in., £4/14/6.

G429—"Home Comfort," White Colonial Wool Blanket, soft and warm, 9-4, 11/6 ; 10-4, 14/6 ; 11-4, 18/6 ; 12/4, 22/6

OUR STORES are closed on WEDNESDAYS at 1 o'clock.

G4210—"Australian Fleece," Dark Grey or Silver Grey Blankets, colonial manufacture, 9-4, 10/6 ; 10-4, 13/6 ; 11-4, 17/6 ; 12-4, 21/-

THE FEDERATION CATALOGUE 45 FURNITURE FOR EVERYONE

FANCY WICKER CHAIRS.

VARIOUS SHAPES AND SIZES.

No. C 676.

No. C 677.

No. C 678.

No. C 679.

No. C 680.

No. C 681.
Nos. C 680 and C 681. Children's Wicker Chairs. Various shapes. White or Stained.

No. C 682.

THE FEDERATION CATALOGUE   47   FURNITURE FOR EVERYONE

No. C 245.
Easy Chairs, superior quality, well upholstered in best quality Saddlebags and Utrecht Velvet of any shade; extra large seat.
Various qualities.
No. C 246. As above, but upholstered with Cretonne.

COUCHES.
No. C 247. Superior quality, faithfully upholstered with best quality Saddlebags and Utrecht Velvet or Plush of any shade.
No. C 248. Upholstered with superior quality Cretonne.
Various qualities.

No. C 249. BOX OTTOMAN.
Superior Finish, upholstered with Cretonne, lined Sateen. Various qualities.

No. C 250.
Easy Chairs, upholstered with Cretonne.
Various shapes and qualities.

COUCHES.
With Spring Seats, Spindle Sides.
No. C 251. Covered with American Cloth. No. C 252. Covered with Cretonne.
With Spring Seats, Upholstered Sides.
No. C 253. Covered with American Cloth. No. C 254. Covered with Cretonne.

EASY CHAIRS.
No. C 255. Upholstered with American Cloth.
No. C 256. " " Morocco Leather.
No. C 257. " " Roan Skin.
Various shapes and qualities.

COLONIAL SOFAS.
No. C 258. Without Cushions. No. C 259. With American Cloth Covered Cushions.
No. C 260. With Cretonne Covered Cushions.

THE FEDERATION CATALOGUE   49   FURNITURE FOR EVERYONE

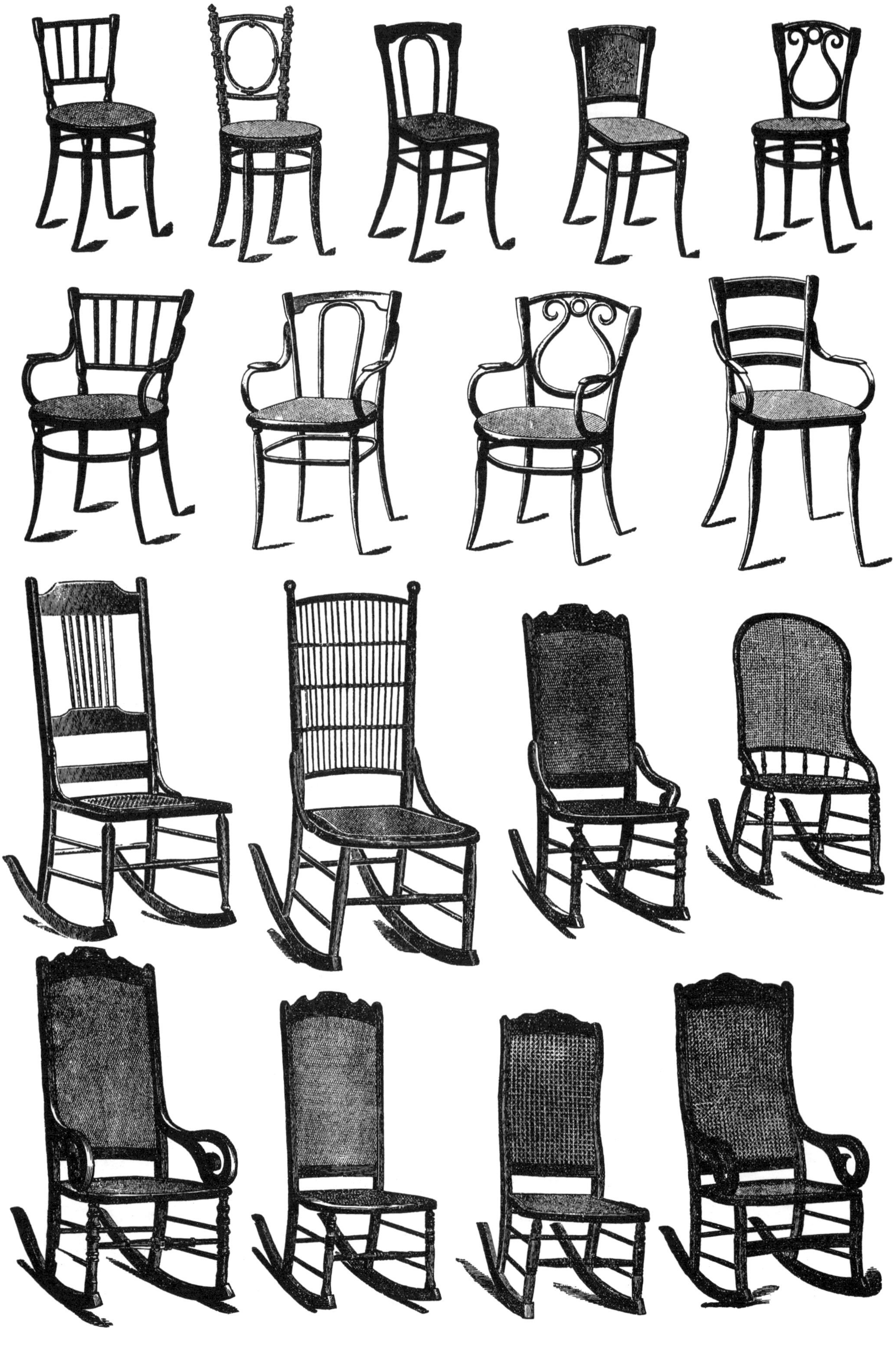

THE FEDERATION CATALOGUE 51 FURNITURE FOR EVERYONE

Wicker Knife Baskets. Baize Lined.
No. C 122. 14 inches, Two divisions.
No. C 123. 16   ,,   Three   ,,
No. C 124. 17   ,,   Four   ,,

Fig. 134.
Butter Prints.
¼, ½ and 1 lb.

No. C 126.
Wood Knife Boxes.

No. C 125.
Polished Striped Wood
Knife Boxes.

No. C 716.
Plate Covers, all White.

Fig. 133.
Butter Prints. (Boxed.)
¼, ½ and 1 lb.

Wood Bread Platters.
Various patterns.
No. C 127. 11 inches.
No. C 128. 12 ,,

No. C 129.
Wood Bread Platters.
11 inches.

No. C 130.
Wood Bread Platters. Octagon.
Various patterns. 11 inches.

No. C 909. Revolving Wood Rolling Pins.
No. C 910.   ,,   Glass   ,,   ,,

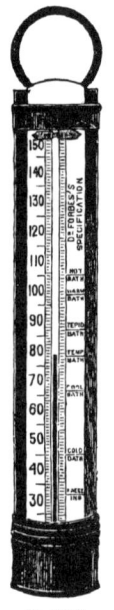

No. C 120. Best quality Copper Thermometer; 8 & 10 inches.

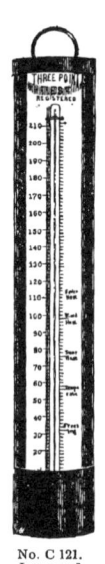

No. C 121. Japanned Thermometer; Best Quality; 3 point test; 8, 10 & 12 inches.

No. C 122. Japanned Thermometer Ordinary Quality; 8, 10 & 12 inches.

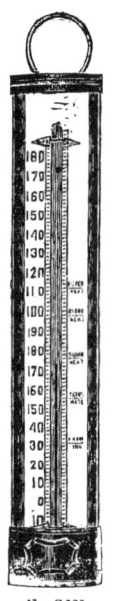

No. C 123. Bright Tin Thermometer; 8, 10 & 12 inches.

No. C 141. Combined Barometer and Thermometer. Polished Oak or Walnut. Various patterns.

No. C 142. Polished Oak or Walnut Barometer. Various patterns.

G722—"Rejane" Massive Enamelled American 8-day Clock, striking hours and half hours on cathedral gong, handsomely finished with metal pillars, 37/6.

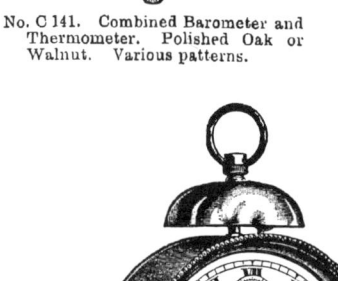

G714—30 Hours' Nickel-plate Alarm Clocks, good time-keepers. "The Queen," 2/9. "The Pirate," 4/6. "The Sunrise," 4/9.

G721—The "Silver King" Alarm, nickel-plated case, opal dial, with fancy centre, plain or Roman figures on dial, 7/11; same Clock, with plain dial, 7/6.

OUR STORES

are Closed on WEDNESDAYS at ONE O'CLOCK.

G718—Handsome American 8-day Clock, strikes at hour and half-hour on cathedral gong, in oak or walnut, 11/6 and 15/6.

G719—"Sorma."—Massive Enamelled American Cathedral Gong Striking Clock, beautifully ornamented, 35/. Slightly smaller and plainer, 30/-

G7110 "Triumph" American 8-day wooden Clock, strikes hour and half hour, beautifully ornamented, two mirrors, one on each side, will last a lifetime, 32/6

No. C 68A.   No. C 68B.   No. C 68C.

No. 68A to 68C.—American Eight-day Wood Clocks. **"Waterbury"** or **"Ansonia."**
Striking hours and half-hours. Six assorted patterns in a case.

No. C 69B.

No. 69A to 69C. American Eight-day Cottage Shape
Wood Clocks. **"Ansonia."**
Striking hours and half hours; six assorted patterns in a case.
We stock several assortments.

No. C 69A.   No. C 69 C.

No. C 70. Small Wood Clock.
One-day time; height, 12 inches.

No. C 71. Small Wood Clock.
One-day time; height, 12 inches.

No. C 72. Small Wood Clocks.
One-day time; height, 12 inches.

FEDERATION CATALOGUE
6. Leisure and Entertainment

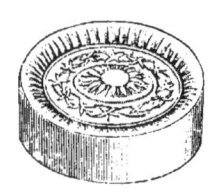

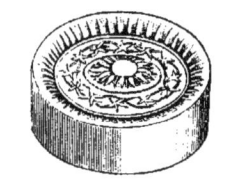

Leisure time, with the chance to have some entertainment, is an important aspect of life for most people in most societies. The degree to which this is achieved has always varied depending on the time, place and individual circumstances. By the turn of the century, conditions in Australia were comparatively good, and even very good when we compare the average family with their counterparts in other developed countries. The eight-hours movement, pioneered in Australia, set each twenty-four hour day into three parts; eight hours' work, eight hours' sleep and eight hours' recreation. Sunday was, in those days, kept fairly strictly as a day of rest and religious observance. Recreation in and around the home covered a long list of possible activities. Gardening, which typically included growing fruits and vegetables, was both work and a leisure-time activity. Hobbies included carpentry, model-building, needlework, wood-carving, painting, metal-work, wire-work, shell-work, china-collecting, weaving, rug-making, poker-work and keeping various sorts of animals. Besides hobbies, there were the leisure activities of reading, writing, playing games and listening to or making music.

Playing musical instruments and singing were traditional forms of household leisure and entertainment which, by the 1890s, were beginning to be affected by the technology of recorded sound. Gramophones or phonographs were the 'sound systems' of the Federation Era. Popular records were purchased and played by those who could afford the machines and their cylinders or disks. For many they remained a novelty only seen and heard at the house of a friend or at community gatherings. Singing to the accompaniment of a piano or other instruments had been the universal entertainment, but when recorded sound came along the 'gramophone selection' was often added to the traditional fare. Player and 'reproducing' pianos first appeared in this era, but were more numerous by the 1920s. They were always a luxury when even ordinary pianos were expensive.

Gramophone records followed the pattern established by sheet music in being an early version of the hit parade or 'top forty'. The latest songs, instrumentals and novelties were snapped up by anyone wanting to be up with the latest. Gramophones or phonographs went from being compact table models to a wider offering of designs which included cabinet models made to complement current furniture fashions. In spite of the 'new-fangled' machines, musical instruments were still bought and played by a broad cross-section of society. Musical sessions at home or out and about were great places to hear fiddles, concertinas, accordions and harmonicas. Mandolins, banjos, guitars, zithers, autoharps, tin whistles and jaw harps were also popular for playing 'homespun' music. The piano and harmonium could be

A rare glimpse of entertainment in the home during the Federation Era.
Courtesy: Ellie Goss.

formal or informal, with the latter being ideal for hymns and sacred songs. German settlers and their families seem to have helped make the accordion one of the prominent items in catalogues.

Photography became an accessible hobby with the introduction of the Brownie box camera in 1900.

With a darkroom set up at home, amateurs could cover all the steps involved in producing family photographs or whatever subjects were of interest. Special papers were available with pre-printed postcard backs. These enabled photographers, both professional and amateur, to offer personalised pictures to send through the mail. Postcards in general had become something of a craze and were soon being collected into albums. Ready-made 'scraps' were carefully arranged in albums or applied to objects, either useful or purely decorative. Découpage was even used to adorn folding screens, proudly displayed in the best room. Designs using shells, stones and pieces of broken ceramic or glass were applied to plant stands, urns, pots and panels. Shells were also applied to picture frames and trinket boxes.

Collectable china could be either old or new. Catalogues offered animals, figures and miniature tea-sets. Miniature china shoes were also keenly sought, just as they are today.

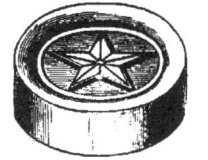

Picnics and cycling were favourite pastimes. *Collection:* the author.

Ceramic, glass or metal souvenirs were another group of items likely to be proudly displayed. Cabinets, sets of shelves, sideboards and mantelpieces were all used for keepsakes and collectables, artfully arranged. Photograph albums were treated as revered objects, not far down the line from the family Bible. Keeping family albums was a genteel pastime, showing pride in the immediate family and extended connections. Entering the births, deaths and marriages in the Bible was another affirmation of the importance of family over succeeding generations. Catalogues offered both family Bibles and photograph albums which were sumptuously bound in embossed leather.

Besides gardening, outdoor activities could include keeping poultry, pigeons, rabbits, ferrets and guinea pigs. Typical caged birds besides poultry were canaries, parrots, blackbirds and thrushes. Cages varied from simple to elaborate in a range of sizes. In the catalogues we find delicate brass or japanned iron cages along with seed cups, baths, water-containers and wire 'nests'. Brass canary cages, including designs for breeding birds, were notable items. Poultry was kept for eggs and meat, but also was one of the many 'backyard' interests which could be rewarded by prizes at the local agricultural show. In the Victorian country town of Merrigum, in 1898, the station master was breeding prize Plymouth Rock fowls and was rivalled by the schoolmaster who had fowls and a 'duckery'. By contrast, the retired schoolmaster had taken up 'Amateur Dentistry' and had the 'latest appliances for pulling teeth'. Treatment was free but it was 'all care and no responsibility.'[1]

Tennis was high on the list of popular games to be played at home. In many places this was simply informal lawn tennis and in dry times when water was scarce it was hard to maintain even a minimal covering of grass. Croquet too had its enthusiasts, usually at the genteel end of the social spectrum. Cricket in the backyard at home had become a much-loved tradition, as had kicking a football. In the Federation Era there were rope quoits with a standard wooden peg and iron quoits thrown toward an iron pin called a hob. Archery was another of the sports needing a reasonable area of ground, and catalogues offered archery sets for both young people and adults. Our modern preoccupation with fitness had its parallels with the turn of the century interest in exercises and drills using Indian clubs and dumbbells. Young women were now being offered a chance to enjoy such pursuits.

House parties and garden fêtes were a chance to socialise and to share the ideal of a well-appointed and well-kept house and garden. For both outdoors and indoor affairs, Japanese and Chinese paper lanterns were likely to offer both light and an exotic character. Many households gave a great deal of their effort and time to bazaars, fêtes, fundraisings and special celebrations. Many wedding breakfasts or receptions were held at home, and required a mass of preparations. The kitchen would be going full steam, while the rest of the house would be specially cleaned and decorated for the occasion.Preparing baked goods, produce, crafts and other goods for sale on stalls was part of being community-minded. One of the treats for private and public occasions was the magic lantern show. These early 'slide shows' included children's stories, novelties, Bible stories and travelogues. Fancy dress or masquerade parties were held on every scale and catalogues offered masks and various materials for costumes. It was also a time when fireworks were available to everyone, and bonfire night at home or at a neighbour's was one of the highlights of the year. For quieter indoor activities, the traditional games such as chess, checkers, dominoes, draughts, ludo and snakes and ladders were played. Card-playing was another popular pastime, except in families where cards, drinking alcohol and even dancing were on the list of unacceptable activities. People and families were varied in their notions of how leisure time should be spent. We may think we have more freedom and more choices, but it is hard to say that we have more fun, or are more contented.

Notes
[1] *Clothing — Plain or Fancy*, Kyabram Free Press, April, 1898.

PIANOS by the world's greatest Manufacturers: Bechstein, Brinsmead, Lipp, Feurich, Ecke and Thurmer. From £42 to 130 guineas.

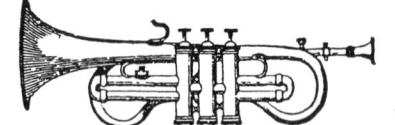

CORNETS—Boosey & Co.'s, London, and all the best makers.

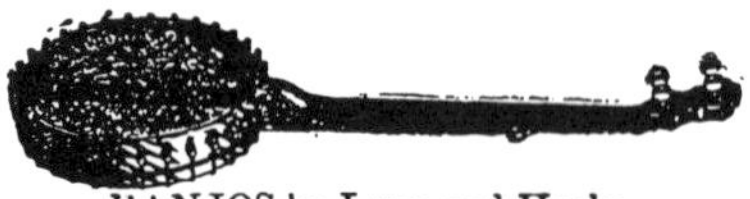

BANJOS by Lyon and Healy, Stewart, Dobson and others. From 25s.

GUITARS. Prices at 25s, 35s, 45s, and upwards.

MUSIC STANDS. For the Table, from 5s. upwards. Telescopic at 10s, 12s 6d & 15s upwards.

ESTEY ORGANS. From £13 10s upwards.

CASES

THE ARTIST MODEL (Allan's Patent)

MANDOLINS at 15s, 25s, 35s, and 45s.

MOUTH ORGANS. From 6d to 10s.

ACCORDEONS From 7/6 to 30s.

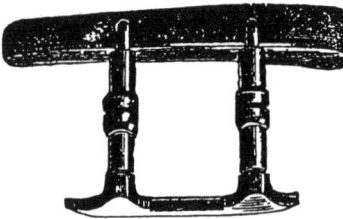

VIOLIN CHIN RESTS at 1s, 2s, 3s and 4s.

BRASS MUSIC STOOLS, With Plush Seats at 60s and 65s. Cheaper Models at 25s, 35s & 45s. Music Stools in Wood, best English make, from 25s to £5.

AUTOHARPS. Muller's, Meinbold's and others. From 15s.

TAMBOS at 1s 6d, 2s, 3s 6d, 5s 6d and 10s 6d.

MUSIC CARRIERS. Prices at 1s 6d, 2s, 2s 6d, 4s, 5s, 6s and upwards. A large selection to choose from.

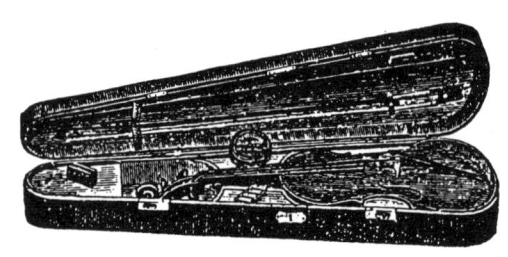

FLUTES from 6s 6d to 25s. Concert Flutes at 45s and upwards.

CLARIONETS Boosey's and other makers from £4 15s.

VIOLINS from 15s to £20.
BOWS from 5s to £10.
CASES from 7s 6d to £5.

PHONOGRAPHS

FROM **25s.** UP.

Including Reproducer, Horn, Records (from 2 up) and Portable Case.

Albert & Son,
118 King-st., Sydney.

Manufacturers of the famous BOOMERANG Mouth Organs.

Largest and Cheapest House in Australia. Catalogues of Violins, Cornets, Mandolines, Flutes, Accordeons, Banjos, Autoharps, Phonographs, Records, Music, Songs, Waltzes. Slot Graphophones and Slot Polyphone Music Boxes Posted FREE.

GRAPHOPHONE.

Very Latest Model.

IT IS A Natural Tone Talking Machine

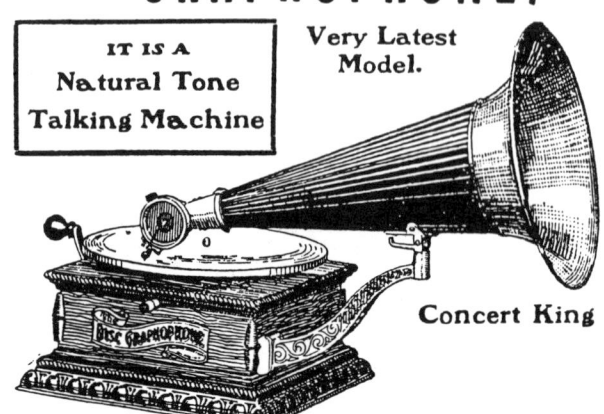

Concert King

THE FEDERATION CATALOGUE   59   LEISURE AND ENTERTAINMENT

No. C 18.
Plain pattern Violin Bows.
Various qualities.

No. C 19.

No. C 20.

Violins in several qualities. Full, half or three-quarter size.

No. C 31.
Violin End Pieces.

No. C 32.
Plain Ebony Violin Pegs.
Various qualities.

No. C 33.
Inlaid Ebony Violin Pegs.
Various patterns.

No. C 34.
Violin Resin.
Oblong shape.

No. C 10.
Nickel Pitch Pipes.

No. C 30.
Violin Bridges.
Various qualities.

No. C 8.
Folding Metal Music Stands.

No. 701.
No. 701.—Top 8¼ x 4¼ ins. 10 keys, 2 stops, 2 sets of reeds.
Black double bellows.
Case Oak or Rosewood, flat top, Nickel valves, Nickel clasps.

Double Row Pearl Keys.

No. 621.
Genuine steel reeds.
Divided reed plates, laid on finest leather, and screw fixed (no wax). Therefore unlimited durability.

Top 13½ x 8 ins.
21 keys, 4 basses, 4 working Wood stops, 4 sets of Steel reeds, 2 Coloured double bellows, Brass corner protectors, **four long bass valves.**

No. 621.
Ebonized panels, Mahogany mouldings, Mother-of-pearl keys, Gilt valves. Leather straps, Patent self acting spring clasps.

No. 619, same as 621, but 19 keys only.

No. 722.
Top 9 x 5¼ ins.
10 keys, 2 working Wood stops, 2 sets of reeds, Black double bellows, Nickel corner protectors.

Ebonized case, Nickel slips round top and bottom.
Improved Nickel valves, Leather straps, Patent spring clasps.
In nicely-finished
solid Mahogany case,
with Leather strap.

No. 722.

No. C 15.
Piccolos.
Various sizes.

No. C 9.
Nickel Tuning Forks.

No. 909.
No. 909.—20 keys, real Walnut case, Bone keys, Anglo Style, real Leather bellows.

No. C 4.
"**George Bauer**" Guitars.
Several qualities.

No. C 2.
"**S. S. Stewart**" Banjos.
In various qualities.

No. C 5.
"**George Bauer**" Mandolines.
Various qualities.

No. 26.

THE "ROYAL STANDARD."

Best Double Rubber.

A special Club Match Cricket Bat.

The pick of well-seasoned willow blades, hand hammered and compressed, fitted with best Rattan Cane and double rubber handle.

Our best selling line.

By Royal Letters Patent.

J. Darling's Patent Steel and Gutta-Percha Driver.
No. 22682.

IN introducing this Cricket Bat to all lovers of our great national game, we can with confidence say that the J. Darling's Patent Handle Cricket Bat is essentially the finest ever produced.

The component parts of this **Patent Handle** are a clever combination of the finest Rattan cane and elastic spring materials, with a highly-tempered forked steel spring.

It possesses unsurpassed resiliency, has a splendid whip and instant recovery.

The Blades are of the Choicest willow, straight grained, well-seasoned, HAND hammered and HAND pressed. Made and finished throughout by our best workmen.

Handles finished either in best russet calf leather, stitched on, or best red rubber cover, firmly solutioned on and bound with red twine at top and bottom, giving the bat a very attractive appearance.

"EVERY BAT BALANCED TO PERFECTION."

No. 17.

THE "AUSTRALIAN FAVORITE."

Selected Single Rubber.

A good driver; fitted with straight-grained blades, well-balanced and medium weight.

No. 9.

THE "POPULAR."

A very popular bat for club use. Handle of best cane throughout, with good sound blades of plenty of wood and straight grain.

Well seasoned and compressed.

Feldheim, Gotthelf & Co.,
SOLE AGENTS FOR
ANGUS & Co.'s
"POPULAR"
AND
"AUSTRALIAN FAVORITE" BATS.

No. C 200.
Iron Dumb Bells. All Weights.

No. C 201.
Wood, ¼, ½, ¾, 1lb.

No. C 198.
Indian Clubs in all weights.

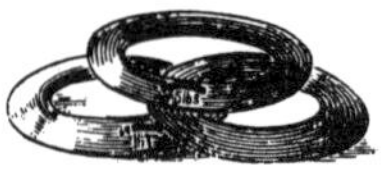

Rope Quoits.
No. C 207. Match size.
No. C 208. Youths' size.

No. C 209A.
Table Croquet, in Wood Boxes.
Various sizes.

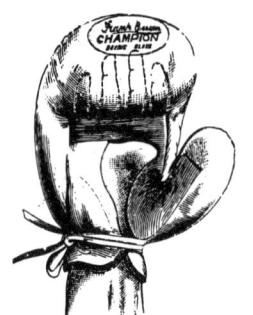

BRYAN'S "CHAMPION" BOXING GLOVES.

No. C 204.
Gold Cape, 4 oz.

No. C 205.
Gold Cape, 6 oz.

WITH OPEN PALMS.

LAWN TENNIS NETS.

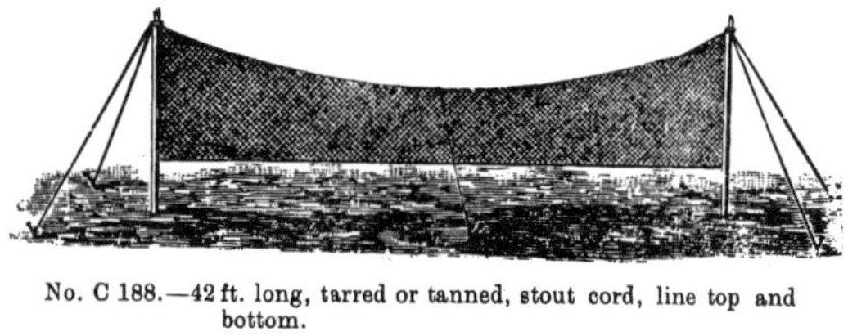

No. C 188.—42 ft. long, tarred or tanned, stout cord, line top and bottom.

No. C. 179.
Rules of Lawn Tennis.
In Cloth Bound Books.

No. C 160.
Australian "Champion."
A high quality Racquet, absolutely perfect in every detail, and recommended to players requiring a first-class Racquet.

No. C 161.
Australian "Federal."
An inexpensive Racquet strung with Best Quality Gut, Frame of English Kent Ash, and made in the best possible manner.

WISDEN'S AUSTRALIAN "FEDERAL" and AUSTRALIAN "CHAMPION" Racquets are made from the best quality materials procurable. They command a ready sale throughout the Commonwealth being specially made to suit this climate. We have been appointed sole Agents for these two Racquets.

Wisden's Racquets.

LAWN TENNIS SETS.

No. C 162.
Four Cedar Bats, 42ft. by 3ft. 6in. Tanned Net, Pine Poles, Lines, Pegs and Runners, Six Balls, complete in Deal Box.

No. C 163.
Four Cedar Bats, 42ft. by 3ft. 6in. Tanned Net, Pine Poles, Lines, Pegs and Runners, Rules and Six Covered Regulation Balls, in Deal Box.

Complete Sets in Wood Boxes.

No. C 164.
Four Best Cedar Bats, 42ft. by 3ft. 6in. Tanned Net, Polished Poles, Lines, Pegs and Runners, Mallet, Rules, Six Uncovered and Six Covered Regulation Balls, in Polished Box.

No. C 165.
Four Cork or Cedar-handled Bats, 42ft. by 3ft. 6in. Tanned Net, Stout Ash Poles, Lines, Pegs and Runners, Mallet, Rules, Six Uncovered and Six Covered Regulation Balls, in Stout Polished Box.

No. C 166.
Four Best Cedar Bats, Best Gut, 42ft. by 3ft. 6in. Tanned Net, Ash Poles, Lines, Pegs and Runners, Polished Four-Bat Press, Six Uncovered and Six Covered Best Regulation Balls, in Polished Box, with Lock and Key.

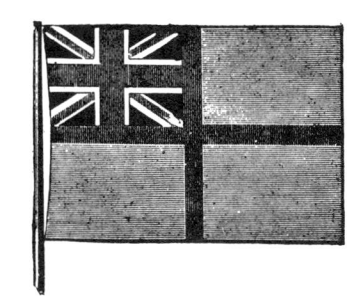

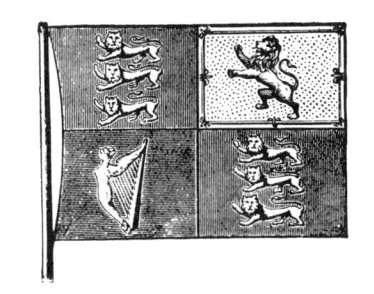

THE FEDERATION CATALOGUE   61   LEISURE AND ENTERTAINMENT

No. C 1. Flags. Various Nations and sizes.
No. C 2. Flags on Sticks. Various Nations and sizes.

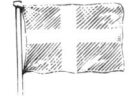

Small Flags for Decorating Christmas Puddings, etc.
No. C 3. Paper.   No. C 4. Gelatine.
Various sizes.

No. C 5.
Crinkled Paper Streamers for Decorating.
Various colors.

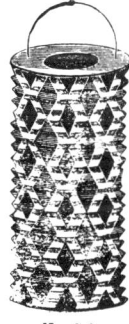

No. C 6.    No. C 7.    No. C 8. 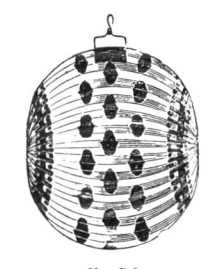   No. C 9.    No. C 10.    No. C 11.    No. C 12.

CHINESE LANTERNS.
A Splendid Assortment in Stock.

No. C 13.    No. C 14.    No. C 15. 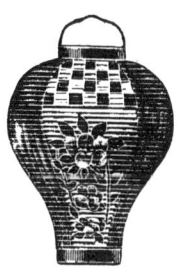   No. C 16. 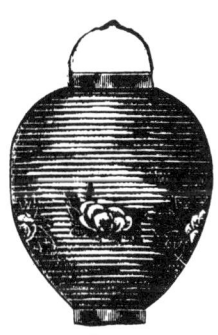   No. C 17.

JAPANESE LANTERNS.
A Large Assortment in Stock. Various shapes and sizes.

No. C 546.
Hand-painted Satin Fans. Various sizes and colours.

No. C 535.
Japanese Folding Paper Fans. Assorted sizes and patterns.

No. C 19.
Fancy Folding Paper Balls. Suitable for
Decorations or Fly Rests.
Various sizes and patterns.

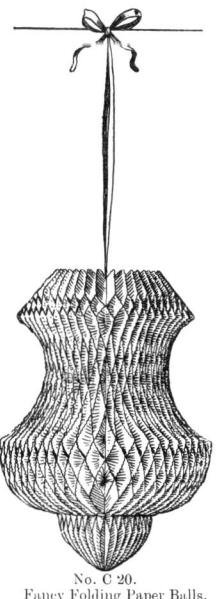

No. C 20.
Fancy Folding Paper Balls.
Suitable for Decorations or Fly Rests.
Various sizes and patterns.
An immense assortment always in stock.

FEDERATION CATALOGUE
7. Clothing — Plain or Fancy

On the question of clothing, in any era, there is always the primary distinction between everyday dress and the accepted fashions for special occasions. If we take those formal photographs in old family albums as being representative of the types of clothing worn by people in their everyday lives we can form a distorted view. There are many informal pictures which tell us that most people did adapt to practical needs, including the demands of climate. The influence of tropical dress from other outposts of Empire was seen in the early decades of European settlement and continued up to and beyond, the Federation Era.[1] This is particularly noticeable in photographs of picnics, tennis parties, sporting events and holiday excursions. Working clothes too were generally practical, the exception being those worn by people in formal occupations who succumbed to a dress code based on Old World demands. Clothes for winter weather in colder regions could logically follow cold climate fashions from Britain or Europe, but in hot summers or in the tropical zones, it was sheer madness to observe European fashion rules. Lighter fabrics such as muslins and cottons were much more sensible. Hats designed for coolness and protection from the sun could be both practical and fashionable.

For women, high fashion in the first fifteen years of the twentieth century meant large or very large hats, typically decorated with all sorts of bands, fabric flowers, feathers and even birds. The favoured body shape was a tiny waist, 'pouter pigeon' bosom and rounded posterior. We can see by the catalogue illustrations that corsets were essential to create the required form, and many brands competed with extravagant claims. If much of the fashionable clothing of the period from 1890 to 1915 seems to be impractical and overly elaborate by today's standards, there was in fact an underlying trend toward rational dress for everyday wear. Apart from the severity of many shirt collar designs, men dressed for offices and white collar jobs in much the same clothes as those worn today. To show their status as being above that of unskilled labourers, skilled workers such as engine-drivers and shopfitters might also wear a collar and tie; but the collar in this case would be a softer type. Waistcoats or vests were favoured at all levels because they were practical. The fob pocket carried a watch on a chain, the essential item for all who needed to keep an eye on the time. If labourers wore waistcoats, they would have an open-necked shirt and might roll up the sleeves. A neckerchief was often seen on workers in both the town and the bush. Women in offices, stores and schoolrooms found blouses and skirts to be practical, with a jacket and hat for travelling to and fro. In fact, almost everybody wore hats outdoors, particularly if they were in public areas.

Catalogues of the Federation Era offered a fascinating

Miss Billie Bourke, a stage celebrity and 'pin-up' girl. *Collection:* John Thompson.

array of hats for men, women and children. Men's hats can be divided into basic types: felt, cloth and straw. 'Hard hats' in black felt of the shape generally described as a boxer or bowler were worn by a wide cross-section of society for both work and recreation. In warm weather and especially for picnics and outings, panamas and straw boaters came into their own. At the upper levels of society, the silk top hat continued to be worn as a mark of distinction. These might also be worn by the clergy, although the traditional low-crown 'clerical' hat and the ordinary black soft felt were also deemed suitable. Tweed peaked caps were worn for driving, cycling and other outdoor activities such as shooting. They were also made for boys, being worn with the standard tweed suit. Sailor hats or tam-o'-shanters were part of the traditional sailor suit, a junior celebration of British naval power. The white tropical helmet, another symbol of Empire, held a place for excursions, travels and particularly for management or government work in the tropics. Drovers and other bush workers, who once wore both cabbage-tree hats and felt 'wide-awakes', now tended to wear wide-brimmed soft felt hats.

Girls in affluent families might wear decorated hats in the styles chosen by their mothers, while more average headwear was simpler. There were wide-brimmed felt hats in black, white and various colours, as well as basic straw models usually with a simple band and bow. The straw boater by Woodrows, seen on page 9, was a popular hat for both sexes. Old-fashioned hooded bonnets with a protective flap behind are familiar from romantic pictures of harvesting scenes in the British Isles and from American pioneer images. They are also well recorded in Australia, and in the Federation Era are seen in picnic and holiday scenes as well as photographs of women and girls at work outdoors.

Female working clothes in less affluent areas, and particularly in isolated bush places, were likely to be very simple and hardwearing home creations, or earlier fashions come down in the world. Poor people had no choice but to make their own clothing or to modify handouts and hand-me-downs. Those better off might make their own clothes to be thrifty, or simply because sewing was a genteel home activity. From the middle to upper levels of society, having clothes made was one of life's pleasures and an important social interaction.[2] The domestic sewing-machine introduced in the 1850s was in a large proportion of households by the Federation Era. Designs for clothing were offered in newspapers, magazines, books and catalogues. The Australian publication, *Weigel's Journal of Fashion*, was highly influential and Madame Weigel's paper patterns found a wide market.

There are as many interesting styles of footwear in old catalogues as there are hats. High button boots were considered elegant for ladies, while lace-up boots for both sexes and all ages were the staple of the trade. Shoes for cycling, tennis and walking were important, as were stout, watertight boots for farmers, labourers, miners and all who toiled in mud and slush. Hardwearing boots and shoes for children were certainly welcome, though not always seen as essential, for many youngsters went barefooted in all seasons. Elastic-sided boots have continued to be made in the designs seen in old catalogues and have become part of Australia's bush and country tradition. Bootmakers who were also boot- and shoe-repairers operated medium to small businesses in every corner of Australia. People also did a lot of their own repairs at home. By contrast, large stores and their catalogues offered ready-made footwear from mechanised factories. American manufacturers provided high-quality boots and shoes which made such inroads into the Australian market that local industry was forced to fight for a share.[3] Other items likely to be imported were shirts, ties, socks and underwear, along with various fashion accessories. On page 70 we can at least be pleased to see an Australian-made sweater for lawn tennis or cycling. This serves as a reminder that woollen sweaters were still mostly worn for sporting activities and the casual jumper as universal leisure wear had not yet taken hold. The woollen cardigan jacket, being more like a coat, was more acceptable. 'Gents Blue Denim Overalls' (see page 70) were strictly work pants and people would have been puzzled by the status of jeans in the latter part of the twentieth century. Much has changed in clothing and accessories over the years and yet it is also surprising to find much that is familiar in these catalogue pages.

Notes
[1] Margaret Maynard, *Fashioned from Penury*, Cambridge University Press, Melbourne, 1994, p.153.
[2] Maynard, p.132.
[3] Maynard, p. 122

Fashionable hats were almost a balancing act. This photograph was taken in North Fitzroy, Victoria, in about 1910.
Collection: the author.

THE FEDERATION CATALOGUE · 65 · CLOTHING — PLAIN OR FANCY

LADIES' RIPPLE BASQUE,

GIRLS' DRESS, WITH SQUARE YOKE.

8559

LITTLE GIRL'S DRESS.

LADIES' JACKET-BASQUE.

1895 - 1900

MISSES' DRESS, WITH FIVE-GORED SKIRT (To be Made with High or Low Neck).

3005

The two Greatest Salesmen on Earth—Quality and Low Price—work for us.

3245

GIRLS' COSTUME.

CHILD'S LONG COAT.

THE FEDERATION CATALOGUE — CLOTHING — PLAIN OR FANCY

G111—Dainty Blouse, in check or fancy flannelette, tucked at sides, box pleat in front, edged in small frills, 4/11, 5/11. In all-wool French or tartan flannel, 8/11, 9/11

G38—Housemaid's Washing Cap, in embroidery, 6d., 9d., 1/-

G256—Good Forfar or Print Apron, same style as shown, 1/-, 1/6, 1/11.

G259—Nurse's Apron, in longcloth, 1/11, 2/3; in drill, 2/6, 2/11; good quality and full size.

D410—"GLENA"—Felt Hat for child, with silk rosettes and strings, 4/11, 5/11; untrimmed, 2/6, 2/11, 3/11.

G223—Maids' Corset, with busk and shoulder straps, in grey, lined, 3/9; without straps, 2/6, 2/11

G365—Daintily Smocked Dresses for Children, in colored cashmere, pretty turn-over collar & smocked sleeves in cream, sky, pink, scarlet, 3/11, 4/11, 5/11; lengths, 19, 21, 24 inches

G322—Very Stylish Costume for young ladies. Russian coat with pretty yoke, turn-over collar of velvet or lace, finished smart buttons, skirt trimmed strappings of material. This costume we make in tweeds, serges and Panama, very special prices, 25/6, 27/6

G358—Splendid range in Children's Coats, nice deep cape, new strap back, stylish sleeve, in all the newest flaked tweeds, in navy, brown, light and dark grey—

24	27	30	33	36	39	42	45 in.
8/11	9/11	10/11	11/6	12/6	13/6	14/6	15/6

Also cheaper line—

24	27	30	33	36	39 in.
6/11	7/11	8/11	9/11	10/11	11/11

G366—Very Effective and Dainty Costume for young ladies, in cream, brown, navy, and black, in serge, cashmere, hopsack, and voile, bodice beautifully trimmed lace, yoke and deep cuffs as illustration, charming skirt with insertions and tucks, lined through, 29/6, 32/6, 35/-

1906

THE FEDERATION CATALOGUE — CLOTHING — PLAIN OR FANCY

1906

G2713 — Infants' Hand-made Wool Bootees, creme or mixed colors 6d., 9d., 1/-, 1/3; Imitation boots, in tan, wool soles, and white wool socks, combined, 1/3, 1/6

G276 — Infants' Wool Jackets in creme, pink & white, blue and white, 1/11, 2/11; hand-made, 2/6, 2/11, 3/11

G2712 — Children's Cloth Gaiters, in all colors, 1/-, 1/6; in wool, cardinal, navy, and fawn, 1/-

G277 — Children's Flannelette Pyjamas, 22, 24, 27in., 1/11; better quality, 2/6, 2/11; 30, 33in., 2/3; better quality, 2/9

G261 — Infants' Dainty Smocked Cashmere Frocks, in creme, white and colors, same as plate, 4/6, 5/11, 6/11; with small turn-down collar, finished with silk feather-stitching, 3/6, 3/11; cheaper line in nun's veiling, 2/11, 3/6

G279 — Pretty Wool and Silk Crochet Hood, ribbon laced through, 3/6, 3/11, 4/11, 5/11; cheaper quality, 1/-, 1/6, 1/11, 2/6, 2/11

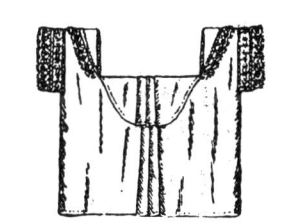

G262 — A Varied Assortment of Infants' Robes, trimmed muslin work and insertion, 10/6, 12/6, 14/6, 16/6, 21/-; cheaper quality, 5/11, 6/11, 7/11, 8/11

INFANTS' LAYETTES.

No 1.	s.	d.	No. 2.	s.	d.
3 Infants' Shirts, 6d.	1	6	3 Infants' Shirts, 7½d.	1	10½
1 doz. Turkish Squares	4	6	1 doz. Squares	4	11
2 Long Flannels, 2/6	5	0	2 Long Flannels, 2/9	5	6
2 Binders, 7½d.	1	3	2 Binders, 7½d.	1	3
2 Day Gowns, 2/3	4	6	3 Day Gowns, 2/6	7	6
1 Wool Shawl	6	11	1 Wool Shawl	6	11
2 Binders, 6d.	1	0	2 Swathes, 6d.	1	0
1 Bonnet	1	6	1 Wool Bonnet	1	6
			1 Robe	6	6
	£1 6	2		£1 16	11½

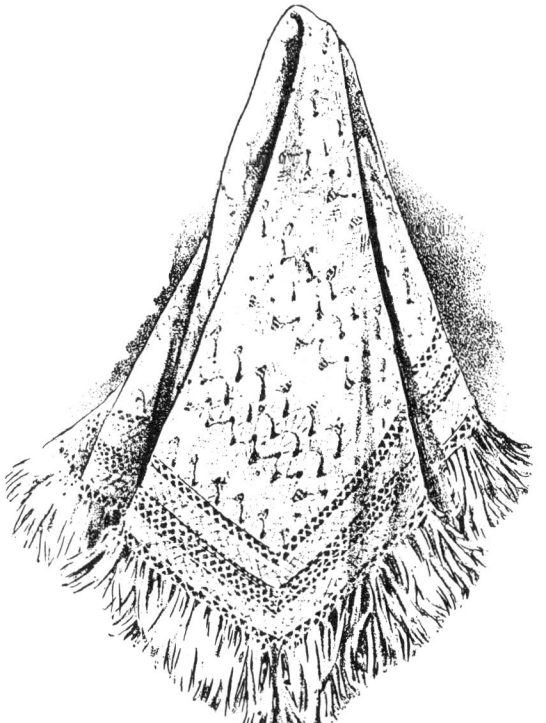

G264 — Infants' Muslin Shirts, trimmed Val. lace, 6½d., 9½d., 1/-

G263 — Infants' Cashmere Pelisses, trimmed embroidery and medallions, 17/6, 21/-; similar to plate, 12/6, 14/6, 15/6; cheaper line, 7/11, 9/11, 10/6

G265 — Infants' White Nainsook or Calico Petticoat, tucked and trimmed with embroidery, 1/11; plain, 1/4½, 1/6; trimmed with lace, 1/9

G266 — Infants' Nainsook Pinafores, trimmed lace and insertion, 1/11, 2/3, 2/6, 2/9, 2/11; cheaper quality, 1/-, 1/3, 1/6, 1/9

G267 — Infants' White Kid Shoes, 1/6, 1/11; in White or Tan Felt, 1/3

G268 — A Large and Varied Assortment of Infants' Wool Shawls, 2/11, 3/11, 4/11, 6/11, 7/11; better quality, 8/11, 9/11, 10/6 to 21/-

G269 — Children's Flannelette or Calico Knickers, with frills, 0 to 3, 9½d.; 4 to 6, 1/-; with lace or embroidery, 0 to 3, 1/3; 4 to 6, 1/6

1906

D11—"ADA"—Lovely Little Felt Motor Hat, for winter wear. Price, 4/11, 5/11.

D15—"VIOLA"—One of the latest shapes in felt. This shape is most suitable for riding or driving. In black, white, and colors. Trimmed with rosette and quill to match. Price, 6/11, 7/11.

D13—"THE STRAND"—Very Smart Felt Shape, in black, white, and colors, trimmed with band of ribbon and quill, 5/11; with wing, 6/11.

D14—"THE SURPRISE"—Something very chic. To be had in felt or straw, in all the leading shades. Drape of silk or velvet round the crown, finished with pretty buckle at the side. Bandeau at the side finished with wing or bird, and ribbon to match. velvet bind on edge of brim. Price, 12/6, 14/6.

G210—"GRACE"—Lovely Little Brown Fur Toque, with lace crown, and bunch of violets or roses at the side, 15/6, 16/11

D16—"LOUISE"—Smart Felt Hat, in all colors. Velvet fold to match, under brim. Trimmed with loops of ribbon round crown; 9/6, 11/6. In velvet, 12/6, 14/6.

We can only show you a few ideas from our immense stock.

We Pack MILLINERY in Boxes, specially made to ensure safe Delivery.

G155—A Stylish Velveteen Blouse, in all shades, with guipure lace yoke, finished with silk bow, tucked front, sleeve full into deep lace cuff, 16/6, 21/-

G156—Ladies' Flannelette Wrappers—large assortment—deep collar, trimmed with insertion, 10/6, 12/6, 14/6

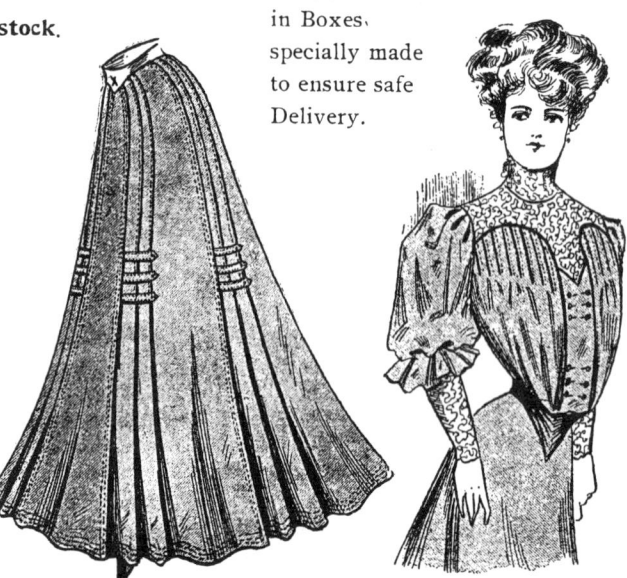

G157—Smart Skirt, in all the new shades of tweeds and cloths, pleated and caught with straps and buttons, 15/6, 16/6, 18/6, 21/-

G158—This charming Blouse in all the new fancy flannels, assorted designs, guipure lace yoke, tucked front, piping of velvet, 10/6, 12/6

THE FEDERATION CATALOGUE — CLOTHING — PLAIN OR FANCY

G691.—Ladies' Glacie Kid Bals., patent caps, facings and back golosh, welted, needle toes, 13/6

G692—Ladies' High Grade Glacie Kid Button Boots, patent toe-caps, 11/6

G693—Ladies' Strong Glacie Hide Bals., plain toe-caps, 5/11; patent caps, 6/6

G694—Children's Best Colonial Calf Bals, 7 to 9, 4/6; 10 to 13, 3/9; toecapped, 3d. extra

G696—Ladies' Fine Glacie Kid Button Boots, patent toecaps, 8/11

G695—Children's Glace Kid Button Shoes, patent caps, 7 to 9, 5/6; 10 to 13, 6/6; 1 & 2, 7/6; in glacie hide, 7 to 9, 3/11; 10 to 13, 4/11; 1 & 2, 5/11; plain lace, 3/6, 4/6, 4/11

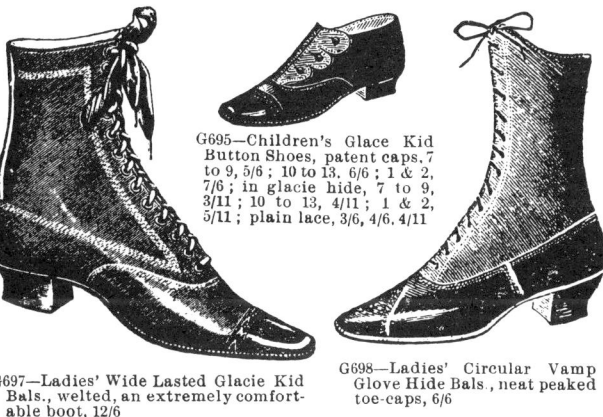

G697—Ladies' Wide Lasted Glacie Kid Bals., welted, an extremely comfortable boot, 12/6

G698—Ladies' Circular Vamp Glove Hide Bals., neat peaked toe-caps, 6/6

SEE HOW FLEXIBLE

G699—Ladies' Finest Glacie Kid Bals., welted, 11/6, 13/6; Button ditto, 9d. extra.

G704—Ladies' Best Grade Glacie Derby Shoes, pumps, 12/6

G709—Ladies' Glacie Hide Oxford Shoe, machine sewn, patent cap, 5/11

G706—Girls' Glacie Hide Sandal Strap Shoes, machine-sewn, 7 to 9, 3/6; 10 to 13, 3/11; 1 and 2, 4/11

G707—Ladies' Glacie Kid 2 or 3-bar Shoe, pumps, 6/11, 8/11, 10/6

G686—Children's Stout Kip Bals., riveted, 7 to 9, 2/11; 10 to 13, 3/6; solid kip, pegged, 7 to 9, 3/11; 10 to 13, 4/11

G687—Men's Best Glacie Kid Bals., welts, a very soft, comfortable boot, 18/6

G688—Best Quality Colonial Box Hide Bals., square or medium toes, 10/6

G689—Men's Machine Sewn Box Hide Bals. wide, medium, or narrow toes 8/11

G6810—Men's Glacie Kid Whole Goloshed Bals., light or medium soles, 11/6

G6811—Youths' Kip Lace Bals, pegged, sizes 1 to 5, 6/11, 8/11

G6812—Men's Colonial Calf Almas, best quality, only 11/6; Ladies' Calf Elastic Sides, 8/11

G6813—Boys' and Youths' Box Hide Whole Goloshed Bals., 10 to 13, 7/6; 1 to 5, 8/11; in stout kip, 6/11, 7/11

G6915—Children's Glacie Hide Shoes, tan or black, 7 to 9, 2/9; 10 to 13, 3/6

G7022—Ladies' Fancy Wool Slippers, 1/9; Gents' do., 2/6

G6815 — Tennis or Gymnasium Rubber Shoes, child's, 5 to 9, 2/6; 10 to 2, 2/9,

G695—Children's Glace Kid Button Shoes, patent caps.

OUR READY-MADE CLOTHING

Is made by the very best artisans, and is in many respects equal in appearance to order work, the difference being principally they are made in large quantities and to regular stock sizes. They are well cut, well finished, and perfect fitting. Special attention is given to the linings and padding, and in all instances are cut from reliable materials only. Special attention is devoted to our Juvenile Clothing, giving a good wearable article at the lowest possible price consistent with quality.

We can supply you with anything you require.

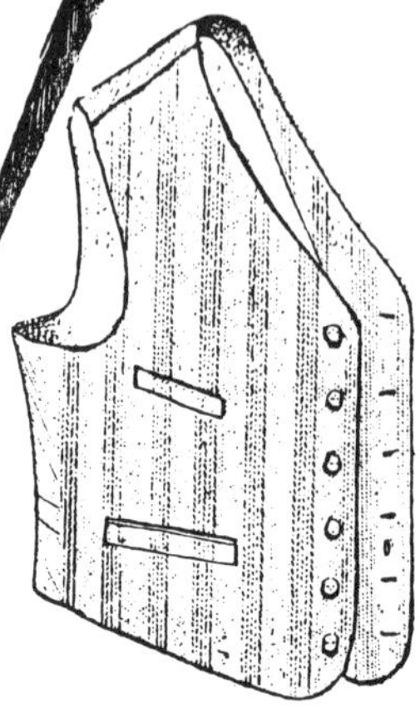

G611—Gents' Sac Suit, made of the famous Doveton Ballarat Tweeds, best Italian linings, padded shoulders, pocket flaps, perfect fitting, 15/6, 17/6, 20/-, 22/6, 25/-, 30/-, 35/-
Gents' Sac Suits, blue vicuna, equal in appearance to order work, 18/6, 21/-, 25/-, sizes 3 to 7
Gents' Blue Serge Sac Suits, fast indigo dye, every size guaranteed a perfect fit, 17/11, 19/6, 21/-
Gents' Sac Suits, in best Ballarat serge, warranted fast indigo dye, special linings and trimmings, 25/-, 27/6, 30/-
Gents' Sac Suits, of fine twill corkscrew, black or blue black, a perfect fit in each size, equal to order work, 30/-, 32/6, 35/-

G612—Boys' 3-Garment Sac Suits, lined knickers, made in fine heavy dark tweeds, strong suits for strong boys, sizes 9 to 13, 8/11, 10/6, 12/6, 14/6, 16/6, 18/6
Boys' 3-Garment Sac Suits, heavy Ballarat serge, fast dye, no end of wear, sizes 9 to 12, 12/6, 15/6, 18/6 ; size 13, 14/6, 16/6, 21/-

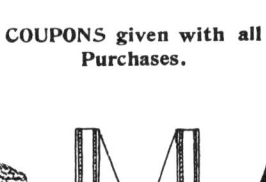

COUPONS given with all Purchases.

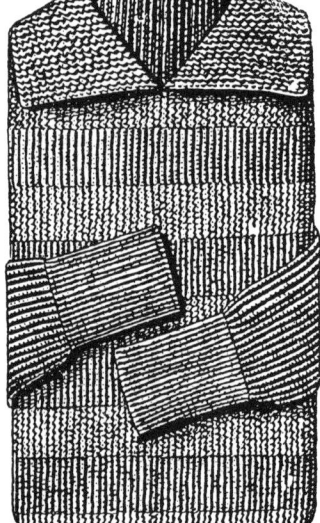

G613—Gents' Cardigan Jackets, black or dark brown, closely knitted, well bound, pockets, cuffs and fronts, 2/11, 3/6, 3/11, 5/6
Special Make, closely knitted, all pure soft wools, 6/11, 7/11, 8/6, 10/6
Gents' Cardigan Jackets, extra large sizes, in best qualities, 6/11, 8/11, 10/6, 12/6, 15/6

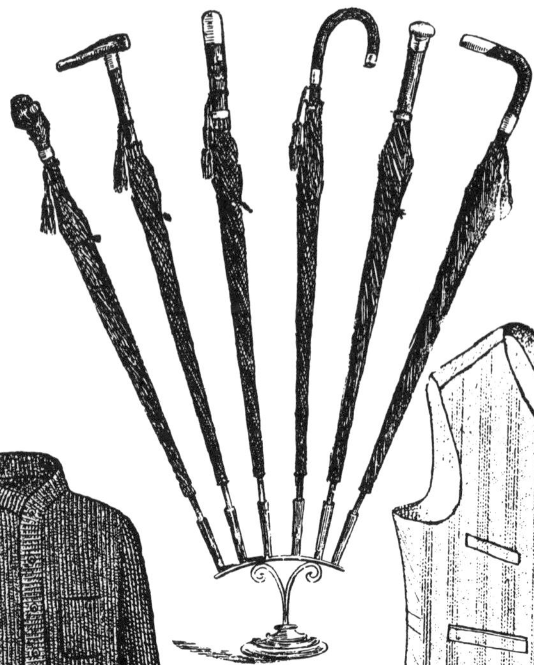

G614—Gents' Umbrellas, fast black silk twill, warranted to keep the color and not split, crook or plain handles, from 3/11, 4/6, 4/11
Special Line—Crook, plain, or horn handles, sterling silver mounts, 5/11, 6/6, 7/6, 10/6
Gents' Needle Point Umbrellas, very fine silk twill, heavy silver mountings, 12/6, 15/6, 17/6

G615—Gents' Vest, made of fine dark tweed, good strong linings and trimmings, sizes 3 to 7, 2/11, 3/6
Gents' Vest, heavy Ballarat serge, fast indigo dye twill, best canvas facings & Italian linings, 3/6, 3/11, 4/6
Men's Mole Vests, for heavy, strong wear, 3/6, 3/11 ; with long calico backs, 4/6, 5/
Men's Mole Vests, long mole backs, best made in the trade, sizes 3 to 7, 4/11, 5/6, 5/11

G668—Bicycle or Lawn Tennis Sweaters, Colonial made, in white, cream, brown, heather, or grey, 4/6, 4/11, 5/11, 6/11, 7/6, 10/6, 12/6. Prices given for racing and fancy sweaters of all kinds.

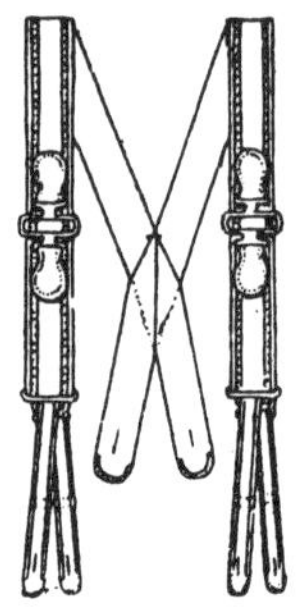

G666—The New French Brace, strong and light, 1/6, 1/11 pair

WHEN ORDERING, State the Colors you prefer.

G617—Youths' 3-Garment Sac Suit, made of dark Ballarat or imported tweeds, cut, finished, and lined like men's suits, sizes 11 to 2½, 13/6, 15/6, 17/6, 19/6, 22/6; also Fine Blue Twill Special Linings, size 11 to 2½, 32/6, 35/- ; Ballarat Serge Fast Indigo dye, 16/6, 18/6, 21/-, 22/6.

G616—Gents' Tweed Trousers, well made, best of trimmings, strong Ballarat tweeds, 4/11, 5/6, 6/6, 7/6. Gents' Striped Worsted Trousers, cut same as order goods, well made and finished, sizes 3 to 7, 5/11, 7/6, 8/6, 10/6, 12/6

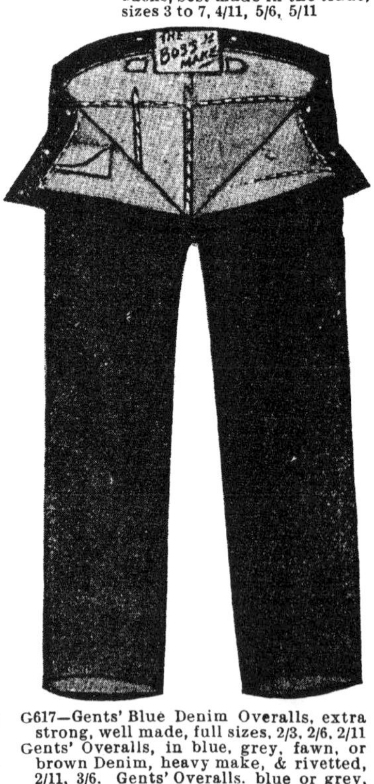

G617—Gents' Blue Denim Overalls, extra strong, well made, full sizes, 2/3, 2/6, 2/11
Gents' Overalls, in blue, grey, fawn, or brown Denim, heavy make, & rivetted, 2/11, 3/6. Gents' Overalls, blue or grey, our special make, double seats and knees, 2/11. Gents' Overalls, for extra heavy wear, double seats and knees, blue, fawn, or grey 3/6, 3/11.

G6511—Insertion Cuffs, for repairing white shirts, 6d. and 10½d. pair

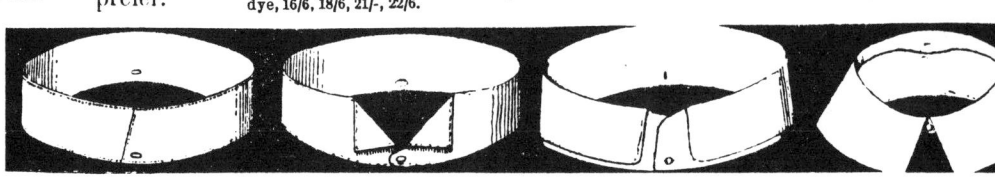

GENTS' CELLULOID COLLARS.

G6524—Military Collar, 2 and 2¼ in. deep, 6d., 8½d.

G6525—Prince Frederick, 2 in. deep, 8½d., 10½d.

G6526—Old Glory, 2 and 2¼ in. deep, 6d., 10½d.

G6527—Boys' Eton Collar, 6d., 8½d., 10½d.

THE FEDERATION CATALOGUE — CLOTHING — PLAIN OR FANCY

G631—Gents' Alpine Hats, wide silk band, wide leaf, in black, brown, and beaver, 3/6, 3/11, 4/6, 5/11, 7/6, 8/6

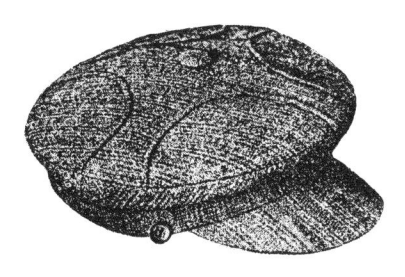

G632—The "Norfolk No. 1" Cap, smart and up-to-date, well finished. 2/6, 2/11

G633—Gents' Best Woodrow Alpine Hats, black, brown, and fawn, 13/6

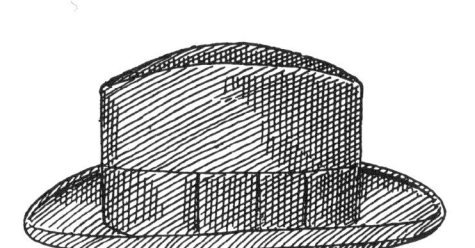

G634—Gents' Alpine Hats, wide silk band, silk bound edge, all fur, grey, fawn, black, or brown, 7/6, 9/6, 13/6

G635—Gents' Alpine Hats, wide silk band, bound edge, in slate or grey, 2/11, 3/11, 4/6, 6/6, 7/6, 8/6

G636—Gents' Black Hard Hats, in all the newest shapes, 3/11, 4/6, 5/6, 6/6

G637—Gents' "Imperial" Caps, best silkette lining, nobby pattern, 2/6, 2/11

G638—The "Canadian," most up-to-date cap now worn, best silk lining, 2/6, 2/11

G639—"Norfolk No. 3"—Gents' Strapped Motor Caps, neat patterns, 2/6, 2/11

G6310—Gents' "President" Hats, in black, fawn, or brown, 2/6, 3/6, 4/6

G6311—The "Seafoam" Black Hard Hats, all fur, 9/6

G6312—Gents' "Pelican" Caps, 1/-, 1/3, 1/6; serge, 1/-, 1/3, 1/6

G6313—Boys' White Felt Tams, wide crown, 1/9; white velvet corduroy, woven name, 2/3, 2/6, 2/11

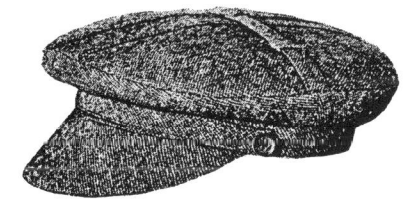

G6314—The "Norfolk No. 2" Cap, the newest shapes, 2/6

G6315—Youths' Alpine Hats, black, brown, cedar, or slate, 3/6, 3/11, 4/6, 4/11

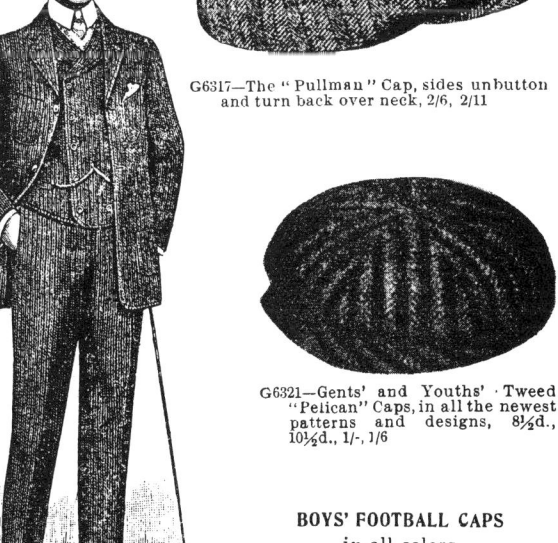

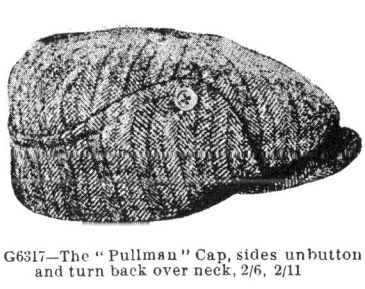

G6317—The "Pullman" Cap, sides unbutton and turn back over neck, 2/6, 2/11

G6318—Boys' Serge and Black Velvet Tams, very wide crown, silk woven name, silk tails, 1/11, 2/6, 2/11

G6319—Boys' Navy Cloth Tams, wide leaf, silk woven band, 1/-, 1/3, 1/6, 1/11; also in navy, fawn, maroon, scarlet, brown or green plush, best make, 2/11, 3/11; also in fawn, brown, scarlet, crimson, or maroon, felt and silk bands, woven name, 1/3

G6321—Gents' and Youths' Tweed "Pelican" Caps, in all the newest patterns and designs, 8½d., 10½d., 1/-, 1/6

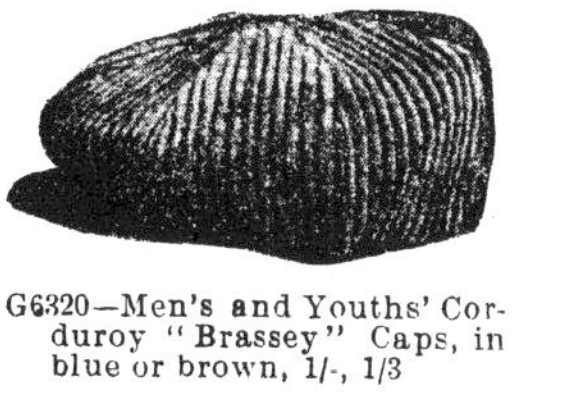

G6320—Men's and Youths' Corduroy "Brassey" Caps, in blue or brown, 1/-, 1/3

G6316—Boys' and Youths' Strapped Motor Caps, in nice selected tweed, 1/6, 1/11

BOYS' FOOTBALL CAPS
.. in all colors ..
4½d. and 6d.; in all-wool flannel,
.... 1/3 ...

1910 - 1915

One of the many striking designs in Imported Costumes of which Craig's are making a speciality.

Comfortable, Stylish, Serviceable

Knitted Coats

Materials Required:
About 1¾ lbs. of Paton's 3 or 4 ply Super Fingering, and four bone needles.

PATON'S
SUPER FINGERING.

Most Dealers stock Paton's Alloa Knitting Wools. If your's doesn't, write us and we will tell you the nearest who does.
Samples of all Paton's Wools sent free on application to

JOHN PATON, SON & CO., (A/sia.) LTD.
230 FLINDERS LANE, MELBOURNE.

One of the season's smartest designs in Day Gowns, produced in Chiffon Taffeta, of which immense variety of shades are available. Vest and winged collar of hemstitched lawn, the belt of fancy silk. Messrs. Craig, Williamson Pty. Ltd. will make this costume to order for £3/17/6 during August.

Maid's Coloured Crepe Costume, white Japanese Silk collar, 26/9. Messrs. Foy & Gibson Pty. Ltd.

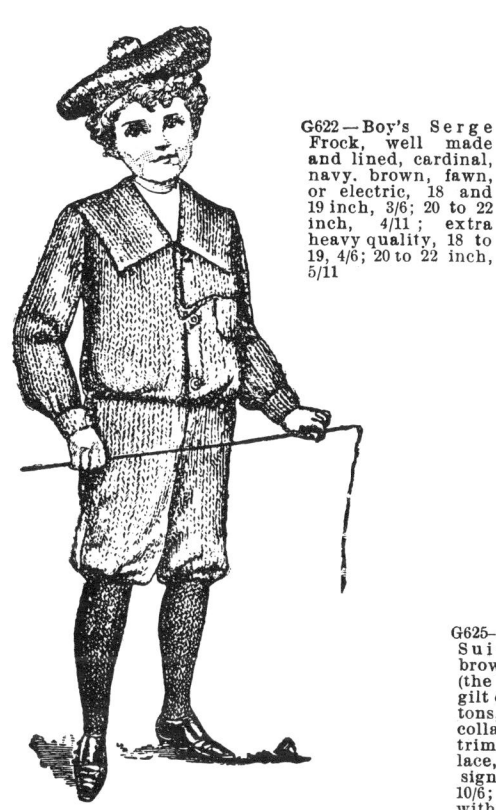

THE FEDERATION CATALOGUE   73   CLOTHING — PLAIN OR FANCY

G622—Boy's Serge Frock, well made and lined, cardinal, navy, brown, fawn, or electric, 18 and 19 inch, 3/6; 20 to 22 inch, 4/11; extra heavy quality, 18 to 19, 4/6; 20 to 22 inch, 5/11

G622.

G625—Boys' Velvet Suits, black, brown, or navy (the Fauntleroy), gilt or pearl buttons, white drill collar and cuffs, trimmed special lace, newest designs, sizes 1 to 3, 10/6; 4 to 7, 13/6; without collar and cuffs, 1 to 3, 9/6; 4 to 7, 13/6

G 74—Children's Frocks, in Fancy Flannelette, 2/11, 3/6; same as illustration—
Lengths— 24in. 27in. 30in. 33in. 36in.
Price—   2/11   3/6   3/11   4/6   4/11

SHOP BY POST

WE PACK CAREFULLY

To Ensure Goods Arriving in First-Class Condition

G621—The "Truefit" Sailor Suit, strong Ballarat tweed, well lined and smartly cut, sizes 2 to 6, 6/6, 7/11, 8/6; 7 and 8, 7/6, 9/6; 9 and 10, 7/11, 9/11, 12/6

WE WANT YOUR TRADE

But we want to feel that we Deserve it. That is why we give you the Most and Best for the :: Least Money ::

G625.

G627—Boy's Serge Tunic, heavy navy serge, box-pleated front and back, lined body and sleeves, sizes 18 to 24 inch, 4/11, 5/11, 6/11; tan or black leather belt, 1/- extra. Boy's Serge Tunic, with lined knickers, extra quality, 6/9, 7/11

G628 — Boys' Sailor Tweed Suits, for strong every-day wear, 3/6, 4/6, 5/11. Tweed Sailor Suits, neat patterns, fine serge fronts and whistle, silk lanyards, sizes 1 to 6, 5/11, 6/11, 7/6; 7 to 10, 6/11 7/11, 10/6. Heavy Serge Sailor Suits, fancy fronts, whistle, and silk lanyard, sizes 2 to 8, 5/6, 6/6, 7/6; 9 and 10, 5/11, 7/11, 10/6. All knickers lined throughout with strong-wearing linings. Best Ballarat Serge, with extra collar and front a pale blue or white, silk lanyard, and whistle, sizes 3 to 6, 8/11, 10/6, 12/6; 7 to 10, 10/6, 12/6, 13/6.

Jersey Suit

for all-round wear. In all-wool, 3 garment (including cap), various colours. 7/6, 10/6, 11/6, 12/6; Norfolk shapes. 15/-

624—Boys' Serge Suits, Duke of York, fast indigo dye, double-breasted vest, white or blue collars, sizes 3 to 10, 11/6, 12/6; sizes 11 and 12, 13/6, 14/6. Boys' Duke of York Suits, in Ballarat serge, very heavy weight, well made, best linings, double collar, sizes 3 to 10, 13/6, 15/6, 17/6; sizes 11 and 12, 15/6, 17/6, 21/-. Same as above, made in dark Ballarat or imported tweeds, specially selected patterns, sizes 3 to 8, 8/11, 10/6, 12/6; sizes 9 and 10, 9/6, 11/6 13/6, 14/6

FEDERATION CATALOGUE
8. Jewellery and Toiletries

Jewellery in the Federation Era was offered in a great diversity of designs, including a wide range of popular symbols. In keeping with the overall interest in Australia's national identity, there were many items which incorporated the word 'Australia' or an Australian map, or both. There were also fashionable 'Southern Cross' brooches with a gem for each star as well as the kangaroo, emu, lyrebird and kookaburra. Aside from these, the general range of jewellery seen in catalogues includes many universal symbols. Stars and crescent moons rivalled swallows and bows on brooches, pins and bracelets. Faith, hope and charity were represented by the cross, the anchor and the heart. The latter was, as ever, the symbol of love and caring, while the padlock suggested fidelity or security. Charms were found on bracelets, watch-chains, brooches and necklaces. Apart from hearts, anchors and crosses, there were wishbones, bells, lucky beans, horseshoes, keys, binoculars, drums, tea kettles, teapots, harps, along with such animals as cats, dogs, sheep, kangaroos and even pigs. Combinations of symbols on brooches and other jewellery included the arrow, crescent and star, the heart, key and diamond and the heart and lovers' knot.

Men were likely to wear 'gentlemen's charms', such as compasses, horses, horseshoes and the symbols of faith, hope and charity. They also wore special emblems if they were members of lodges or societies. The Masonic, Oddfellows and Buffaloes lodges were all represented in jewellery designs.

Keeping pictures of loved ones in lockets or brooches ensured a constant offering of suitable designs in gold and silver. Hair was also placed in jewellery and was even braided to form watch fobs. The jewellers were given enough of the loved one's hair to serve the purpose, and then added gold or silver mountings, including the toggle and swivel to attach to the pocket-watch. Other 'gentlemen's watch fobs' were made from silk, leather or woven wire. Watch-chains, either plain or ornamental, were called fob, vest or Albert chains. Open-faced watches for both men and women saved the need to release a cover to see the time. In a move toward the modern wristwatch, there were expanding 'watch bracelets'. Ladies might wear an open-faced watch suspended from an enamelled metal bow. American brands such as the Waltham watch ranged from high-quality, expensive pieces to models within the reach of the average pocket. Swiss watches, as ever, were held in high esteem. Ornate silver mounted stands were available, to best display a fine watch on a bedside or dressing table. As with all jewellery, there was a confusing list of terms devised to convince people they were buying a quality product when solid gold or solid silver were not used. 'Gold-filled', 'rolled gold', 'gold-plated' and

Miss Madge Lessing, a typical Edwardian 'belle', coiffed and dressed in the height of fashion.
Collection: John Thompson.

'gilt' were all used to describe layers of gold of varying thickness over a less valuable metal. The name 'Canadian' gold was used to describe gold-plated jewellery which would 'wear gold colour throughout'. Then there was 'Albo Silver', 'Mexican silver', 'Amnora silver' and the ubiquitous electroplated nickel silver. Various 'white metals' were used to avoid the obvious plated quality when brass or copper began to show.

Jewellery sections in old catalogues can display an extraordinary gathering of items and decorative designs. Besides the rings, necklaces, pendants, brooches and bracelets, there are belt clasps, hair ornaments, and all sorts of pins for hair, hats, scarves, ties, cuffs, lace collars and so on. For men there were collar studs and cufflinks; the best in gold with diamonds, others in silver, with or without precious or semi-precious stones. Anyone who considered himself or herself of some social standing would carry a small case for visiting cards. Some cases were in mother-of-pearl inlay, others were of silver. There were purses made to carry gold sovereigns and also sovereign cases. Women of fashion had chatelaine bags which were pinned to their costume or delicate 'wrist bags'.

Ornamental jewellery boxes were likely to be seen on dressing-tables, along with pin-cushions, pin-trays, hair tidies, manicure sets, scent bottles and puff boxes. Catalogues offered ceramic toilet sets consisting of a tray on which sat one or two candlesticks, a ring tree, a powder jar, a pin-holder and one or two bottles for scented water. Silver-backed brush, comb and mirror sets were widely used, with the 'plastic' material 'Xylonite' also finding a place. There were silver-mounted or silver-plated cloth, hat and nail brushes and toilet sets with nail file, cuticle knife, shoe-horn, button hook, as well as a nail brush and hand brush. Fitted dressing rolls and cases contained hair and clothes brushes and manicure sets. Glove and handkerchief sachets were yet another boudoir item. Men's shaving gear was offered in catalogues in an extensive range from basic needs to elaborate cased sets suitable for both home and travel. The safety razor appeared in the early 1900s but in Australia the 'cut-throat' type kept its popularity for a long time. Ceramic or metal shaving mugs came in a host of designs and have become collectors' items. Shaving brushes produced a lather from shaving cream or soap. Some soap came in the form of shaving sticks in printed tin containers.

Dental care would have been of no interest to many people, while others were showing the concern which has become almost universal in more recent times. Sadly, bad nutrition due to poverty and ignorance saw many with bad teeth. These were often completely removed at an early stage. Collectors have been reminded of dental care in past eras by the survival of ceramic containers for Cherry Tooth Paste. A number of London firms made cherry-flavoured toothpaste, including Gosnell's, Maw's and Breidenbach's. There was also Calvert's Carbolic Tooth Paste, bottles of Colgate's Liquid Dentifrice and tin boxes of Fletcher's tooth powder in three flavours: carbolic, cherry and camphorated chalk. Toothbrushes were offered with metal, bone or composition (early plastic) handles and claims were already being made for various arrangements of bristles. Hair combs were made in metal, bone and ivory and in 'plastic' materials such as 'Xylonite', 'Vulcanite' and 'imitation tortoise-shell'.

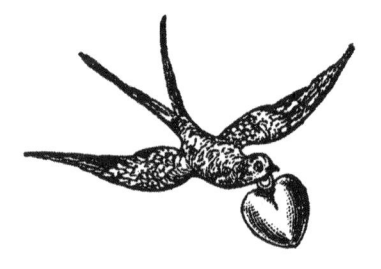

Toiletries such as soaps and perfumes benefited greatly in their presentation from advances in colour printing. During the Federation Era, lavish packaging was used to capture expanding world markets for mass-produced household needs. Full colour labels on bottles, boxes, tins, wrappings and seals created an impression of lavish production and a first-quality product. Toilet soaps from British, European and American manufacturers were often presented in superbly decorative wrappers and boxes. Perfumes were in ornamental bottles, sometimes of fine quality, often with ribbons and fancy seals in keeping with their sumptuous labels. Eau de Cologne and lavender-water were similarly packaged. Rose, violet, sweet peas, wallflower, apple blossom and many other fragrances were used for fashionable perfumes. Fragrant powders were another important item, especially face powders. Perfumes had an important role to play in a world where disagreeable odours might be far more prevalent. Making do with regular washes and a ritual weekly bath was a well-established tradition. Showers were not very common and for many people, baths or showers were an irregular event. The fully-equipped bathroom was a showpiece in affluent households and for the rising middle class a fully-plumbed bathroom attached to or within the house was not a part of suburban expectations. Those who could afford diamonds and pearls could also afford the best French toiletries, while others chose the popular, less expensive signs of gentility.

THE FEDERATION CATALOGUE — JEWELLERY AND TOILETRIES

No. E6797.—New Elegant Design, 9c. Gold Brooch, Set Diamond, Ruby and Sapphire, 14s 6d.

No. E7364.—New Lucky Bean Pin Charm, 9c. Gold, 4s 6d.

No. 111.—New Bar Brooch, Amethyst, and 9c. Gold, 10s. 6d.

No. E7364.—New Lucky Bell Pin Charm, 9c. Gold, 4s 6d.

No 512.—Heart and Lovers' Knot Brooch. Artistic Design, Amethyst and 9c. Gold, 18s 6d.

No. 184A.—Keeper, 18c. Gold, £1 7s 6d.

No. 162.—3 Fine Diamonds, 18c. Gold, £4 17s 6d.

No. 165.—2 Rubies, 1 Diamond, 15c. Gold, £1 5s.

No. 183.—Elegant Carved Keeper, 18c. Gold, £2.

No. 172.—Fine White Diamond, £4 10s. Larger, £5 10s.

No. 176A.—Lady's or Gent's 18c. Gold Band Ring, £1 1s, £1 10s, £2.

No. 171.—18c. Gold, 9 Diamonds, 3 Sapphires, £3 10s.

No. 160.—1 Diamond, 2 Rubies, 18c. Gold, £2.

No. 178.—Wedding Ring, 18c. Gold, £1 1s.

No. 150.—15c. Gold Bracelet, 1 Diamond, 2 Rubies, £4 7s 6d.

No. 208.—15c. Gold Heart, 10s 6d. 9c. ditto, 6s 6d.

No. 139.—9c. Gold Bracelet, Ruby Centre, £1 2s 6d.

No. 217.—15c. Gold Heart, Diamond and Sapphire, £1 5s.

No. 134.—15c. Gold Bracelet, set 2 Diamonds, 3 Sapphires, £7 10s.

No. 153A.—Daisy Brooch, 8 Fine Diamonds, 3 Rubies, £4 17s 6d.

No. 125.—15c. Gold Brooch, 4 Diamonds, 3 Rubies, £2 15s.

No. 115A.—9c. Gold Two Bar Brooch, Amethyst Centre and Heart, £1 5s.

No. 117.—Pretty 15c. Gold Bar Brooch, 1 Diamond, 2 Rubies, £1 7s 6d.

No. 157.—Elegant Scroll Brooch, 14 Fine Diamonds, 2 Whole Pearls, 3 Rubies, £6 15s.

No. 130.—15c. Gold Opal and Diamond Bracelet. New and Handsome Design, £12 10s.

No. 108.—The "Little Pet's" Bracelet, 9c. Gold, 15s. 6d.

No. 148.—Solid Gold Bracelet, 3 Diamonds, 4 Rubies, £4 4s.

No. 756.—The New Lucky Bells. Latest London Novelty. 9c. Gold 5-Bell Bracelet, £1 10s. Ditto, 3-Bell, £1 5s.

No. 201.—Set Links. 9c. Gold £1 1s ; 15c. Gold £2 Silver, 6s 6d.

No. 194A.—Set Links. 9c. Gold, £1 5s ; 15c. Gold, £2 10s. Silver, 4s 6d.

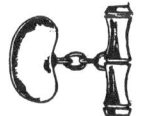

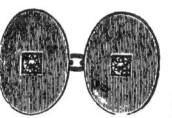

No. 124A.—15ct. Gold and Amethyst Brooch, Special Value, £1 7s 6d.

No. 193A.—Set Links. 9c. Gold, 12s 6d ; 15c. Gold, £1 5s. Silver, 3s 6d.

No. 120.—15c. Gold, Diamond, and Ruby Brooch, £2.

No. 130.—Set Heavy 18c. Gold Links, Set with Fine Diamonds, £8 10s.

No. 199A.—Set Links. 9c. Gold, 18s 6d ; 15c. Gold, £1 17s 6d ; Silver, 5s 6d.

No. 242.—15c. and Pearl Wish-Bone, 10s 6d.

No. 235.—15c. Heart, Key and Diamond, £1 12s 6d.

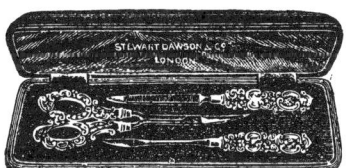

No. 233.—15c., set Pearls, 15s 6d.

No. 240.—Double Shoe, set Pearls, £1 5s.

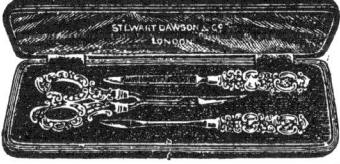

No. 286.—Elegant Photo. Frame, Solid Silver, Cabinet size, 16s 6d. Plain Silver, Midget size, 4s.

No. 311.—Solid Silver Bon-Bon Dish, 6½in. by 5in., £1 7s 6d. Other Designs, £1 10s.

No. 268A.—Set of Solid Silver Manicure Instruments; Nail File, Scissors, and Cuticle Knife, in Case, 17s 6d.

No. 316.—Solid Silver Sweet Dish, 3½in. long, 12s 6d. Others, 18s 6d and £1 1s.

No. 298.—Solid Silver Serviette Ring, 6s 6d. Best Silver Plate, 3s 6d and 4s.

No. 246.—Telescopic Pencil, very Special Value, Finest Finish. 9-c. Gold, £1 15s. Sterling Silver, 10s 6d.

No. 245.—Sterling Silver Cedar Pencil Case, 4s. Heavy 9c. gold, £1 15s.

No. 290.—Silver Mounted Toilet Salts Bottle, 2¼in. high, 6s 6d. Larger, 7s 6d and 10s 6d.

No. 297.—Solid Silver Thimble, Steel lined, 3s 6d. Others, 1s and 1s 6d.

No. 285.—Finest Cut Glass, Silver Mounted Salts Bottle, 16s 6d. Size larger, 18s 6d. Small sizes 3s 6d & 4s 6d

No. 282.—Silver Boot Button Hook, 8s 6d. Shoe Lift to Match, 10s 6d. Glove Button Hook, 2s 6d.

No. 284.—Cut-Glass Puff Box, with Solid Silver Top, 3in. high, £1 1s.

No. E7121.—Best Silver-plated SMOKER'S COMPANION, comprising Tray, Cigar Holder, and 2 Ash Holders, £1 10s.

No. 302A.—Two Solid Silver Gent.'s Hair Brushes, in Case, £3 3s.

No. 253.—Solid Silver Match-Box, 10s 6d. Plain, 8s 6d.

The "Triumph" Watch for Gentlemen or Youths is a Gigantic Triumph over any other low-priced Watch already in the market. Polished Nickel, Keyless, Short Wind, 18s 6d.

Heavy Solid Silver Clasps, New and Elegant Designs, 16s 6d, 18s 6d, £1 1s. (DRAWN HALF-SIZE).

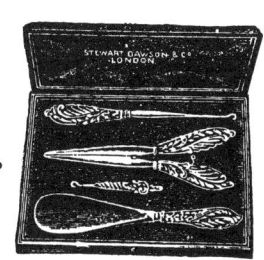

No. 321.—Silver Glove Stretcher, 6½in. long, Shoe Lift, and Button Hooks, in Morocco Case, £1 10s.

D731—Double Bar Brooch, set with 11 Pearls, 2 Rubies or Sapphires, 9ct. gold, 20/; 15ct. 32/6.

D732—Double Bar Brooch, set with Ruby or Sapphire, 9ct. gold, 14/6; 15ct., 21/.

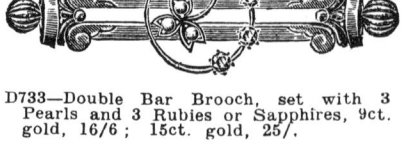

D733—Double Bar Brooch, set with 3 Pearls and 3 Rubies or Sapphires, 9ct. gold, 16/6; 15ct. gold, 25/.

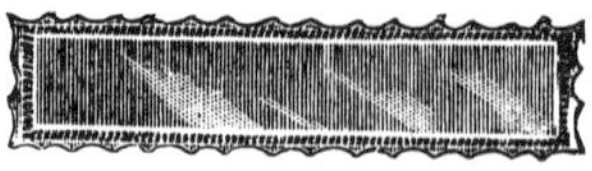

D734—Bell Brooch, chased, 9ct. gold, 10/; 15ct. gold, 15/.

D735—Beautiful Arrow and Crescent Brooch, set with 35 Pearls, 30/.

D736—Bar Brooch, 9ct. gold, 6/; 15ct. gold, 10/6.

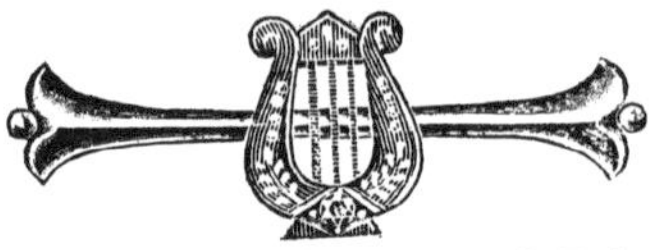

D737—Swallow Brooch, set with Pearls and Rubies or Sapphires, 9ct. gold, 12/6; 15ct. gold, 19/6.

D7310—Pretty Design, set with Ruby or Sapphire, 9ct. gold, 7/6.

D7311—Set with 8 Pearls, 9ct. gold, 11/; 15ct. gold, 17/6.

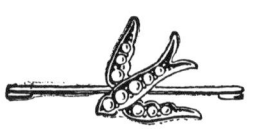

7312—Safety Pin Brooch, Swallow, set with 11 Pearls, 9ct. gold, 7/11.

D738—Star Brooch, set with 42 Real Pearls, 15ct. gold, £2/12/6.

D739—Star Brooch, set with 39 Real Pearls, 15ct. gold, 60/.

D7313—Double Bar Brooch, Swallow, set with 5 Pearls and 7 Rubies or Sapphires, 9ct. gold, 14/6.

ALL BROOCHES

are guaranteed as represented, are neatly packed in small boxes, and sent Post Free per registered post.

D7314—Double Bar Brooch, set with 2 Pearls and Sapphires or Ruby, 9ct. gold, 15/; 15ct. gold, 22/6.

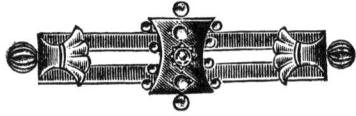

D7315—Double Bar Brooch, set with Ruby or Sapphire, 9ct. gold, 11/; 15ct. gold, 17/6.

D7316—Swallow Brooch, set with 9 Pearls, 9ct. gold, 15/6; 15ct. gold, 25/6.

D7321—Double Bar Brooch, set with 2 Pearls and Ruby or Sapphire, 9ct. gold, 13/6.

D7318—Single Bar Harp Brooch, set with 2 Real Pearls and Sapphire or Ruby. 9ct. gold, 14/; 15ct. gold, 21/.

D7317—Double Bar Brooch, set with 2 Pearls and Ruby or Sapphire, 9ct. gold, 11/; 15ct., 18/6.

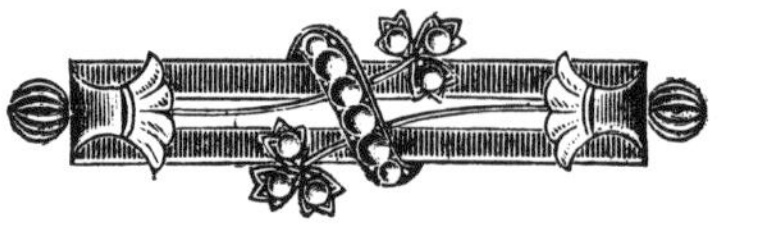

D7319—Neat Design Brooch, set with Ruby or Sapphire, 9ct. gold, 10/6; 15ct. gold, 13/6.

D7320—Crescent Brooch, set with Ruby or Sapphire, 9ct. gold, 10/; 15ct. gold, 16/6.

D7322—Neat Design Shield Brooch, set with Ruby or Sapphire, 9ct. gold, 7/6; 15ct. gold, 12/6.

D7323—Pretty Design Brooch, set with Ruby or Sapphire, 9ct. gold, 10/; 15ct. gold, 15/6.

D7324—Double Bar Brooch, set with 12 Real Pearls, 9ct. gold, 15/6; 15ct. gold, 22/6.

D7325—Double Bar Greenstone Brooch, set with 8 Pearls, 9ct. gold, 15/6.

G7218—Dress Ring, set with Ruby or Sapphire, 20/.

G7219—Dress Ring, set with 6 Diamonds, 45/.

G7220—Engagement Ring, set with 2 Diamonds and 3 Rubies or Sapphires —18ct. gold, 52/6.

G7221—Dress Ring, set with 6 Rubies or Sapphires, 1 Diamond, and 4 Roses —15ct. gold, £2/15/.

G7222—Dress Ring, set with Sapphire or Ruby and 2 Roses, 15ct. gold, 27/6.

G7223—Dress Ring, 4 Pearls and Ruby— 9ct. gold, 15/; 15ct. gold, 40/; set with 5 Diamonds, 60/.

THE FEDERATION CATALOGUE — 79 — JEWELLERY AND TOILETRIES

G741 — Gold Locket, beautifully finished, 9 ct. gold, 27/6; 15 ct. gold, £2/5/-.

G742 — Gold Medal, neat design, 9 ct. gold, 10/6; 15 ct. gold, 17/6.

G743 — Gold Locket, 9 ct. gold, 20/-; 15 ct. gold, 30/-.

G744 — Gold Medal, pretty design, 9 ct. gold, 15/6; 15 ct. gold, 22/6.

G745 — Gold Pendant, Masonic emblem, 9 ct. gold, 8/11; 15 ct. gold, 15/6.

G746 — Gold Medal, handsome design, 9 ct. gold, 17/6; 15 ct. gold, 27/6.

G747 — Cross Pendant, beautifully chased, 9 ct. gold, 6/11; 15 ct., 10/6.

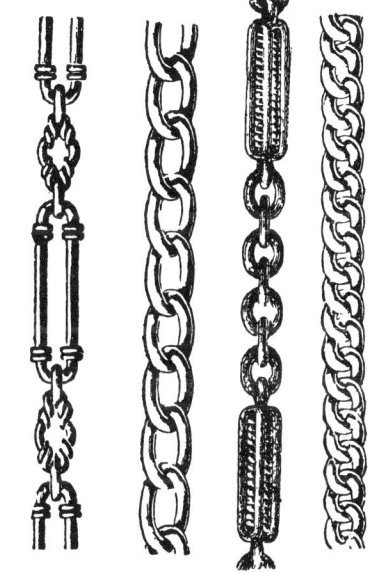

G748 — Gents' Double-pocket Watch Chains; we can do any of the above in silver, at 8/6, 10/6, 12/6; in 9 ct. Gold, 80/-, 85/-, 90/-; in 15 ct. gold, 110/-, 120/-, 130/-.

G749 — Gents' Sleeve Links, 9 ct. gold, set with opal, 18/11; with ruby or sapphire, 17/6; 15 ct. gold, set with opal, 33/6; with ruby or sapphire, 32/6.

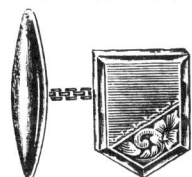

G7410 — Gents' Sleeve Links, 9 ct. gold, 16/6; 15 ct gold, 28/6.

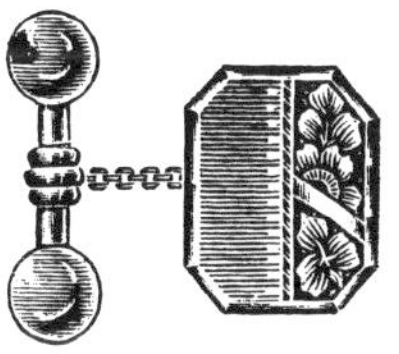

G7411 — Gents' Sleeve Links, 9 ct. gold, 15/6; 15 ct. gold, 27/6.

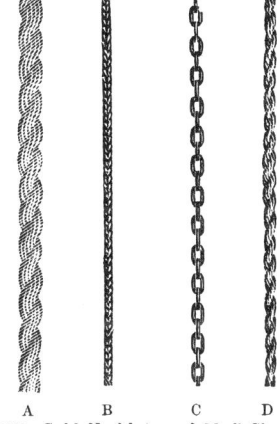

G7412 — Gold Necklets and Muff Chains. A — Necklet, 9 ct. gold, 21/-; Muff Chain, 9 ct., 60/-. B — Necklet, 9 ct gold, 12/6; Necklet, 15 ct. gold, 20/-; Muff Chain, 9 ct gold, 45/-; Muff Chain, 15 ct gold, 67/6. C — Necklet, 9 ct. gold, 13/6; Necklet, 15 ct. gold, 24/6; Muff Chain, 9 ct gold, 42/-; Muff Chain, 15 ct. gold, 67/6. D — Necklet, 9 ct. gold, 6/11; Necklet, 15 ct. gold, 17/6; Muff Chain, 9 ct gold, 29/6; Muff Chain, 15 ct. gold, 50/-.

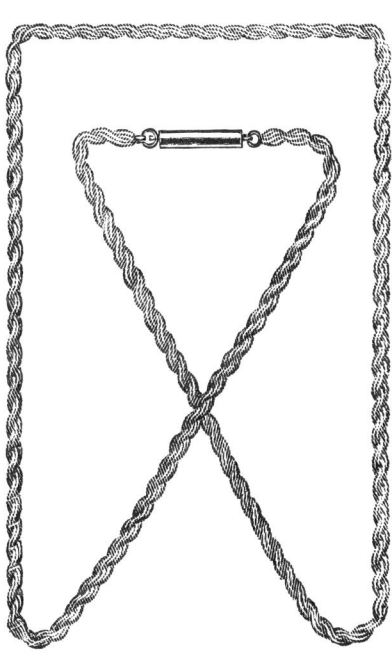

G7413 — Very Neat Pendant, 9 ct. gold, 8/6; smaller size, plain circle, 4/11.

G7414 — Collar Stud, 9 ct. gold, 4/-; 15 ct. gold, 7/6; 3 Front Studs, 9 ct. gold, 10/6; 15 ct. gold, 15/6.

G7415 — Evening Dress Stud, plain top, 9 ct. gold, 2/9; set with ruby, 4/6.

G7416 — Set with two pearls and two rubies or sapphires, 15 ct. gold, 10/6; set with two pearls and two diamonds, 13/6.

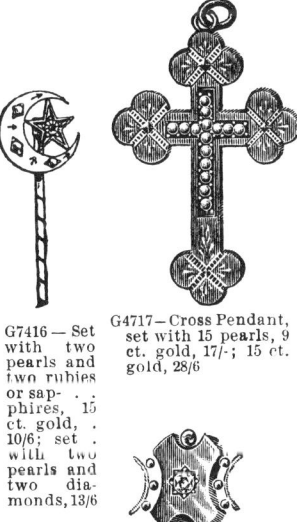

G4717 — Cross Pendant, set with 15 pearls, 9 ct. gold, 17/-; 15 ct. gold, 28/6.

G7418 — Very Pretty Photo Pendant, set with 4 pearls, or pearls and rubies or sapphires, 9 ct. gold, 14/11; 15 ct. gold, 22/6.

G7419 — Massive Chain and Padlock Bangle, 9 ct. gold, 28/6 and 45/-; 15 ct. gold, 50/- and 70/-; extra heavy, 9 ct., £2/17/6; 15 ct., £4/5/-.

G7420 — Greenstone Pendant, twice the size of illustration, 9 ct. gold mounting, 7/6.

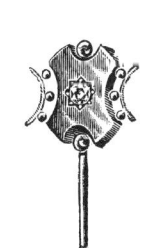

G4721 — Scarf Pin, pretty design, set with ruby or sapphire, 9 ct. gold, 9/6; 15 ct. gold, 13/6.

G7422 — Clasp Bracelet, set with 4 Pearls and 1 ruby or sapphire, 9 ct. gold, 42/6; 15 ct. gold, 65/-.

G724 — Plain Gold Band, extra heavy — 9ct., 18/6; 15ct., 25/; 18ct., 30/.

G725 — Plain Gold Band, medium — 9ct., 16/6; 15ct., 20/; 18ct., 27/6.

G726 — Plain Gold Band, ordinary — 9ct., from 14/; 15ct., from 17/6; 18ct., from 20/.

G727 — Gold Keepers — 9ct., 10/6 to 20/; 15ct., 15/ to 25/; 18ct., 17/6 to 27/6.

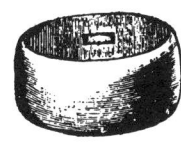

G728 — Gold Wedding Ring, extra heavy — 9ct., 17/6; 15ct., 22/6; 18ct., 28/6.

G729 — Gold Wedding Ring, wide and heavy — 9ct., 14/6; 15ct., 18/6; 18ct., 23/6.

G7210 — Gold Wedding Ring, medium — 9ct., 13/6; 15ct., 16/6; 18ct., 20/.

Narrow Widths, 10/6, 15/, 17/6.

THE FEDERATION CATALOGUE   80   JEWELLERY AND TOILETRIES

No. C 710. Tusk Brooches. Rolled Gold Mounted.

No. C 711. Oxidised Watch Brooches.

No. C 712. Enamelled Watch Brooches.

No. C 713. Gilt Name Brooches. Various patterns.

No. C 714. No. C 715. Gilt Twin Brooches with Chain. Various patterns.

No. C 716. No. C 717. Gilt Twin Brooches with Chain and Heart Pendants. Various patterns.

No. C 718. Gilt Brooches with Double Pendants. Assorted patterns.

No. C 719. Fancy Pads, containing one dozen Paste Brooches. Assorted patterns.

No. C 720. A large Assortment of novel designs in stock.

No. C 721.

No. C 722. Bent Glass Top Show Case, containing one dozen Bar Shape Gilt Brooches. Assorted patterns.
No. C 723. Same as above but Rolled Gold.

No. C 724. No. C 725. Hall Marked Silver Brooches. Assorted patterns.

No. C 726. Bent Glass Top Case, containing one dozen Bar Shape Paste Brooches. Assorted patterns.

No. C 727.   No. C 728.   No. C 729.   No. C 730.

No. C 731.   No. C 732.   No. C 733.   No. C 734.

No. C 727 to No. C 734. Black Horn Brooches. A large variety, on Cards or in Boxes of one dozen.

No. C 735.
No. C 736.
No. C 737. Jet Brooches with Gilt and Pearl Settings. Assorted patterns.

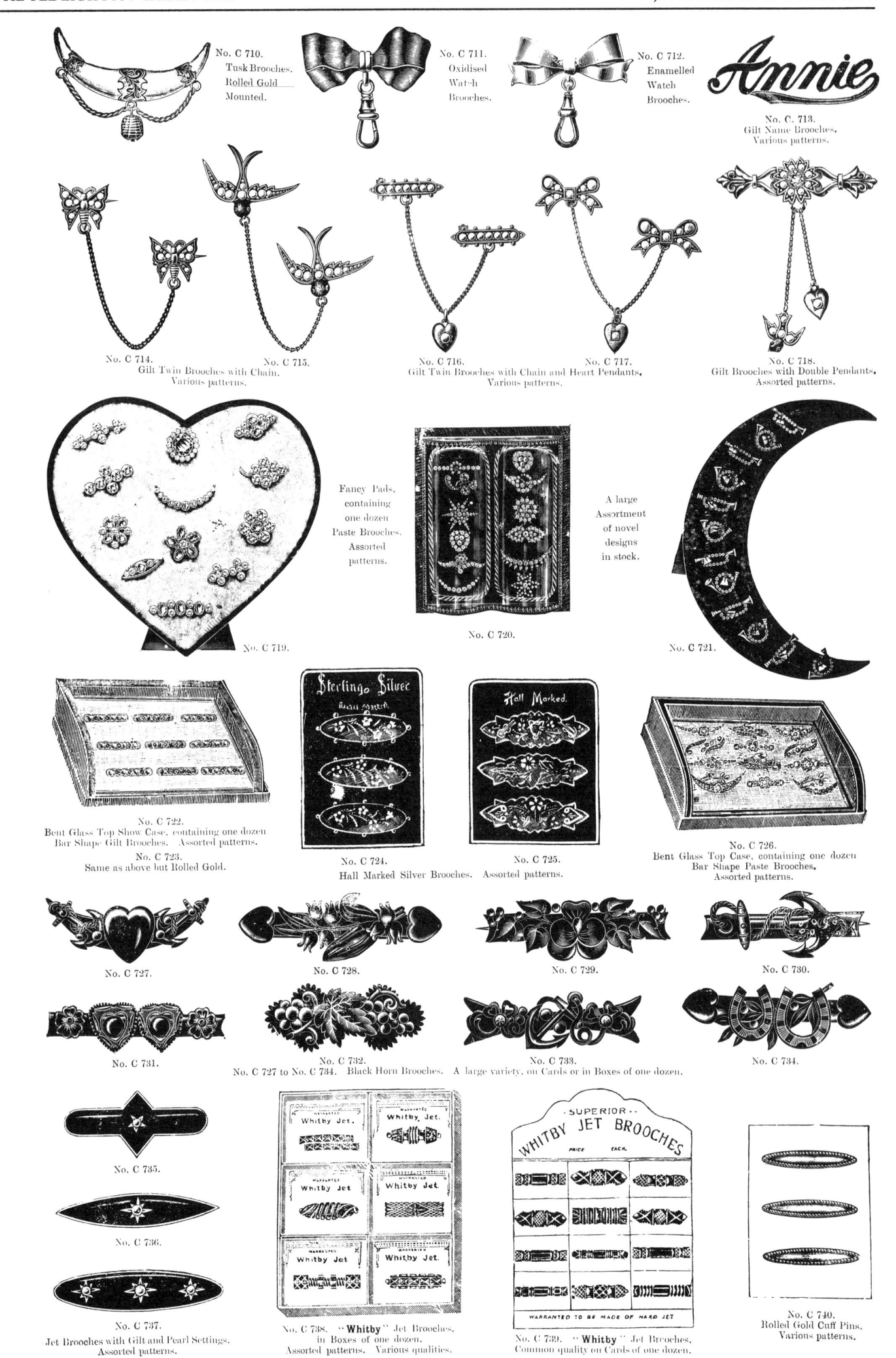

No. C 738. "Whitby" Jet Brooches, in Boxes of one dozen. Assorted patterns. Various qualities.

No. C 739. "Whitby" Jet Brooches. Common quality on Cards of one dozen.

No. C 740. Rolled Gold Cuff Pins. Various patterns.

THE FEDERATION CATALOGUE — JEWELLERY AND TOILETRIES — 81

A. SAUNDERS.
Strong, Cheap Reliable Levers. Unrivalled, 20s; Silver, 35s; Hunting, £2. London Keyless Lever, 25s; Silver, £2 2s; Hunters, £2 10s.

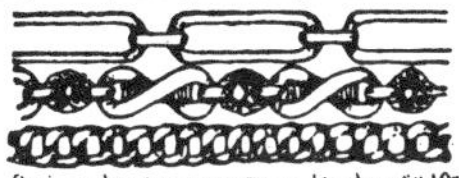

Solid Gold Chain, Single or Double, £2 10s, £3, £3 10s, £4, £4 10s, £5. 15c. Solid Gold, £5 10s, £6, £6 10s, £7, £8, £10. Pure Silver, 10s, 12s 6d, 15s, 20s.
Send for Price Illustrated Book.

A. SAUNDERS' 2-Bird and Heart Brooch, 8s 6d. Special Value.

A. SAUNDERS' Pearl Set Bird, 3 Bells and Chain Gold Brooch, 13s 6d; 15c. Gold, 25s.

9c. Gold, 2 Love Birds, Chain and Heart, 10s. Special Value.

A. SAUNDERS. Gold, 2 Ivy Leaves and Heart Mizpah Brooch, 12s 6d. (Six similar patterns.)

A. SAUNDERS. Gold Good Luck Brooch, 10s 6d. 15c. Gold, 21s.

15c. Gold, Diamonds and Rubies, with Ivy Leaves, 25s. Very Cheap.

POST FREE. POST FREE.

A. SAUNDERS. Special made Gold Waltham, ¾ Keyless Lever, 20 years' guaranteed, £4 4s; 14c., ditto, £5 5s; 25 years' guarantee, extra jewelled, high-grade works, £6 10s; Pure Silver, £2 10s, £3, £4. Perfect Timekeepers. Extra strong, Solid Gold, £8 10s, £10 10s, £12 10s, £15, £20.

A. SAUNDERS. Registered 9c. Gold Amethyst Brooch, 17s 6d; 15c. Gold, 30s; 18c. Gold, 35s. Our Latest Motto Brooch.

9c. Gold, Heart Amethyst Brooch, 7s 6d.

A. SAUNDERS. 3-Bar, Red Stone Centre, 20s; 15c. Gold, £2.

A. SAUNDERS. New Style 2-Bar Diamond-cut Amethyst, 22s 6d; 15c. Gold, £2. Very Strong and Pretty.

A. SAUNDERS. Large Size 2-Bar Gold Brooch, Diamond-cut Amethyst, 25s; 15c. Gold, £2 5s.

A. SAUNDERS. 15c. Gold, Bird 2-Bar Ruby and Diamond, 35s. Send for Illustration.

9c. Gold 2-Bar Diamond-cut Amethyst, 20s; 15c., £2.

A. SAUNDERS. 2 Twist Gold Brooch, Ball and Chain, 12s 6d. Heart Amethyst, 13s 6d.

A. SAUNDERS. 2-Bar Gold Scroll, Pearl Set, Red or Blue Stones, 20s.

A. SAUNDERS. 15c. Solid Gold Pure Diamonds and Sapphires or Rubies, £12 10s; all Diamonds, £15. A Nice Xmas Present.

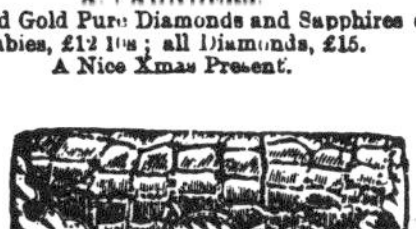

Pure Silver-mounted Purses, 15s, 20s, 25s. Cheap styles, 5s, 7s 6d, 10s.

Gold Heart Locket. Plain, 8s 6d; Chased, 10s.

A. SAUNDERS' Amethyst & Pearls Heart Charm, 17s 6d; 15c. Gold, 25s.

A. SAUNDERS' Pure Solid Silver Matchboxes. Gold-mounted, 10s, 15s, 17s 6d; Silver, 4s 6d, 6s 6d, 10s.

Links, 9c. Gold, 21s; 15c. Gold, 35s and 45s; Silver, 4s 6d. Other style, 10s 6d, 12s 6d, 15c, 20s. Silver, 2s 6d, 3s.

HAT PIN. Pure Silver, Parisian Diamonds, 4s 6d; Turquoise, 3s. Any Initial. Latest style.

Heart and Dumbbell Gold Links, 10s 6d; with Initials, 12s 6d; 15c. Gold, 22s 6d.

A. SAUNDERS. 9c. Gold, 10s 6d; 15c. Gold, 25s. Silver, 2s 6d and 3s.

A. SAUNDERS. New Name Bracelet, 25s. Any name or Initials Free. 15c. Gold, £3; narrower, £2 and £2 10s. 9c., 17s 6d, 20s, 30s, £2. Post free.

Gold Horseshoe. Silver, 5s; Locket, 20s and 25s. Silver and Gold, 7s 6d and 10s.

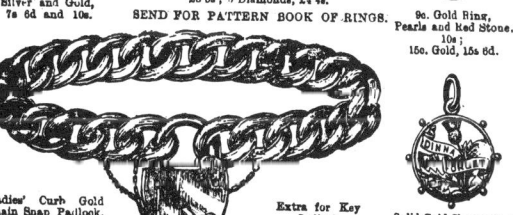

Ladies' Curb Gold Chain Snap Padlock. 25s, 30s, 35s, £2 5s, £3; 15c., £2 10s, £3, £4, £4 10s, £5, £6, £10.

Registered "Gold ..." and Spray Brooch, 13 Pearls, Ruby or Sapphire, and Diamond, 25s. Without Diamond, 15s 6d. Latest Ladies' Rage.

SEND FOR OUR COMPLETE BOOK OF JEWELLERY

A. SAUNDERS. 9c. Solid Gold Raised Flowers, 5s 6d. Silver, 2s 6d.

A. SAUNDERS. Gold Brooch, Pearl Set Bird and Heart Amethyst, 21s; 15c. Gold, £2.

A. SAUNDERS. 15c. Gold 2-Bar Pure Double-cut Diamond, £2. Splendid Value.

A. SAUNDERS. Gold Secret Brooch, 25s; 15c. Gold, £2. Diamonds, £2 10s and £3. Any Name or Motto Free.

A. SAUNDERS (Registered). Good Wish Gold Brooch, 13s 6d; 15c. Gold, 25s; Silver, 4s 6d.

A. SAUNDERS. Registered 9c. Gold Amethyst Brooch, 17s 6d; 15c. Gold, 30s; 18c. Gold, 35s. Send for Pattern Book.

A. SAUNDERS. 15c. Gold 2-Bar Scroll, Diamonds and Sapphires or Rubies, £2 10s. Very Strong.

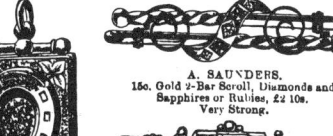

A. SAUNDERS. 15c. Gold, 4 Diamonds, Ruby, and 4 Pearls, £3 5s; 5 Diamonds, £4 4s.
SEND FOR PATTERN BOOK OF RINGS.

Extra for Key Padlock. All with Safety Chain.

Solid Gold Charm that charms, 10s 6d. Procured only at A. SAUNDERS.

Gold Bird with Bell, 6s 6d; with Amethyst, 7s 6d.

A. SAUNDERS. Solid Gold, 20s, 25s; 15c. Gold, 35s, £2. Monogram on, 2s 6d extra. Solid Silver, 5s.

Diamond-cut Amethyst Gold Bangle, 30s.

9c. Links, 10s 6d and 12s 6d; 15c. Gold, 21s and 25s. Silver, 3s and 4s 6d.

A. SAUNDERS. 18c. Gold, Diamond, 2 Rubies or Sapphires, £2 10s.

A. SAUNDERS. Hand-made, 18c. solid Gold, 6 Opals, £2 10s; larger, £3 10s.

18c. Gold Diamond, 2 Rubies or Sapphires, £2; 3 Diamonds, £3.

Pure Diamond Band Rings, 15s., 30s; 15c., £2, £2 10s, £3, £3 10s.

Curb Rings, solid Gold, 15s, 20s, 25s, 30s, £2. Price to quality of Gold.

A. SAUNDERS. 18c. Gold, pure Double-cut Diamond, £5; Larger, £6 6s, £7 10s, £8 10s, £10, £12 10s, £15, £20.

Any Name, 9c. Gold, 12s 6d, 15s; 15c., 20s, 25s; 18c., 25s, 30s, 35s, £2.

18c. Gold, 3 Opals, Sapphires, or Rubies, 4 Diamonds, £3 and £4. Send for size card.

9c. Gold Ring, Pearls and Red Stone, 10s; 15c. Gold, 15s 6d.

ALL ARTICLES POST FREE. Watch Repairs Guaranteed. All Guaranteed. Ladies' Short-wind Keyless O.K., 20s. Silver Hunting Keyless, £2, £2 10s, £3; Key, 25s, 30s, 35s. Solid Gold Keyless, £4, £5. Superior Quality, £6, £7, £8, £10. All guaranteed.

A. SAUNDERS. 3-Bar, 4 Diamonds and Ruby, 20s. Very Neat and Pretty.

9c. Gold, 12s 6d; 15c. Gold, 22s 6d. Set Pearls and Rubies, 20s; 15c. Gold, 35s.

15c. Gold 2-Bar Scroll, Diamonds and Rubies, £2.

15c. Gold Wishbone and Forget-me-nots, only 15s.

A. SAUNDERS (Registered). Gold Secret Name Brooch, 15c. Gold, Diamonds, £2 10s and £4. Any Name or Motto Free. Six different patterns, similar

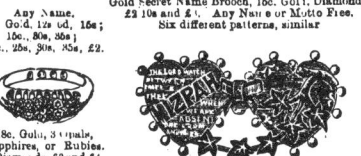

A. SAUNDERS. Gold, 2 Hearts and Ivy Leaves Brooch, 12s 6d. (Six similar patterns.)

A. SAUNDERS' Ivy Wishbone and Arrow Gold Brooch, 12s 6d; Ivy Leaf, 10s.

A. Saunders. Hand-made Wedding Rings and Keepers, 9c. Solid Gold, 5s 6d, 7s 6d, 10s each; 15c. Gold, 15s; extra heavy, 25s; 18c. Gold, 20s; extra heavy, 30s, 35s, 40s. Send for card. Quality of Gold and Finish First-class. For size cut hole in cardboard.

A. SAUNDERS' ROTHERHAMS! ROTHERHAMS! STRONG, RELIABLE ENGLISH LEVERS. Hand-finished, full-capped English Levers, £3 10s. Strongest, cheapest, and best timekeepers ever made. Extra quality, £4, £4 10s, £5, £5 10s, £6, £7, £8—3, 4, 5, and 6 years' written guarantee. Silver Hunting Key or Keyless, £2 and £2 10s Open Face, 25s and 30s. Shortwind Keyless, 7s 6d, 10s 6d, 12s 6d, 15s. Extra quality, 20s, guaranteed Gold, £4 4s, £5 5s, £7 10s, £8 10s, £10, £12 10s, £15, £20. Direct Agents for Rotherhams and Waltham Levers. Send for Price List.

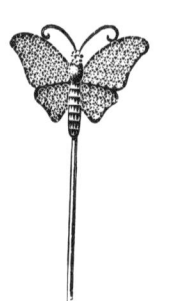

THE FEDERATION CATALOGUE   82   JEWELLERY AND TOILETRIES

| No. C 848. Bright Cut. | No. C 849. Imitation Pearl Enamelled Leaves. | No. C 850. Enamelled Shamrocks. | No. C 851. Sweet Pea Tints. | No. C 852. Enamelled Body. | No. C 853. Amethyst or Topaz Blows. | No. C 854. Shamrock Paste. | No. C 855. Enamelled Fish. |

HAT PINS IN ENDLESS VARIETY.

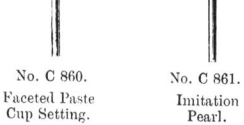

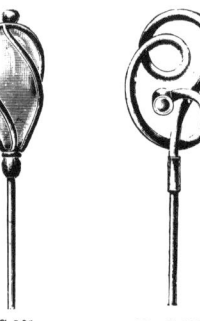

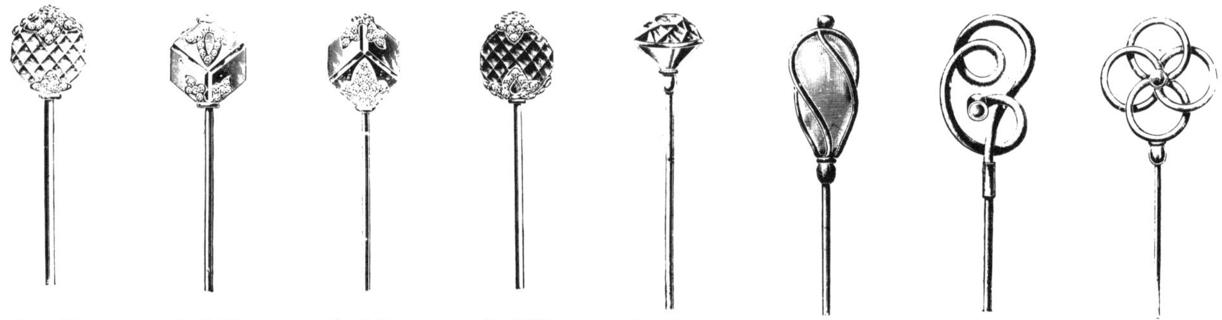

| No. C 856. | No. C 857. | No. C 858. | No. C 859. | No. C 860. Faceted Paste Cup Setting. | No. C 861. Imitation Pearl. | No. C 862. Imitation Turquoise Set. | No. C 863. Imitation Turquoise Centre. |

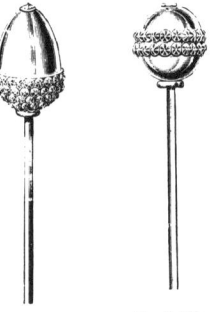

Sterling Silver Bright Cut Mounts.   Assorted Coloured Pastes.

| No. C 864. Sterling Silver. | No. C 865. | No. C 866. | | | No. C 867. | No. C 868. | No. C 869. |

Silver Gilt and Bright Cut Mounts.   Sterling Silver Bright Cut Mounted Pastes.

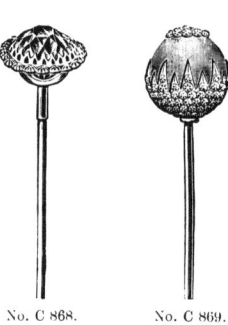

We are continually receiving NOVELTIES in HAT PINS and always have a large assortment in stock.

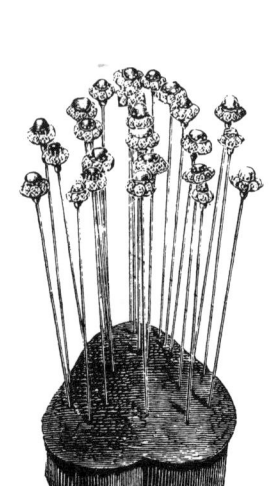

No. C 870. Heart-shape Pad containing two dozen assorted Hat Pins.

No. C 871. Gilt Hat Pins, Coloured Stone Tops.

No. C 872.

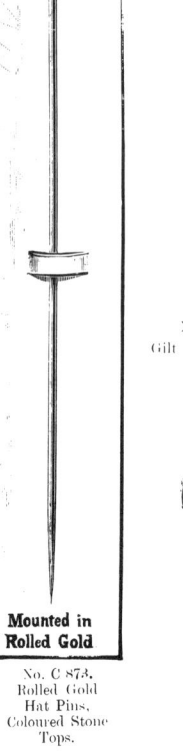

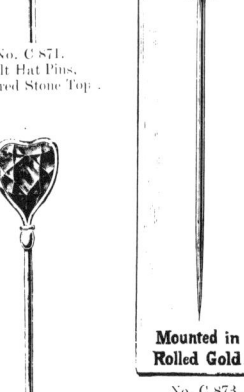

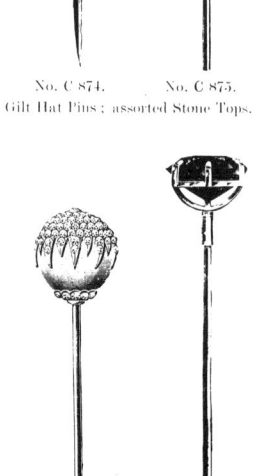

No. C 873. Rolled Gold Hat Pins, Coloured Stone Tops.

No. C 874.   No. C 875. Gilt Hat Pins; assorted Stone Tops.

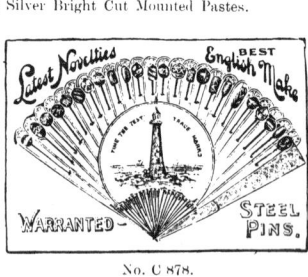

No. C 876.   No. C 877.

No. C 878. Card containing two dozen Hat Pins. Assorted patterns.

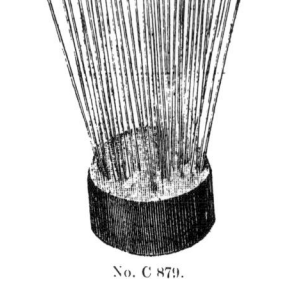

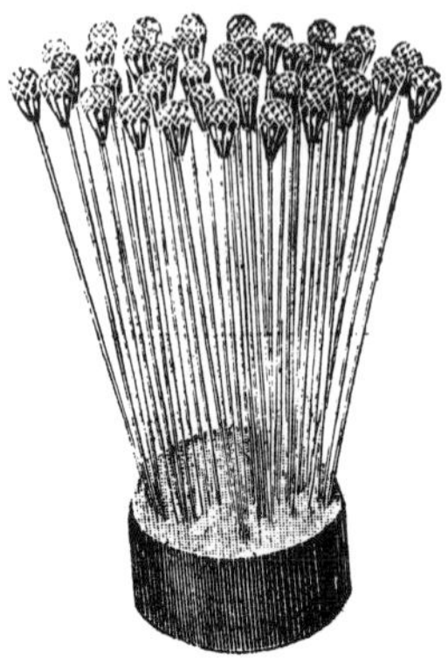

No. C 879. Fancy Pad, containing two dozen assorted Hat Pins.

JEWELLERY AND TOILETRIES

LOVELY GOLD BANGLE. Set with 16 First Water Diamonds and 16 Rubies or Sapphires, £17 10s.

Solid Gold Kangaroo Pendant, 12s 6d.

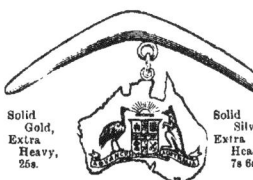

AUSTRALIAN BOOMERANG BROOCH. Solid Gold, Extra Heavy, 25s 6d. Solid Silver, Extra Heavy, 7s 6d.

Solid Gold Emu Pendant, 12s 6d.

SOLID GOLD BELL BANGLES. 3-Bell, plain, 24s; engraved, 25s; 5-Bell, plain, 30s; engraved, 31s 6d.

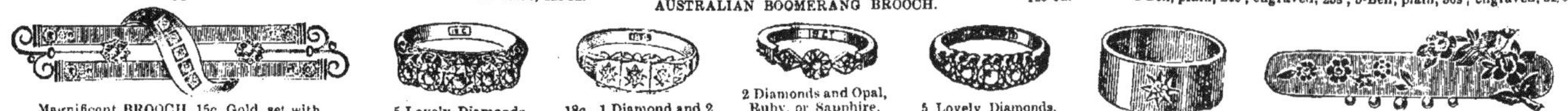

Magnificent BROOCH, 15c. Gold, set with 5 Diamonds and 2 Rubies, Sapphires, or Opals, 70s.

5 Lovely Diamonds, from £10 to £40 each.

18c., 1 Diamond and 2 Rubies or Sapphires, 27/6.

2 Diamonds and Opal, Ruby, or Sapphire, 18c. Gold, 75s.

5 Lovely Diamonds, from £3 to £35.

Diamond, 18c. Gold, 40s, 60s, 80s.

NEW GOLD BROOCH, With Spray of Forget-me-not or Name 10s 6d.

2 Gold Bars, set with 2 Diamonds, 17s 6d.

Solid Gold and Real Opal, 17s 6d. With Ruby or Sapphire, 20s. 50 other Patterns.

Garnet PENDANT and Gold Bird SAFETY PIN, 5s 6d. Without Pendant, 3s.

Christmas Presents and New Year's Gifts

Thousands of Latest Novelties.

Solid Gold TIE and HEART BROOCH, 5s.

Real Amethyst or Topaz Links, Extra Strong, 5s 6d pair.

NEW GOLD CROSS BROOCH, With Raised Mizpah and Bird, 12s 6d.

SOLID GOLD BROOCH, Any Name or Motto, with Raised Lucky Wishbone and Bell and Chain Pendant.

POST FREE

9c., 17s 6d, 20s, 25s; 15c., 35s, 40s, 45s. Silver, 4s, 5s pair. With Monogram, 2s 6d extra.

Finest Enamel on Silver Gilt. Souvenir of Sydney. STAMP CHARM, 3s 6d.

LUCKY SHAMROCK CHARM, Set with 1 Pearl, 2 Amethyst, and 1 Topaz or Obsidion, 4s.

POST FREE

Solid Gold, 14s pair. With any Monogram. 50 other Patterns.

Solid Gold MOTTO BROOCH, 11s 6d. Also, same style in Souvenir, Regard, Good Luck and Mizpah

Our New Wild Boar's Tusk BROOCH, with Chain and Bell Pendant. Silver Mounted, 5s 6d. Gold Mounted, 14s.

Solid Gold and 3 Opals, 25s; Solid Gold and 1 Opal, 15s.

18c., 14 Lovely Diamonds and 3 Rubies or Sapphires, £7 10s.

9c., 10s, 12s 6d, 15s, 20s; 15c., 20s, 22s 6d, 27s 6d; 18c., 21s, 25s, 30s. With any Name or Motto, 1s extra.

5 LOVELY OPALS. 10c., 42s, small size, 35s. 15c., 50s, „ „ 45s. 18c., 55s, „ „ 50s.

Our QUERY RING. (Note of Interrogation) 18c., set with 11 First-water Diamonds, £8 and £9 10s.

Gold XMAS BELL BROOCH, 10s 6d.

Latest Design. 15c. Gold Brooch, 1 Diamond and 2 Rubies or Sapphires, 42s.

Our Gold Novelty BROOCH, 17s 6d, with octagon Amethyst and Pearl Bird.

OUR NEW GOLD BAMBOO BANGLES. 22s 6d; Broader, 32s 6d; Children's Size, 14s.

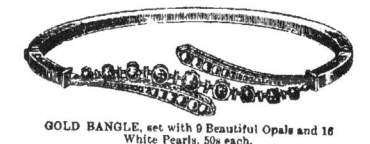

LATEST LONDON NOVELTY TIE CLIPS. Plain Gold, 8s 6d pair. Set with Opals, Pearls and Turquoise, 15s pair.

MAGNIFICENT GOLD BROOCH, Set with 13 First-water Diamonds, 1 Pearl and 15 Rubies or Sapphires, £13 10s.

GOLD BANGLE, set with 9 Beautiful Opals and 16 White Pearls, 50s each.

18ct. Gold, with 1 Diamond and 1 Ruby or Sapphire, £1 10s.

18ct. Gold. 1 Ruby or Sapphire and 6 Diamonds, £2 10s.

18ct. Gold. 5 fine Opals, £2 10s.

15ct. Gold. Opals and Diamonds, £4.

18ct. Gold. 3 Opals, 4 Diamonds, £5.

18ct. Gold. 1 Opal, 10 Diamonds, £10.

18ct. Gold. Opal Heart and 14 Diamonds, £10 10s.

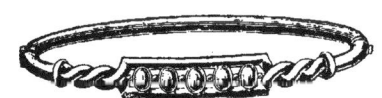

15ct. Gold. 5 Opals, £3 15s.

15ct. Gold. With beautiful Opal and fine Diamonds, £22 10s.

15ct. Gold and fine Opals, £9 9s.

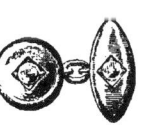

Sleeve Links, set with Opals. 9ct. ... £1 10 0 15ct. ... £2 0 0

New Curb Chain Bangle, 15ct. Gold, set with Opals, Turquoise, or Pearls, £5

Sleeve Links. 9ct., £1; 15ct., £1 7s 6d.

15ct. Bow and Heart Brooch. All Pearls, £2. With Diamond Heart, £2 10s.

Fine Pearl Necklet, 15ct. Gold, £12 10s.

Handsome Opal and Pearl Brooch. 15ct. Gold, £5 5s.

Handsome Opal Necklet, 15ct., £9.

15ct. Pendant, set with fine Pearls, £4 4s.

Amethyst and Pearl Pendant, 15ct., £2 15s.

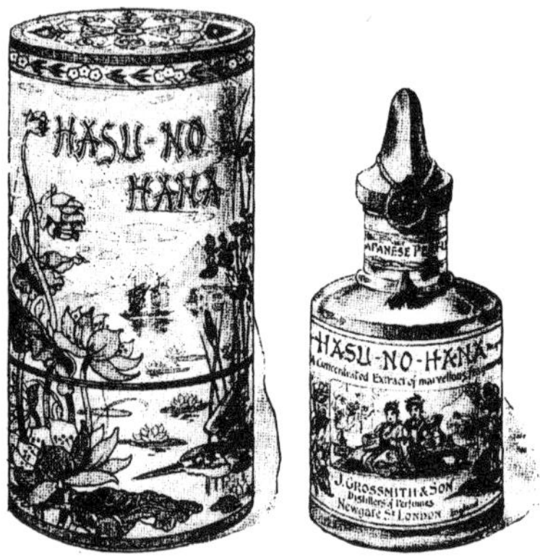

THE FEDERATION CATALOGUE   84   JEWELLERY AND TOILETRIES

No. 290s.
The New Japanese Perfume "**Hasu-no-hana**" (Registered). The distinctive odour of the fragrant Lotus of Japan.

No. 305s.
The New Indian Perfume "**Phul Nana**" (Registered), Bouquet of Indian Flowers.

No. 380.
An Entirely New Perfume, "**Florodora**" (Registered). Sweetest of odours. Remarkably refreshing and distinctly Floral in character.

PREMIER VINOLIA SOAP.
Unsurpassed for the Complexion.
For Family Use.
In Boxes of 3 and 36 Tablets.

VINOLIA CREAM.
For Itching, Face Spots, Sunburn, Eczema, and all Skin Irritation.
It Relieves Itching at once.
In four sizes.

VINOLIA POWDER.
For Redness, Roughness, Toilet, Nursery, etc.
In white, cream, and pink tints.
In four sizes.

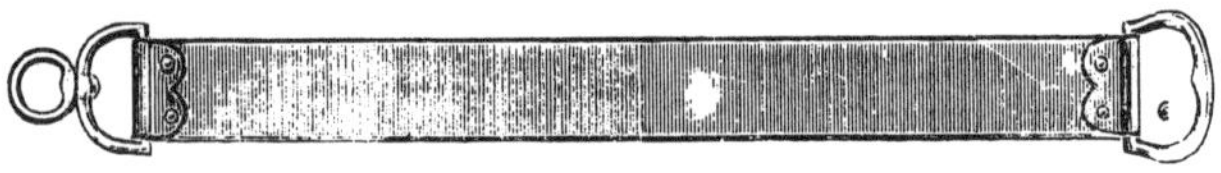

No. C 15.
Plain Leather Razor Strops, Canvas Back with Swivel. Various qualities.

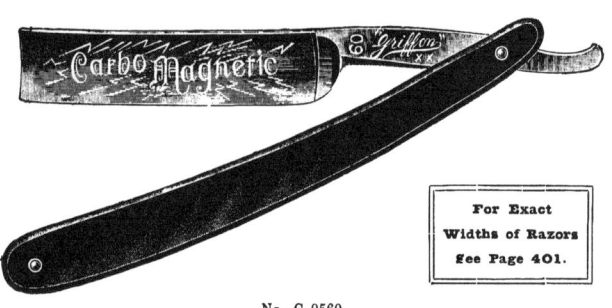

For Exact Widths of Razors See Page 401.

No. C 9560.
Carbo-Magnetic Razors. Black Handles. Can be had with Round or Square Points. ½, ⅝, and ¾ inches wide.
THE CARBO-MAGNETIC RAZORS.
Electrically Tempered. Full Hollow Ground. Always ready for use.
No Honing! No Grinding! No Smarting after Shaving.
With ordinary careful use will keep an edge for years without honing.

No. C 7806.
No. C 7814 contains One Safety Frame with Seven Blades, put up in elegant satin-lined Morocco Case.

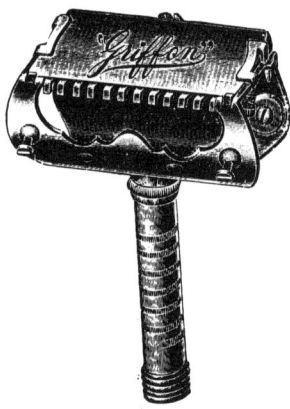

No. C 7804.
The New Improved "**Griffon**" Safety Razor, Ready for Use. Keen, Clean. The only one instantly adjustable for close or ordinary shave. Guaranteed.

No. C 40.
Colgate's Shaving Sticks.

No. C 41.
Premier Vinolia Shaving Sticks.
We also stock (No. C 42) Pears' Shaving Sticks.

No. C 294.

No. C 295.
Electro-plated on White Metal Shaving Mugs and Brushes. Assorted shapes.

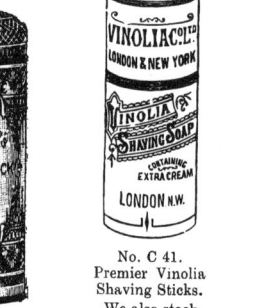

Bone Handles.
No. C 210. Real Badger.
No. C 211. Imitation Badger.
No. C 212. Hog Hair.

Bone Handles.
No. C 213. Real Badger.
No. C 214. Imitation Badger.
No. C 215. Hog Hair.

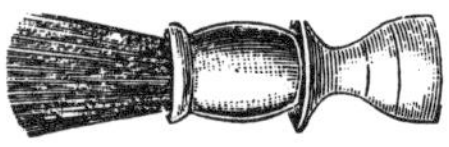

Nickel Handles.
No. C 216. Imitation Badger.
No. C 217. Hog Hair.

Nickel Handles.
No. C 218. Imitation Badger.
No. C 219. Hog Hair.

BREIDENBACH'S

No. 1280. Queen's Violet.

No. 918. Glycerine and Cucumber Soap.

No. 1142. Geisha Bouquet.

CHOICE ENGLISH PERFUMES

No. G1. Assorted Odours.

No. 1452. Sweet Pea.

Nos. 1300 & 1301. Lavender Water or Eau de Cologne.

The remarkable achievement in the manufacture of this subtle odour was made by the late F. H. BREIDENBACH, about the year 1832, and although the title has been adopted by various makers, it is generally admitted that the peculiar secret of the manufacture of the veritable Wood Violet Perfume has never been discovered by its imitators.

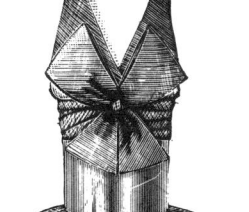

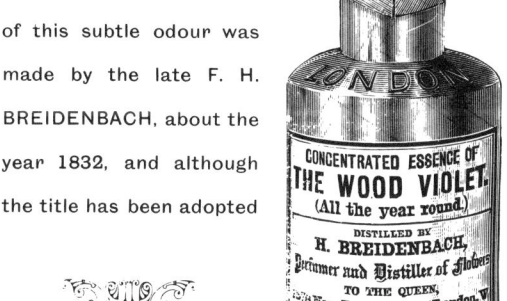

No. 47. The Wood Violet.

Nos. 133 & 132. Eau de Cologne or Lavender Water.

AND REFINED TOILET SOAPS.

No. 1760. Assorted Odours. Leatherette.

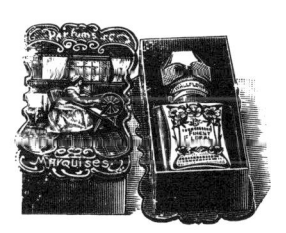

No. 1761. Assorted Odours. Registered Design.

No. 1465. Rose Sublime.

No. 1127. "Buttermilk" Soap.

No. 1423. Trefle (Clover).

A Large Variety of Messrs. BREIDENBACH & CO.'S Productions kept in stock by FELDHEIM, GOTTHELF & CO.

FEDERATION CATALOGUE
9. Children and Childhood

Photographs of healthy, bright-eyed children and scenes of holidays and leisure-time might suggest an unbalanced view of childhood in the Federation Era. It is always difficult to summarise a period in history, and historians continue to offer fresh insights based on new evidence or re-evaluations. As stated earlier, in comparison with other times and many other places, Australia in the period from 1890 to 1915 offered a reasonable standard of living for a large percentage of the population. Children in affluent or relatively affluent circumstances might expect the best of the toys seen in the following pages, while poor souls in the slums of the cities or heartbreak rural settings would be delighted with a rag doll or a homemade cricket bat. Most children were expected to make their own fun if they did have time to themselves. Having allotted tasks around the house or about the farm varied from family to family, but many children were relied upon to contribute their labour. Some began full-time work at a relatively young age, with exploitation a possibility in the workplace, or as outworkers based at home. Highpoints in the weekly round could be the freedom to ramble home from school, time at weekends to play favourite games and evening activities such as reading or being read a story. High days and holidays stood out like beacons in the yearly round. A trip to the seaside, the agricultural show, a visiting circus and the annual picnics were savoured in that age when entertainment was generally far less accessible than it has since become. Silent movies were rapidly gathering popularity in the early 1900s, but radio in the home was ten to twenty years away and television far in the future.

Ingenuity has always been an essential ingredient for making childhood fun out of whatever was available. Sliding down grassy or muddy hillsides on pieces of wood or sheets of metal is a timeless favourite. The billycart needed a bit of work to create but was a longtime source of endless fun. In the Federation Era the billycart was likely to be a two-wheeler drawn by a goat (often a billygoat) or even by a dog. Homemade carts used discarded pram wheels and scrap timber, contrasting with the small carts made by toy manufacturers and coachbuilders. All sorts of wheeled toys were offered in stores and catalogues, including pull-along wagons, self-propelling wagons, doll carriages and a whole range of tricycles. Toy wheelbarrows came in various sizes, as did horses on wheels with carts behind. On page 6 there is a photograph of two bright-eyed boys with a wonderfully elaborate 'horse and cart'. Such toys would be seen in an affluent household, but in this case it was probably a photographer's prop. Wooden steam engines and carriages were often homemade but sophisticated factory and workshop products were also widely distributed. Pull-along animal figures on wheels were another popular toy which

A favourite doll. Photograph: Verey, Castlemaine. *Collection:* Ashley Tracey.

could be either purchased or made as a one-off present for a particular child.

A category of toys which tended to reflect both affluence and adult interest were the finely-crafted model steam engines. Typically these were 'stationary' engines which might power other toys or constructions. The 'live steam' model locomotive was another area of interest which could captivate both young people and adults. On page 93 we can see that besides stationary engines and locomotives, there were also model steamboats 'guaranteed to work well'. Magic lanterns, which worked in the same manner as larger-scale adult models, were another quality toy which, like the steam engine, needed some adult supervision. Both required the use of flammable fuels, and the engines creating steam under pressure needed working safety-valves.

Toys scaled down from everyday life in the adult world represented a fair proportion of all of those offered in the period from 1890 to 1915. Carpentry sets and gardening tools were both likely to be seen as constructive toys. Miniature stoves, cooking utensils, tea-sets and small-scale furniture answered the child's desire to follow adult models, or encouraged the sex-role stereotypes to the satisfaction of parents. Playing house is a traditional pastime, and make-believe shops have also been around for a few centuries. Dolls have long been part of such activities, and catalogues offered dolls' furniture, including bedsteads and cradles made of wood or metal. The 1905 Feldheim Gotthelf catalogue from Sydney offered toy carpet-sweepers, toy wringers, dolls' perambulators and doll's houses in a range of sizes. Doll's houses were one item which could be made at home, and we know from surviving examples that they varied from humble creations to grand affairs of multiple rooms and finely-crafted details. The dolls themselves varied in size from a few centimetres to quite large. Plain types of wood or fabric contrasted with lifelike models with china heads and real hair. On page 90 we can see indiarubber dolls, jointed wooden dolls, jointed china dolls and china bathing dolls. There are also dolls' stockings and shoes in various sizes. Examples of dressed dolls are seen on page 91, including dressed rag dolls.

For boys there were clockwork locomotives with sets of carriages and lines. The best examples included stations and other details. Motorcars soon appeared as clockwork toys, while clockwork horses and carts continued to challenge them, just as they did in real life. Model boats for sailing outdoors worked by windpower, clockwork or were steam-driven. Most working models of yachts could be made by someone at home if the luxuries from the store or catalogue were out of reach. Whirlygigs activated by the wind were another home craft which in turn brings to mind all the

Best outfit and a tricycle.
Photograph: Verey, Castlemaine. *Collection:* Ashley Tracey.

designs of kites which have been made over the years. Humming-tops and peg-tops are familiar to older generations, but the use of tops for games has disappeared, as has the wooden hoop rolled along with a stick. To keep adults on their toes there were toy musical instruments including trumpets, drums and tambourines. Books for children and young adults often included games to play and things to make. Card tricks and conjuring or simple chemistry were just some of the topics presented. Marbles or alleys was predominantly a boys' game and the collecting of fine specimens a real challenge. The list on page 91 gives some indication of the riches to be had. Who would not covet an 'Onyx Cornelian', a 'Red Agate', an 'Opal' or a 'Tigers Eye'. Painted or glazed china and coloured stone alleys have gone off the market, but twisted glass ones are still available. The true 'alley' was made of the purest marble, often being beautifully variegated. Traditional games were Long Taw and Ring Taw, the word 'taw' being used for a treasured marble even in Shakespeare's time.[1]

Books for young people may not have been available in the kind of range seen in stores at the present time, but they probably had a powerful impact when there were no distractions such as radio or television. Children in the Federation Era benefited from advances in printing technology in the greater use of colour and of affordable mass-produced books. Annuals such as *Boys' Own*, *Girls' Own*, *Chatterbox* and *Little Folks* found a ready market as did the classic tales, *Alice's Adventures in Wonderland*, *Robinson Crusoe* and *Puss-in-Boots*. Grimm's and Andersen's fairy tales were there to scare and delight, while *Children's Stories from Dickens* stirred the social conscience. The year 1894 brought *Seven Little Australians* by Ethel Turner, a realistic picture of family life which suggested that Australian children had their own character and identity. This was followed by *The Family at Misrule* (1895) and, in turn, many others. *A Little Bush Maid* by Mary Grant Bruce, which first appeared in 1910, was again part of a new nationalist tradition in Australian children's books.[2] Young people could readily identify with the free-spirited and resourceful characters, quite different to those presented to them in English books. Young Australians, like the nation at large, were finding an identity.

Notes:
[1] George Forrest, *Everyboy's Book*, G. Routledge & Co London, 1855, p. 18.
[2] Brenda Niall, *Mythmakers of Australian Childhood*, This Australia, vol.1, no.1, Summer 1981-82, p. 72.

George and Nellie Bulger were photographed in Bendigo, Victoria in 1910. *Courtesy:* Avis Cox.

No. C 244.
Wood Hoops, with Sticks.
5, 6, 7, 8, 9, and 10 feet circumfrence.

No. C 245.
Iron Hoops, with Crooks.
20, 22, 24, 26, 28 inches diameter.

No. C 246.
Oval Shape Water Cans. Two sizes.

No. C 247.
Round Shape Water Cans. Two sizes.

No. C 248.
Wood Spades. Several sizes.

No. C 249.
Polished Handle Garden Sets. Various sizes.

No. C 250.
Plain Handle Garden Sets. Several sizes.

No. C 251.
Polished Handle
Iron Spades.
Several sizes.

No. C 252.
Painted Iron Buckets.
Several sizes.

No. C 253.
Decorated Tin Buckets.
Several sizes.

No. C 254.
Leather Whips
Various sizes.

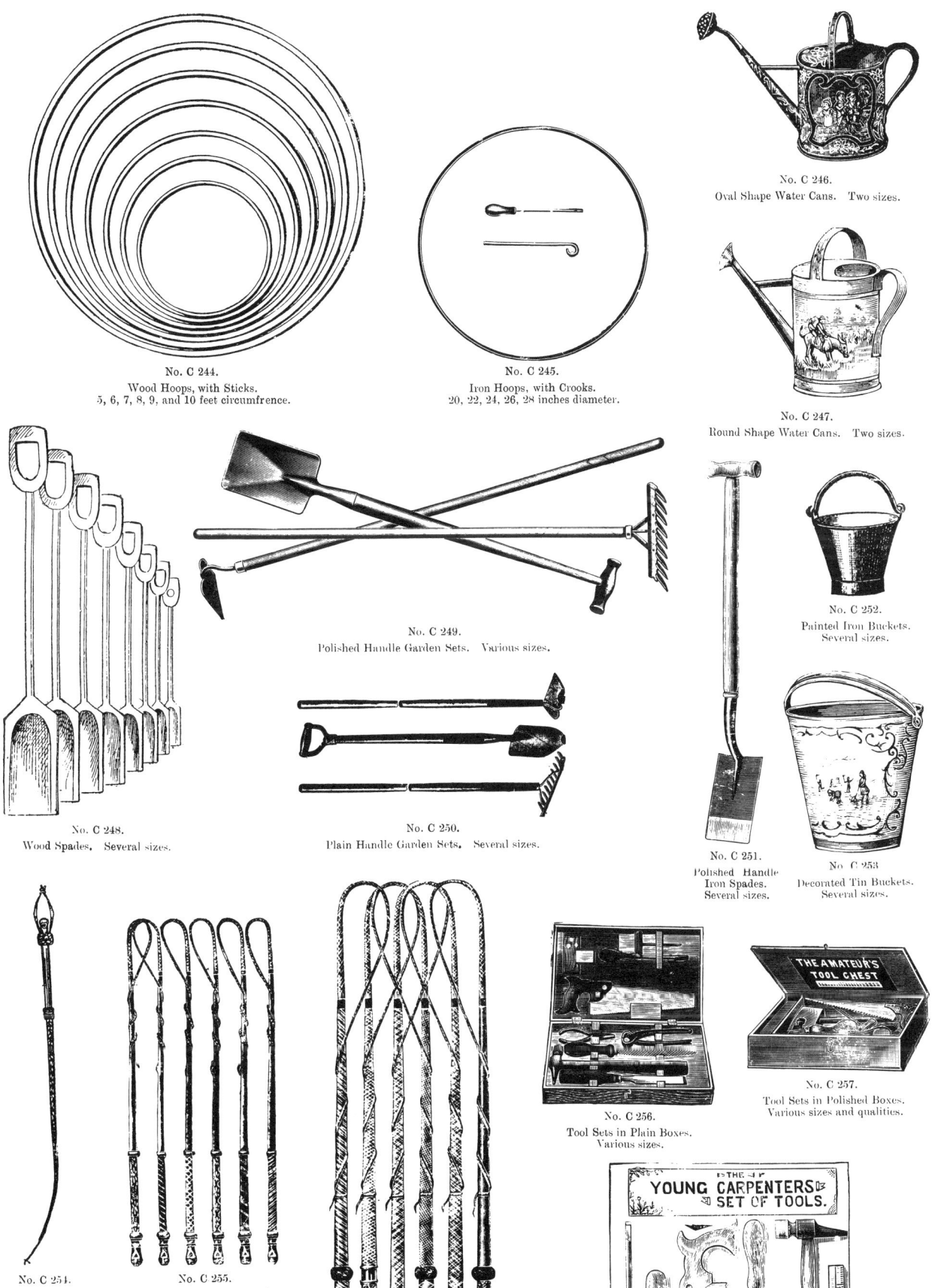

No. C 255.
Small Whips on Assorted
Cards. Various sizes.

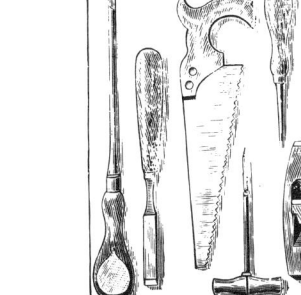

No. C 256.
Tool Sets in Plain Boxes.
Various sizes.

No. C 257.
Tool Sets in Polished Boxes.
Various sizes and qualities.

No. C 258.
Leather Whips with Wood Handles.
Several sizes.

No. C 259.
Whips on Assorted Cards.
Various sizes.

No. C 260.
Tool Sets on Cards. Various sizes.

THE FEDERATION CATALOGUE — 90 — CHILDREN AND CHILDHOOD

| 2¼ inch. | 2½ inch. | 2¾ inch. | 3 inch. | inch. | 3½ inch. | 3¾ inch. | 4 inch. | 4½, 5, 6, 7 inch. |

COLOURED HOLLOW BALLS.

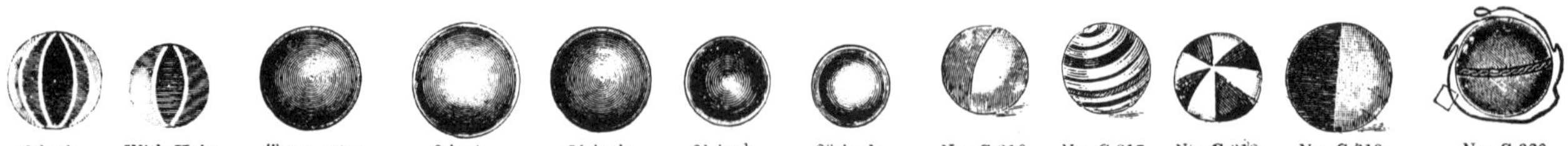

| 2 inch. | With Hole. No. 4. Coloured Hollow Balls. | Terra-cotta Balls. 2½ inch. | 2 inch. | 2¼ inch. | 2½ inch. | 2¾ inch. | No C 316. | No. C 317. Celluloid Balls. | No. C 318. Assorted colours and sizes. | No. C 319. | No. C 320. Celluloid Balls on Elastic. Two sizes. |

GREY HOLLOW BALLS.

No. C 321. India-rubber Toys. Assorted patterns.

No. C 322.

No. C 323. India-rubber Animals. Various shapes and sizes.

No. C 324.

No. C 325.

No. C 326. | No. C 327. | No. C 328
Dressed India-rubber Dolls. Various sizes.

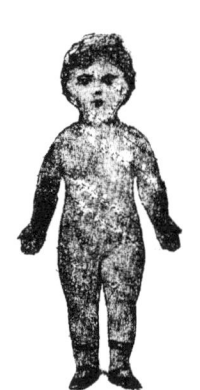

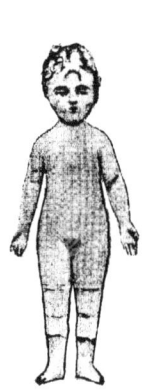

No. C 329. | No. C 330.
Naked India-rubber Dolls. Several sizes.

No. C 331. | No. C 332.
India-rubber Figures. Assorted patterns and sizes.

No. C 333. China Dolls' Heads. Various sizes.

No. C 334. Jointed Dolls' Heads. Various sizes.

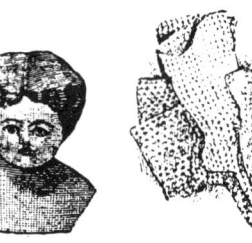

No. C 335. | No. C 336. Washable Dolls' Heads. Various sizes.

No. C 337. Dolls' Stockings. Various sizes.

No. C 338. Dolls' Shoes. Various sizes.

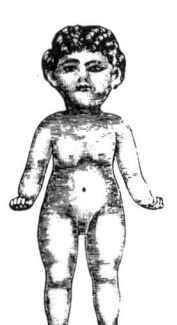

No. C 339. Small Size Jointed Various sizes.

No. C 341. Small Size Jointed China Dolls, with Long Hair.

No. C 342. Small Size Jointed China Dolls.

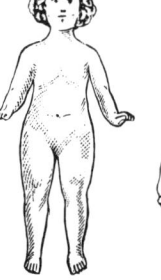

No. C 343. China Bathing Dolls. Various sizes.

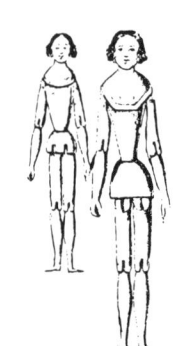

Nos. C 344.

No. C 345. | No. C 346. Wood Dolls. Various sizes.

No. C 347. Squeaking Dolls on Sticks. Assorted patterns.

No. C 348. Clapper Dolls. Assorted sizes and patterns.

No. C 393.

No. C 394.

No. C 395.

Dressed Rag Dolls. Assorted patterns and sizes.

No. C 390.
Best Quality Jointed Dolls.

No. C 391.
Dressed Jointed Sailor Dolls.

No. C 399.
Small Size Fancy Dressed Jointed Dolls, in Boxes of half a dozen. Various assortments.

No. C 400.

Dressed Nankeen Dolls.

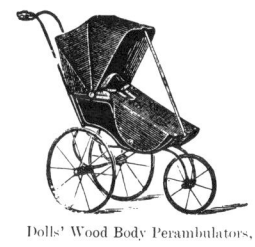

Dolls' Wood Body Perambulators.

No. C 293.
Dolls' Wood Mail Carts, with Iron Wheels.

No. C 294.
Dolls' Wicker Body Mail Carts, with Iron Wheels.
Several qualities and sizes.

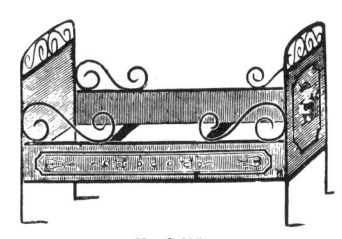

No. C 295.
Dolls' Wire Bedsteads.
Several sizes.

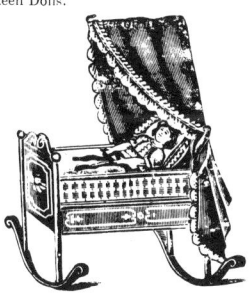

No. C 296.
Dolls' Tin Bedsteads or Cradles.

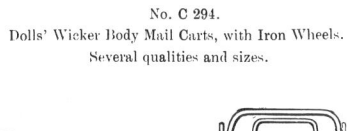

No. C 297.
Dolls in Perambulators.
Various sizes.

No. C 298.
Cane Toys.
Assorted patterns.

No. C 299. Dolls' Houses.
Various sizes.

No. C 300.
Toy Carpet Sweepers.

No. C 301.
Toy Wringers.

MARBLES

Coloured Stone	... ...	In Bags of 1000
Blood Alleys	... ...	In Boxes of 100
Twisted Glass	... ...	Size. 0, 1, 2, 3, 4, 5, 6, 7, 9
China (Painted)	... ...	,, 0, 1, 2, 3
,, (Glazed)	... ...	,, 0, 1, 2, 3
Pebbles	... ...	,, 0, 1, 2, 3
Opal (Assorted Colors)	... ...	Size 0, 1, 2, 3
Tiger's Eye	... ...	,, 0, 1, 2, 3
Red Agates	... ...	,, 0, 1, 2, 3
Cornelians	... ...	In Boxes of 12 and 25 (Various Sizes).
Onyx Cornelians	... ...	In Boxes of 12 and 25
Goldstone Cornelians	... ...	In Boxes of 12 and 25

No. C 111. Whip Tops.
Several sizes.

474

No. C 110.
Top Cords. Two sizes.

No. C 758.
Postage Stamp Albums, with Fancy Embossed Covers, assorted patterns.

No. C 798.
Juvenile Invitation Cards.
The patterns of Children's Invitation Cards are very high-class in design, and include printed invites for Tea Parties, Dances, etc. Complete with Envelopes. In Boxes containing Eight Cards.

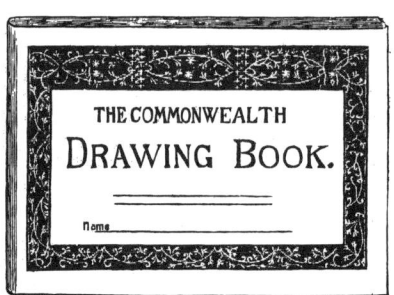

"The Commonwealth" Drawing Books.
Royal Oblong Quarto, 12½ by 9¾ inches. Interleaved.

Every Boy His Own Toy Maker

Just the Book for Clever Boys. It brightens the ideas of every Boy. Tells how to make a Steam Engine, a Photo Camera, a Windmill, a Microscope, an Electrical Machine, a Galvanic Battery, Telegraphic Apparatus, Telephones, a Kaleidoscope, a Magic Lantern, an Æolian Harp, Ships and Boats of all kinds, Kites, Balloons, Bows and Arrows, Fishing Tackle, Bird and Animal Traps and many other things. 200 illustrations. Only EIGHT PENCE, posted. UNION CO. 299 Elizabeth St., Melbourne

THE CHAMPION DANCER OF THE WORLD

TIM NIMBLEFOOT

Only 1/3 Complete including delivery to any address.

Size 14 ins. high.

PERFORMS
JIGS, HORNPIPES,
REELS,
STEP DANCES,
FLIP FLAPS and
BREAKDOWNS
PERFECT TIME
Wonderful Agility.
Marvellous Heel and
Toe Work.

YOU have only to beat time for any kind of Step Dance and Tim Nimblefoot will "shake his legs" in the most amazing way. You never saw finer dancing in your life. The most perfect time is preserved and the endless variety of "steps" Tim performs is surprising and far excels the best efforts of the most expert professional dancers. Everybody admires Tim Nimblefoot's remarkable agility and grace. This clever toy is an unfailing source of amusement for old and young, grave and gay. It is very strongly made of wood and there is nothing about it to get out of order, even with the roughest handling. A smaller toy of the same kind, but with a comical Japanese dancer. NINE PENCE, carriage paid

The Union Co., 299 Elizabeth St., Melb

FUN Fast & Furious FUN
FIGHTING ROOSTERS
7d. per Pair,
Carriage paid.

PERFECTLY FEATHERED MODELS OF GAME FOWLS

WITH very little practice you can make these little Game Roosters imitate a fierce Cock Fight in the most life-like manner. You will puzzle and amuse your friends. Printed directions sent with each pair of Roosters.

THE FINEST AUSTRALIAN TOY.

The JUMPING KANGAROO

AMUSES YOUNG AND OLD
Strong and Durable
Nothing to get out of order

Nine Pence, Posted.

THOUSANDS of these Kangaroos are selling in the streets of Melbourne and Sydney. Everyone is delighted with them. You merely place the 'roo at the top of a sloping board and he jumps and jumps and keeps on jumping in a very quaint and life-like way, until he reaches the bottom. By having two or more Kangaroos you can arrange quite exciting races.

THE CACKLING HEN
A WONDERFUL IMITATION.
The Real Cackle and a Real Feathered Bird
Four Pence each, posted.

Just draw the string through your fingers and the Hen loudly proclaims the production of a new-laid egg.

SPECIAL BARGAIN: Roosters, 2/- posted Hen and Two Kangaroos all for 2/- anywhere

The Union Co., 299 Elizabeth St., Melb

OSBORN & JERDAN

Opticians, Electricians,
Photographic Stock Merchants & Model Makers,

438 GEORGE STREET, SYDNEY
(opposite Lassetter's).

Wish to bring under your notice a few Models, etc., specially suited for the Xmas season.

Note.—All Steam Models are fitted with Safety Valves. and are absolutely safe, and guaranteed to work well.

The Grandest Present in the World for Children.

Our "ALADDIN" Lanterns are the cheapest and the best to be obtained anywhere, and not mere toys that look showy but show nothing on the screen. They are strong, well-made instruments, made entirely of Russian iron rivetted together (no solder). They show a perfectly distinct and brilliant picture on the screen, because they are fitted with a complete set of good lenses and powerful kerosene oil lamps. The slides are beautifully colored, and good, well-chosen subjects, calculated to amuse the children. Each lantern is enclosed in a nice strong case, with 12 slides (four pictures on each slide), and full instructions for use. Made in five sizes.

No.		Price.	Post.	Extra Slides, per doz.
8000.	Shows picture 2½ft. diam.	5/-	-/11	1/3
8001.	" 3½ft. "	7/6	1/2	1/6
8002.	" 4ft. "	10/6	1/5	2/-
8004.	" 5ft. "	15/-	1/11	3/6
8006.	" 6ft. "	20/-	2/2	5/-

Vertical Engine.
Japanned Boiler, 3" Flywheel, Brass Cylinder, with Lamp in box, 2/-; post, 6d.

Model Locomotives.
Japanned Boilers. "The Fury." 7/6 each ; post, 8d.
Copper Boilers, all Brass Fittings. 10/6 each ; post, 11d.

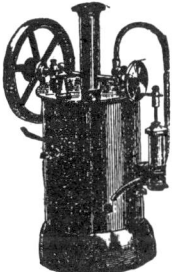

Vertical Engines.
Pretty Models, all Brass. In Two Sizes.
2½" Fly-wheel ... 10/6
3" " ... 15/6

Our Famous "Dover" Engines.
10" Long Copper Boilers, 6 Wheels. All Brass Fittings. Work beautifully. 18/- each ; post, 1/-.

Vertical Engine.
Handsome Design. Copper Boiler. 10/6; post, 6d.

Model Engine Fittings of all kinds.

New Model—Just arrived.
10/6 ; post, 1/-

"The Thunderer."
14in. long. Very powerful. £1 12s. 6d. ; post, 1s. 8d.

Model Yacht Fittings in Stock.

A New Hand Camera. Simple, Cheap, and takes splendid pictures. Size, 3¼ x 3¼. Magazine holds six plates. Price, £1 2s. 6d. Plates, 1s. 3d. dozen.

Small Electro Motors.
Work well, with very little battery-power.
4/9 ; post, 6d. Larger size, 6/-

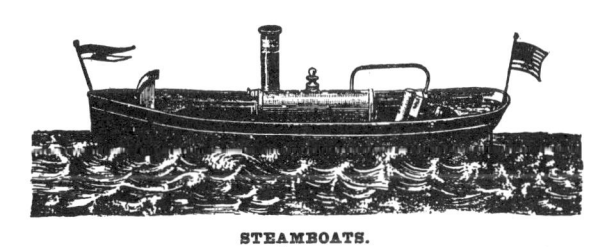

STEAMBOATS.
Pretty, Well-finished Models. Small size, 12in. long, 10/6 ; 20in. long, 20/- Guaranteed to work well.

The "Unique" Electro Motors.
Powerful and Well-Made.
7/6 each ; post, 8d.

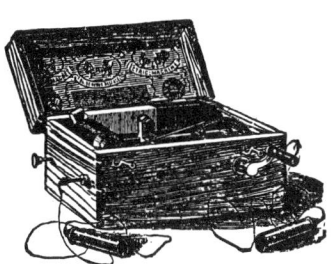

Magneto Electric Machines.
A Special Shipment at Very Reduced Prices.
No. 1. Usually sold at a Guinea 12/6
No. 3. " Two Guineas 32/6

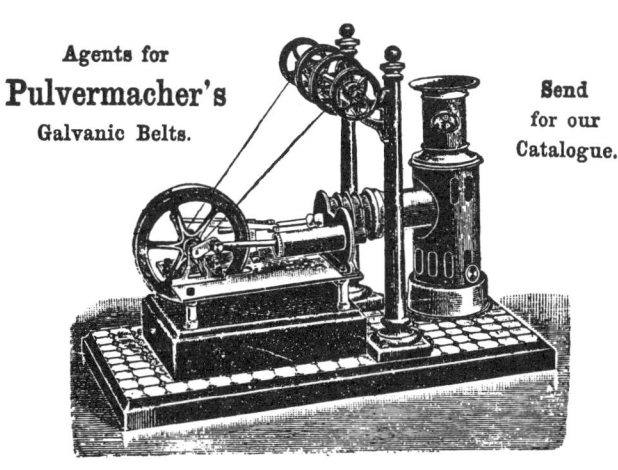

Agents for **Pulvermacher's** Galvanic Belts.

Send for our Catalogue.

HOT AIR ENGINES.
No water necessary ; work with a Spirit Lamp only. In four sizes.
No. 334 ... 12/6   No. 336 ... 25/-
No. 335 ... 18/6   No. 337 ... 35/-

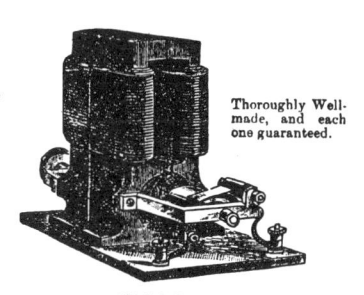

Thoroughly Well-made, and each one guaranteed.

Model Dynamos.
For working with small Steam, Gas, or Water Engines.

No. 1. Four Volts ... 20/-
No. 2. Eight " ... 25/-
No. 3. Ten " ... 35/-

A SELECTION OF CHILDREN'S TOY BOOKS.

"Father Tuck's" Washable Calico Series. 6d. to 2s. 6d.   Printed direct on Tuck's Washable Calico. Practically Indestructible. Each Book contains 12 coloured pictures.

No. C 1105.	No. C 1010.	No. C 1201.	No. C 1006.	No. C 1106.
OUR ANIMALS	Baby's ABC	OUR RAILWAY BOOK	 THE DOLLS' HOUSE ABC	 OUR BOOK OF GAMES

UNTEARABLE TOY BOOKS. Popularly known as Linen Toy Books. 6d. to 2s.   Postcard and other Painting Books. 1d. & 3d. to 1s.

No. C 6669. Linen, 2s.	No. C 6654. Linen, 1s.	No. C 6636. Linen, 6d.	No. C 4012. Painting, 6d.	No. C 2544. Painting, 1s.
THE CATLAND ABC	FATHER TUCK'S OLD RHYMES ABC	JACK AND THE BEANSTALK	CATS AND DOGS PAINTING BOOK OF POSTCARDS	FATHER TUCK'S CRAYON PICTURES

All these Books contain 12 Pages fully illustrated.

The 6d. Books contain 12 Postcards.
The 1/- Book, 24.

CHILDREN'S STORIES FROM DICKENS. 6d. Cloth-covered Books. 64 Pages.   One Shilling Series of Stiff-Covered Books. 18 full-paged Illustrations in Colour.   **"THE MIGHTY MIDGET" SERIES.** Illuminated Board Covers. 6d. and 1s.

No. C 7.	No. C 11.	No. C 6560. Stiff-Covered Books, 1s.	No. C 150.	No. C 151.
LITTLE DAVID COPPERFIELD	LITTLE PAUL DOMBEY	IN THE FARMYARD	 THE LAD WHO ALWAYS DID HIS BEST	THE BOY THE PIANO AND THE BABY

The Name of the Firm and the Trade Mark "The Easel and Palette" appear on every "TUCK" Publication.

No. C 642.	No. C 643.	No. C 644.	No. C 645.
CIRCUS AND MENAGERIE ABC	PLAY AND LEARN ABC BOOK	THE ARABIAN NIGHTS	PUSS IN BOOTS
1s. 6d. Toy Books. Profusely Illustrated, with Varnished Board Covers.	1s. Toy Books. Splendidly Illustrated, with Varnished Board Covers.	6d. Toy Books. Nicely Illustrated, with Varnished Board Covers.	1s. Toy Books. Nicely Illustrated, with Coloured Linen Covers.

We have an immense variety of Toy Books in stock in various sizes and qualities.

No. C 646.	No. C 647.	No. C 648.	
ROBINSON CRUSOE	Simple Simon & Bo Peep	BABY'S OWN ABC	FROGGY'S LITTLE BROTHER
6d. Toy Books. Nicely Illustrated, with Coloured Linen Covers.	1s. Toy Books. Nicely Illustrated, with Paper Covers.	6d. Toy Books. Nicely Illustrated, with Paper Covers.	Toy Books. Nicely Illustrated, with Paper Covers. No. C 649. 3d. lines. No. C 650. 2d. ,, No. C 651. 1d. ,,

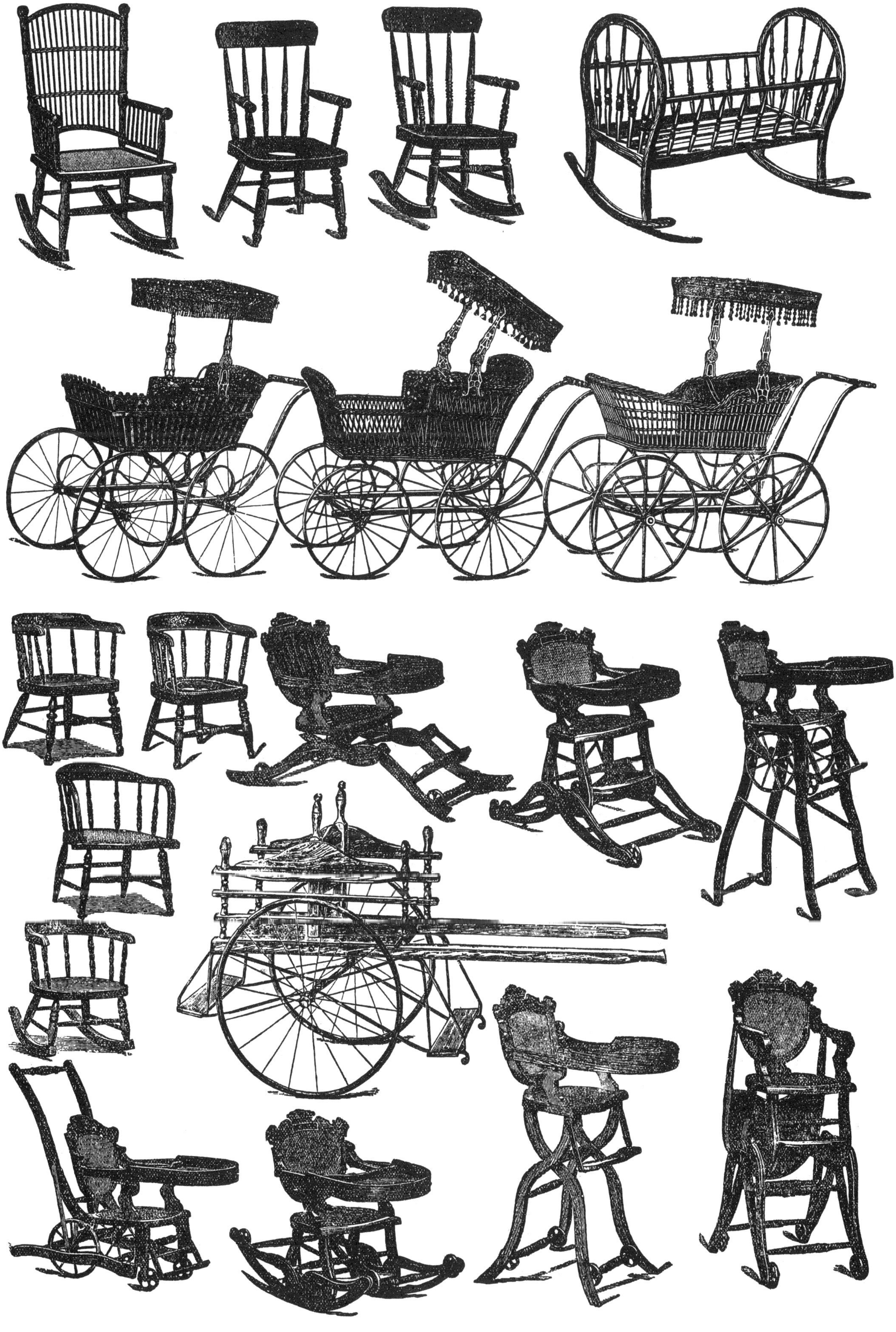

FEDERATION CATALOGUE
10. Pictures, Cards and Keepsakes

Miss Billie Bourke, popular Edwardian stage celebrity. *Collection:* John Thompson.

Every picture really was worth a thousand words in earlier times, when most of the population was illiterate. However, universal education had progressively altered the balance in the second half of the nineteenth century and, by 1890, there were few people under thirty who could not read or write. Words became important to more and more people, but images on walls, in books, magazines and newspapers and in all kinds of printed ephemera were a powerful medium. As technology allowed the reproduction of photographs as well as colour printing at an economical price, pictures or illustrations combined with words reached an ever-widening audience. Narrative paintings mostly seen as popular prints continued to find a place in Australian households, as did the often simpler sentiments of pictures taken up by companies as part of a product promotion. Pears prints are the best-known example of the latter. Newspapers and journals also offered attractive prints to their readers, and these were often reproductions of well-known Australian paintings. Particular favourites were those which offered a heroic or nostalgic view of bush life. For urban Australians, these were an important part of a growing mythology, a way of belonging to the bush and countryside, which many had not long left behind. Even people just beginning the struggle of pioneering new settlements needed such visions to reassure themselves.

By contrast, imported images of Old World scenes were more idealised and rarely suggested the hardships so many settlers had escaped. Painters in England in the second half of the nineteenth century were often attracted to the changing countryside where they captured or created images of idyllic cottages in rambling gardens. Such scenes became popular prints, as did romantic European landscapes and splendid views in North America. Exotic places in other parts of the British Empire, stirring scenes of great battles and pictures of royalty or notable people were also offered in stores and catalogues. Animals too were likely to engender strong sentiment, and as horses were still such a part of everyday life, it is not surprising that horse prints were popular. The faithful dog minding a flock of sheep captured many a heart, and different species of animals seen together in harmony was an ancient theme.

Richly-coloured reproductions which suggested oil paintings would naturally appeal to those who could never hope to own a good-quality original work. Oleographs followed in the tradition established by the famed Baxter prints, with rich colours used to dramatic effect. The most common themes were European landscapes with a stream or lake, a house, or other architectural element and forest with mountains. Some were snow scenes with bold contrast between the light and the dark. Affordable oil paintings were also available for the mass market. Typically these were in pairs and usually in a vertical format. Bush scenes were included as were Old World views, but most were production-line works painted for overall effect, with little merit as individual works. All kinds of flower pictures are noted in old catalogues; some were painted on wood or metal panels, others on canvas and some on opaline or white glass. The latter were offered as 'hand painted opal glass florals'.

In keeping with the popular taste for ornamentation, the manufacturers of cards, souvenirs, albums, birthday books and decorated mottos used all of the advances on printing to create a seemingly endless supply of brightly-coloured keepsakes and ephemera. Greeting cards could be gorgeous confections of printed, embossed and perforated paper, card, silk or celluloid, with wishes and sentiments in fine calligraphy or fancy typefaces. Pictorial elements used include flowers, foliage, fruit, romantic scenes and popular symbols. There were angel and anchor designs, hearts and anchors, doves and angels, air balloons, automobiles, bicycles, baskets of flowers and lucky horseshoes. Birthdays, Christmas, New Year and special remembrances were all represented. Far removed from such frivolity were the bereavement or mourning cards with their black-bordered envelopes.

Postcards entered their golden age in the Federation Era and were an essential part of the increasing expectation of holidays and day excursions. With an efficient mail service, and in many places twice-daily delivery, postcards were a readily-available means of easy communication at a time when telephones were mostly confined to affluent households. Cities, towns, resort areas and beauty spots were represented on cards, as were sentimental pictures, romantic scenes and gently humorous scenes of courtship and holiday fun. These became keepsakes, alongside less ephemeral souvenirs such as plates with views printed on them or

Australian scenes were among the most popular subjects for postcards. *Collection*: the author.

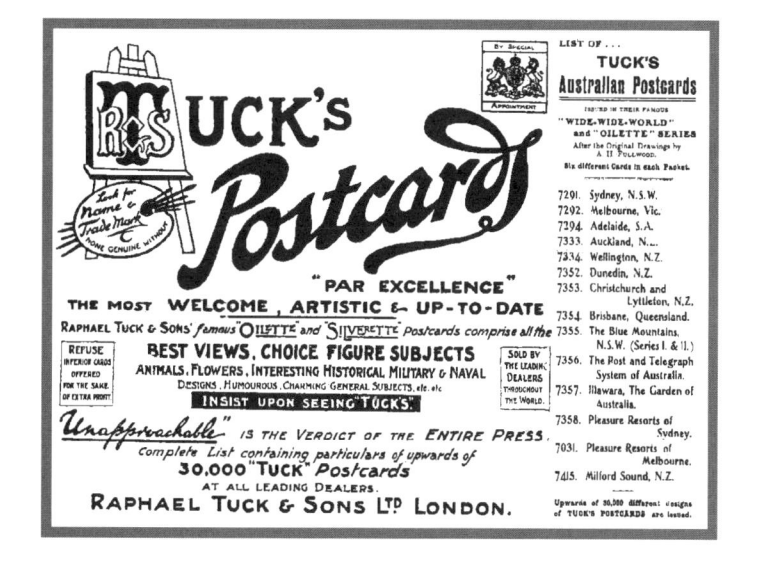

objects decorated with shells. Other keepsakes were the kinds of knick-knacks seen in catalogue pages: small ceramic figures, ornamented photo frames and fancy cups and saucers.

Keepsakes include all the objects to which special memories are attached, including gifts for different occasions or as an expression of love, admiration or service to a cause. Wedding presents are amongst the things most likely to survive from earlier times. This is because such things are usually treated with reverence and, in many cases, are carefully set aside and brought out only for special occasions. With a return to prosperity after the turn of the century, weddings were generally large-scale events and many were quite lavish. Settlers who counted themselves as successful, on selections taken up some twenty or thirty years earlier, were keen to celebrate their progress; this accounted for many a daughter launched in high style. Weddings in the Federation Era were reported in great detail in the local papers in both town and country. Detailed descriptions were given of the bridal party's outfits and those of all the women guests, as well as the wedding breakfast. A complete list of wedding guests, together with their presents, was also included. Silver and silver-plated items were most popular. Butter dishes, cream jugs, sauce ladles, jam-stands, cake dishes, sugar scoops, egg-stands, breakfast cruets, toast-racks, table rings, salt-cellars and fancy cutlery all found a place. Silver candlesticks, fine-quality kerosene lamps, marble clocks, sets of vases, jug and basin sets, trays, framed fretwork, biscuit barrels, pickle jars, photo albums and various items in cut-glass or crystal are proudly listed. Many of these country wedding breakfasts were held at home after the ceremony in a nearby church. It was not uncommon for a dance to be held after the couple had been farewelled at the railway station.

Catalogues of the period 1890 to 1915 offer an extraordinary range of stationery, including the paper and envelopes used for wedding invitations, letters of thanks and all the other social niceties. There were tinted papers in floral boxes and sedate cream or grey for formal correspondence. The 'Court Mourning Cabinet' was a boxed set of paper and envelopes with black borders. Church and Sunday school were central to the lives of many families. Children were given text and reward cards, most of which were decorated with floral or other elements. Religious wall mottoes, such as 'The Lord Giveth Wisdom' and seasonal greetings such as 'A Merry Christmas' were printed in rich colours with ornamental lettering and decorative details. 'Home Sweet Home' must have sold in the millions and was an important statement in the light of Australia's growing commitment to a home of one's own.

POSTCARD ALBUMS
IN NEW DESIGNS AND EXCEPTIONAL VALUE.

THE enormous increase in Illustrated Postcards in this country and throughout the world has led to a growing demand for suitable Albums to contain collections of these Postcards. Such collections become very valuable and interesting, recording and illustrating as they do the travels of friends and relations in all parts of the world. The New Series of Postcard Albums we now offer are exceedingly well adapted for their purpose. The binding is strong and good, and, at the same time, artistic and elegant; the leaves are nicely ornamented, and have suitable slits for inserting the Postcards.

Please note that all our Albums are very well bound and contain plenty of guards to allow for the thickness of Postcards.

Upright Shape Postcard Albums in various qualities. All with Dark Green leaves.

We have a Splendid Assortment of Postcards and Postcard Albums.

Designs in Cheap Quality.
No. C 689. To hold 100 Cards.
No. C 690. ,, 150 ,,
No. C 691. ,, 200 ,,
No. C 692. ,, 300 ,,
No. C 693. ,, 400 ,,
No. C 694. ,, 500 ,,
No. C 695. ,, 700 ,,
Assorted Colour Covers, with various Fancy Designs.

Designs in Medium Quality.
No. C 696. To hold 100 Cards.
No. C 697. ,, 150 ,,
No. C 698. ,, 200 ,,
No. C 699. ,, 300 ,,
No. C 700. ,, 400 ,,
No. C 701. ,, 500 ,,
No. C 702. ,, 700 ,,

Best Quality Art Linen.
Assorted Colour Padded Covers, with various Fancy Designs.
No. C 703. To hold 100 Cards.
No. C 704. ,, 150 ,,
No. C 705. ,, 200 ,,
No. C 706. ,, 300 ,,
No. C 707. ,, 400 ,,
No. C 708. ,, 500 ,,
No. C 709. ,, 700 ,,

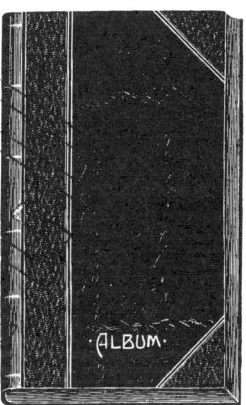

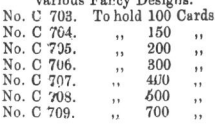

Half-Bound Cloth.
Various Colours and Qualities.
No. C 710. To hold 100 Cards.
No. C 711. ,, 150 ,,
No. C 712. ,, 200 ,,
No. C 713. ,, 300 ,,
No. C 714. ,, 400 ,,
No. C 715. ,, 500 ,,
No. C 716. ,, 700 ,,

FISHING FOR JACK.
After D. Downing.
Size, 14 in. by 16¾ in., upon Mount 30 in. by 22 in.
Artist's Proofs, £1 11s. 6d.;
Unsigned Proofs, £1 1s.; Prints, 10s. 6d.

ELAINE.
After W. A. Breakspeare.
Size, 15 in. by 17 in., upon Mount 32 in. by 24 in.
Artist's Proofs, £2 2s.; Prints, £1 1s.

GENERAL VISCOUNT KITCHENER.
After H. W. Koekkoek.
Size, 12½ in. by 17 in., upon Mount 24 in. by 35 in.
Artist's Proofs, £2 2s.; Prints, £1 1s.

CARRIAGE FOLK.
After J. C. Dolman.
Size, 16¾ in. by 12½ in., upon Mount 32 in. by 22 in.
Artist's Proofs, £1 11s. 6d.; Prints, 10s. 6d. In Colours, double price.

ENGRAVINGS.
PHOTOGRAVURES.
RELIEFS.
ART NOVELTIES.
POSTCARD ALBUMS.
Etc., etc.

DANGER.
After D. Downing.
Size, 17 in. by 11½ in., upon Mount 30 in. by 20 in.
Artist's Proofs, £1 11s. 6d.;
Unsigned Proofs, £1 1s.; Prints, 10s. 6d.

Christmas and New Year Cards.

WE have been noted for many years past throughout the whole of the Australasian Colonies for our Special Series of Christmas and New Year Cards, which are stocked in endless variety, and of which we make a special study.

Our annual display of Christmas and New Year Cards is well known by all buyers as offering to the trade a collection of Special Lines altogether unique, and we invite a comparison of our assortment in Cheap, Medium, or High-class Cards, with those of any other house in the Colonies. Our collection comprises Novelties in Style, Design and Colouring of the highest order, selected from the best publications of each season.

A New Collection for each Season.

BIRTHDAY CARDS.

MADE IN A LARGE VARIETY OF PATTERNS.

No. C 845. 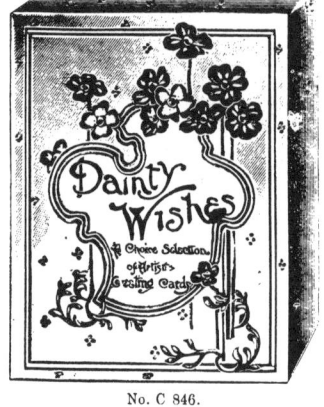   No. C 846.    No. C 847.

A well-selected assortment of all the Latest Designs always in stock; they are chosen with great care and sold at remarkably low prices. It is impossible to describe these goods, as they vary so greatly from season to season; but we make it our business to find out and procure the newest patterns that are produced. Stocked as under:—

Folding Birthday Cards with Leaflets, in endless variety.   Celluloid Birthday Cards with Leaflets; a large assortment.

Boxes containing Twelve Assorted Birthday Cards—

No. C 848. Common Quality.   No. C 849. Medium Quality.   No. C 850. Best Quality.

No. C 812.
Angel with Anchor Cards, With Flowers.
10¼ by 6¼ inches.

No. C 813.
Heart and Anchor Cards, with Flowers.
5¼ by 5 inches.

No. C 815.
Air Balloon Card, with Flowers.
7½ by 4½ inches.

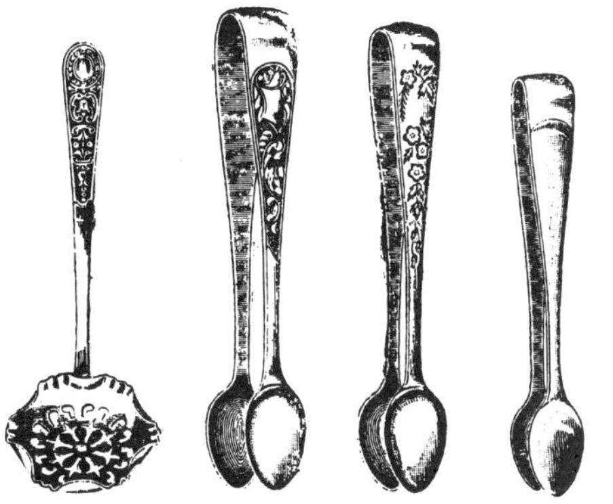

THE FEDERATION CATALOGUE　　　　　　　　101　　　　　　　　PICTURES, CARDS AND KEEPSAKES

Sugar Sifters.
Fancy Handles.
No. C 554.
Electro-plated.
No. C 554/1.
Hall-marked
Silver.

Sugar Tongs.
Plain.
No. C 555.
Electro-plated.
No. C 555/1.
Hall-marked
Silver.

Sugar Tongs.
Assorted Engraved Patterns.
No. C 556.   No. C 557.
Electro-plated.   Electro-plated.
No. C 556/1.   No. C 557/1.
Hall-marked   Hall-marked
Silver.   Silver.

No. C 292.
Electro-plated on White Metal Card Receivers.
Various patterns.

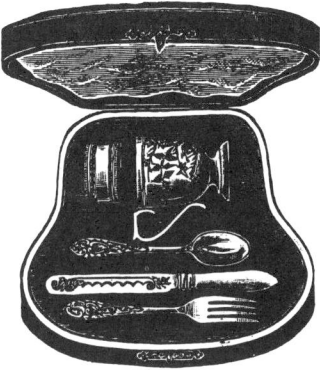

Electro-plated Knife, Fork, Spoon, Mug, and
Serviette Ring, in Case.
No. C 426. Xylonite Handle.   No. C 427. Pearl Handle.

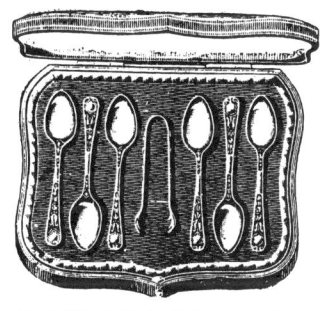

No. C 532. Satin-lined Leatherette Case,
containing six Hall-marked Silver Tea Spoons
and Tongs. Assorted patterns.

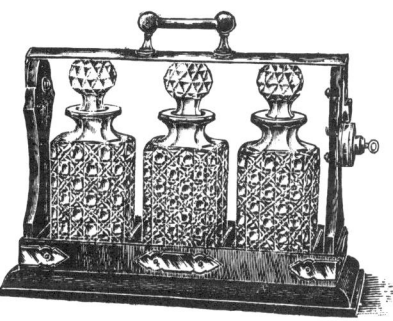

No. C 214.
Oak Spirit Frames, with Electro-plated Mounts
and 3 Full-Cut Bottles.

No. C 347. Moulded
Glass Marmalade Jars,
Electro-plated Mounts.
Various patterns.

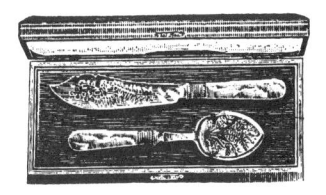

Leatherette Case, containing Jam Spoon and
Butter Knife.
No. C 558. Pearl Handles.
No. C 559. Xylonite Handles.

No. C 330. Electro-plated Wire
Frame Jam Dishes, with various
pattern Fancy Glasses.

No. C 331. Electro-plated
Wire Frame Oval Jam Dishes,
with White Glasses.

No. C 332. Electro plated
Jam Dishes, with White Glasses.
Assorted patterns.

No. C 100.    No. C 101.
Decorated China Biscuit Barrels. Electro-plated on Nickel
Silver Mounts. Assorted patterns.

No. C 126.
Electro-plated Cruets with Six Moulded Bottles.

No. C 127.
Various patterns.

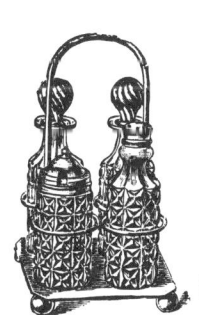

No. C 130.    No. C 131.
Electro-plated Cruets with Four Moulded Bottles.

No. C 132.
Various patterns.

No. C 148.    No. C 149.    No. C 150.
Electro-plated Breakfast Cruets with Three Decorated China Bottles.
Assorted patterns.

No. C 151.    No. C 152.    No. C 153.
Electro-plated on Nickel Silver Breakfast Cruets with Three Decorated China Bottles.
Assorted patterns.

FEDERATION CATALOGUE
11. Practical Considerations

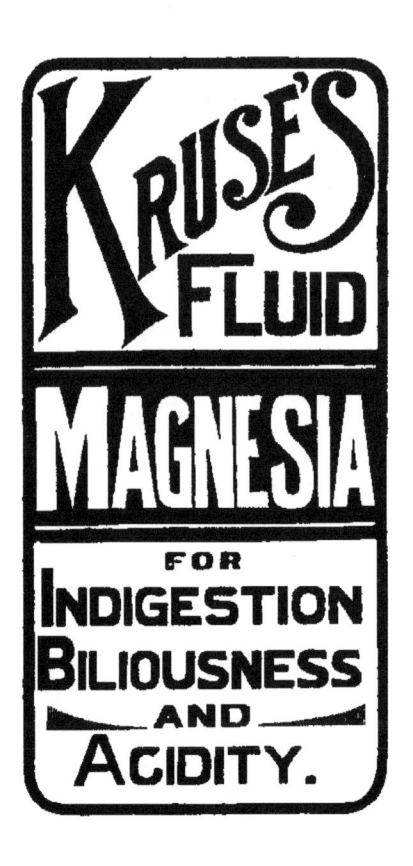

A comparison of ordinary household life in the Federation Era with conditions at the present time offers many similarities and as many contrasts. Some things were simple then, and yet many tasks were complicated compared to our modern labour-saving age. Getting through the family washing was then quite a production, as was running an efficient kitchen or cleaning floor-coverings. Household gadgets were likely to be useful hand-operated devices such as apple-peelers or carpet-sweepers. While electricity had been applied to kettles, radiators and fans, such items did not come into general use until the Interwar Era. The first really efficient vacuum cleaners came into production prior to World War I, but the electric vacuum cleaner as we know it did not achieve widespread use for some decades. Most people continued the old routine of taking rugs and carpets outside and beating them, or would clean them *in situ* with a patent carpet-sweeper. On page 105 we can see three designs by Bissells and a Ewbank Number 10. Such sweepers are still in use, being a relatively efficient device needing only human energy.

One of the useful items seen in catalogues was the combined nursery lamp and food-warmer. Small nursery lamps were widely used and here was one which would keep a container of liquid warm. There were also gadgets for heating irons on a primus stove and curling-tong lamps for home hair-styling. Cast-iron gas rings fed by a flexible gas hose were very useful when a full gas stove was not available (see page 112). Apart from pressure stoves such as the Primus and the Jewel, there were small non-pressure types such as the Beatrice, the Triumph and the Frizzler. Taller models such as E.M. Miller's 'Perfection' smokeless Kerosene Heating Stoves were also given a flat top for heating a kettle or a pot. Anyone who has used kerosene for heating or lighting will know that the pump seen on page 112 was a clean and simple way to fill lamps, stoves and heaters.

Cast-iron stoves on legs were based on traditional American designs, and could be freestanding. They generally had good-sized cooking tops and ovens of varying capacities. On page 106 we can see the standard Colonial oven in two designs. These models were set into a hearth with a fire on top or a fire both above and below. There were also Colonial grates made especially to sit on these ovens. Cast-iron cooking ranges were available in varying sizes from small compact models right up to great leviathans with central fire boxes, two ovens, hot water tanks and full cast-iron surrounds.

Cooking, heating and lighting were all essential considerations although, in some parts of Australia, heating was never a need and in most places it was a seasonal concern. The pots, pans, kettles and griddles are just some of the items seen in catalogues which were used on stoves or with an open fire. In many places people still used iron cranes or chains hanging from a bar to cook over an open fire. Others would stand a kettle or a pot on iron bars which reached from hob to hob. Some would use a camp oven bush-style, simply placing it close in to the fire with coals heaped on top. On page 112 we see house bellows offered in eight different sizes. I can well remember my grandfather, gently encouraging the open fire. In cities and towns where coal and coke were used, there was a need for 'coal vases' (see page 107) to sit beside the fireplace. To carry the fuel from a backyard storage there were helmet-shaped coal hods and coal scoops.

Replacement grates and ashpans were also important items in catalogues. Page 107 gives us a wonderful selection of fenders, spark guards, fire-dogs and fire-irons.

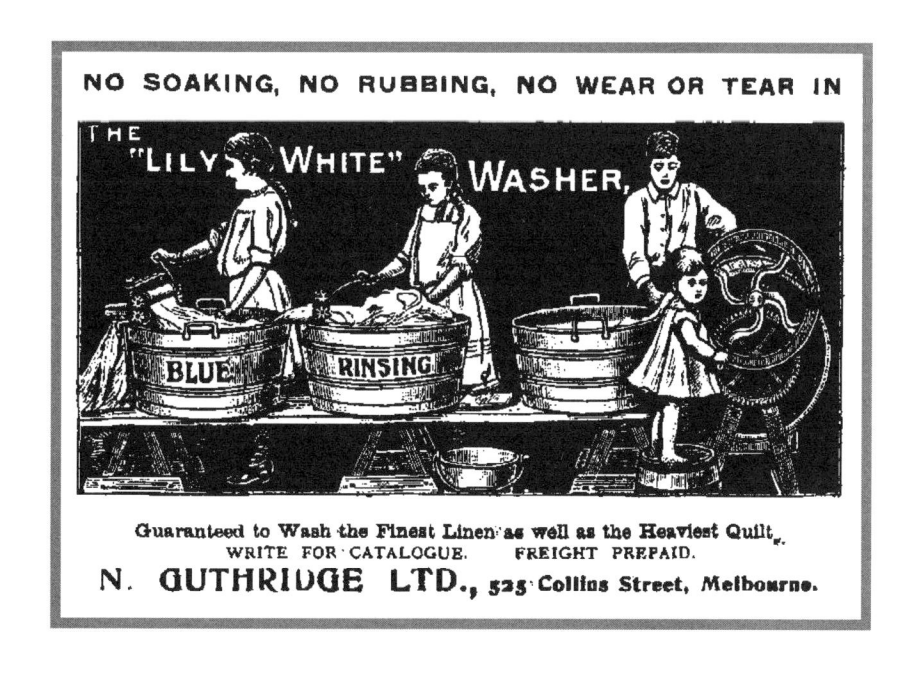

Lighting in the home was governed by a number of factors, including availability and affordability. If available, gas was a much-improved option after the introduction of the incandescent mantle in the late 1880s. Karl Auer von Welsbach patented this important invention in 1885. Not only did it make gaslights many times brighter; it was soon applied to kerosene lamps, and in this field made a difference to rural life for decades to come. By contrast, gas-lighting reached its peak efficiency just as electricity was beginning to take hold, and in time it was completely overtaken. Candles and simple kerosene lamps continued to play an important role in many households. Candles could now be bought at a reasonable price and were a practical form of portable household lighting. People who had the material to make their own could buy the traditional metal candle moulds. Pillar and hand-held candlesticks were standard items in catalogues of the Federation Era and, as we have noted, silver candlesticks were often given as wedding gifts. Kerosene lamps came in three basic types: the table, wall and suspension models. The range of patent types, specific designs and decorative character was a testimony to the manufacturers in America, Britain and Europe. Some were perfectly refined in their plain, functional design, others were richly ornate and others again were grotesque by any standard. While at times gas and oil lamps might share decorative design elements, gas-lighting, with its tubing, was perfectly suited to the sinuous curves of Art Nouveau. By adding flowers and foliage, all sorts of exotic forms were created. The shades too could be flower-like to add to the effect. With the wiring passed through tubes and stems, electric lighting could follow the same design path. Influence from the American Craftsman movement set a very different trend and resulted in an entirely geometrical approach.

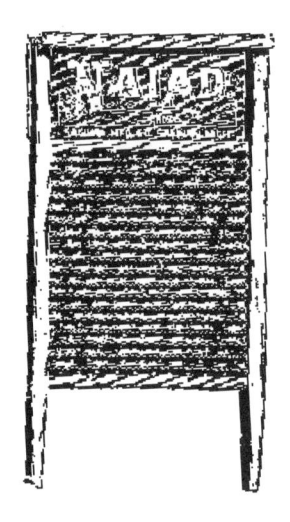

Cleanliness being next to godliness was an adage fervently followed by respectable folk, and meant a great deal of scouring and scrubbing, dusting and polishing. Brooms and brushes take up pages in old catalogues, with a design for every purpose. Whitewash or distemper brushes were frequently put to use in some households. Water-based paints brightened up rooms, while whitewash gave simple exterior walls a fresh look, and poultry pens a well-tended air. Varnish brushes applied a rich glow to woodwork and to wooden furniture. Scrubbing brushes and sand soap or pumice made kitchen tabletops, dressers, and draining-boards creamy white. There were stove brushes, hearth brushes, saucepan brushes and special shapes for bannisters and cornices. Feather dusters were as popular as feathers on fashionable hats and mostly shifted the dust from one place to another.

Baths of cast iron and galvanised sheet were reasonably common; the very affluent might have marble or copper baths. Portable tubs had to suffice for many families, being the only choice where the fully-fledged bathroom had not yet arrived. Plunge baths were large coffin-like devices, and sponge baths small shallow affairs designed to catch the drips. Hip baths even came with arm rests, and travelling baths with lids. Galvanised-iron tubs could be used for washing children or for doing the laundry. Washing machines could be wooden tumbling barrels or tubs on legs with simple hand-cranked agitators. In ordinary households the copper, a pair of strong arms and a wooden copper stick mostly did the job. Patent ringers were seen as labour saving. Turning handles was a way of life for many people as they churned butter, minced meat, whisked eggs, ground coffee, polished knives, sifted flour and worked up a tub of icecream. Then there was the ironing to think about, and if you had a set of 'Mrs Potts sad irons' with an interchangeable walnut handle you felt much better off than people with plain old flat irons.

No. C 1013.
The "**Ewbank**" Carpet Sweepers.
A high-class Sweeper, superior to many others of a similar nature which are sold at a higher price.

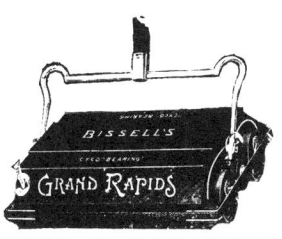

No. C 1014. Bissell's "Cyco" Bearing
"**Grand Rapids**" Carpet Sweepers.
A high grade Sweeper. This is the most popular Sweeper in the world. More of this brand have been sold during the past fifteen years than all other makes combined. The "Grand Rapids" contains all the latest patented improvements, such as "Cyco" bearings, dust proof axle tubes, anti-raveling collector, etc.

No. C 1015.
Bissell's "Cyco" Bearing "**Gold Medal**" Carpet Sweepers.
An extra high grade Sweeper. This Sweeper has the largest sale of any nickel-plated Carpet Sweeper in the world. The "Gold Medal" is one of the finest patterns, and contains all our latest patented improvements such as "Cyco" bearings, dust proof axle tubes, anti-raveler, etc.

No. C 1016.
Bissell's "**Crown Jewel**" Carpet Sweepers.
This is the best low-priced Carpet Sweeper on the market. It is strong and durable and has all the essentials of a high-grade Sweeper. The "Crown Jewel" has a gracefully curved top, and the case is made of birch finished in natural and imitation mahogany. This Sweeper contains all the best features of a modern Carpet Sweeper such as a complete broom action, self-adjusting brush, reversible bail spring, automatic dump, etc.

No. C 797.   No. C 798.
The "Perfection" Smokeless Kerosine Heating Stoves are absolutely safe and reliable.

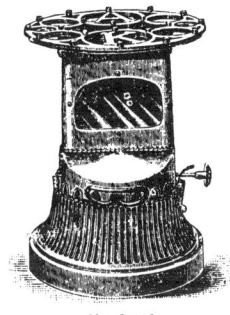

No. C 819.
Oil Stoves. Round. One Burner. Various qualities.

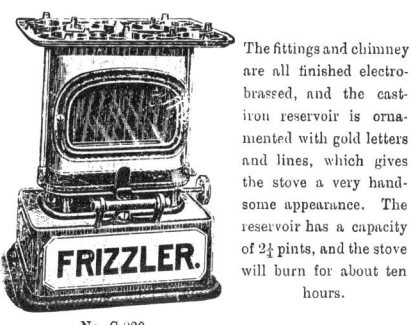

No. C 820.
"The Frizzler" Oil Stoves, with Extinguisher.

The fittings and chimney are all finished electro-brassed, and the cast-iron reservoir is ornamented with gold letters and lines, which gives the stove a very handsome appearance. The reservoir has a capacity of 2¼ pints, and the stove will burn for about ten hours.

No. C 822.
One-Flame Oil Stoves, Black Body.
No. C 823.
Two-Flame, Black Body.

No. C 824.
"The Quick" Spirit Stoves, Polished Brass Oil Container, with Galvanised Feet.

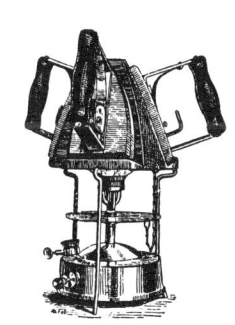

No. C 825.
"The Primus" Iron Heaters.

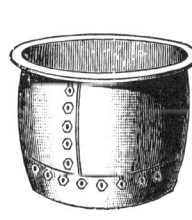

All parts of our Stoves are standardised .... and kept in stock, and can be replaced ..... when necessary.

Fig. C 803.
Rivetted Copper Washing Boilers. 10, 12, 14, 16, 18 and 20 Gallons.

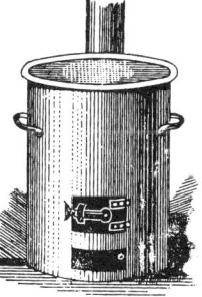

Fig. C 805

No. C 821.
"The Jewel" Atmospheric Stoves.

Burns without a wick. Gives a greater heat than any other Stove. Boils a quart of water in three minutes. Broils chops to perfection. Makes toast better than any other Stove. Simmers beautifully, and people who understand cooking know how important that is.

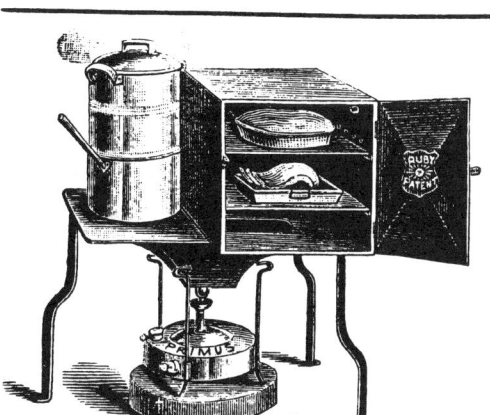

THE RUBY "PRIMUS" • AN ABSOLUTELY PERFECT COOKER.
KEROSENE GAS COOKING APPARATUS.

NOTHING BETTER FOR SUMMER COOKING.   WONDERFULLY ECONOMICAL
MANAGED WITH GREATEST EASE.

Made in six sizes at 38/6, 47/6, 52/6, 57/6, 60/-, 65/-.

All Particulars on application to

CHAMBERS & SEYMOUR,
IRONMONGERS, SWANSTON STREET, MELBOURNE.

THE FEDERATION CATALOGUE   106   PRACTICAL CONSIDERATIONS

THE ..
BEEHIVE
ONE-FIRE
COOKING STOVE.

SAVES TIME,
SAVES LABOUR,
SAVES FUEL.

Cooks and bakes to perfection.
Can be used inside or outside of the house.
Firing Door is the whole length of stove, avoiding all danger of the wood falling on the hearth.
The strongest made and most ingeniously constructed Stove on the market.
When you buy a Stove, we want you to tell your neighbour how satisfied you are with it.

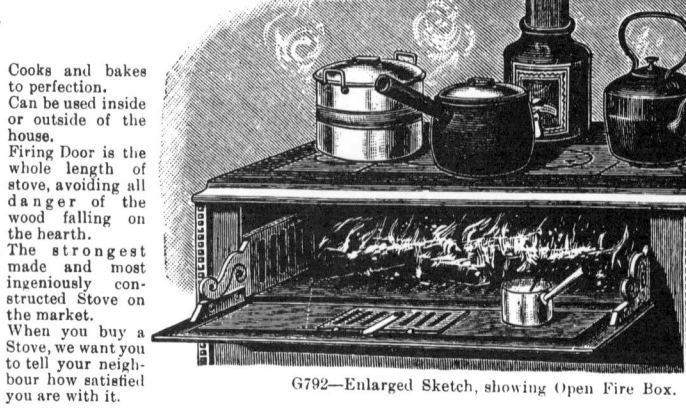

G791

G792—Enlarged Sketch, showing Open Fire Box.

THIS STOVE is constructed on an entirely new principle, the design and finish being equal to the best American Ranges. The Oven Door is made of Best Cast Iron; the polishing being superb. Fitted with loose ash-pan, thus ensuring cleanliness. A strong Copper Boiler, tinned inside, with Tap, can be fitted at an extra cost of 27/6, adding 6in. to the length. We can confidently recommend this as the most Economical and Perfect Cooking Stove in the Colonies. Each Stove is supplied with 8ft. of Piping, a Rake, and Lifter.

OUTSIDE MEASUREMENT.

	LENGTH.	DEPTH.	HEIGHT.
No. 1—	24in.	x 18in.	x 27in.
No. 2—	30in.	x 18in.	x 27in.
No. 3—	36in.	x 18in.	x 27in.

DIMENSIONS OF OVENS.

LENGTH.	DEPTH.	HEIGHT.		PRICE.
20in.	x 14in.	x 12½in.	Burns 20in. Wood	£2/18/6
24in.	x 14in.	x 12½in.	Burns 24in. Wood	£3/14/6
30in.	x 14in.	x 12½in.	Burns 30in. Wood	£4/11/6

Nos. 2 and 3 Stoves Fitted with Double Doors, no Extra Charge.
No. 1 Fitted with Double Doors, 2/6 extra.

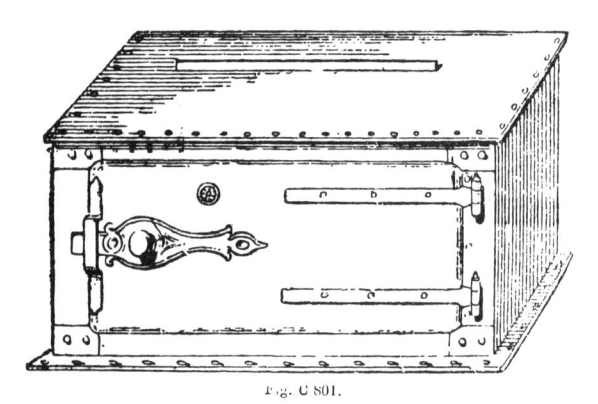

Pardon me! Have you seen Our **BRITANNIA ONE FIRE STOVE?**

Fig. C 801.

COLONIAL OVENS.

ORDINARY SIZES.

	Wide. Inches.	High. Inches.	Deep. Inches.			Wide. Inches.	High. Inches.	Deep. Inches.
No. 1	18	9	15	No. 13	...	24	16	15
,, 2	18	10	15	,, 14	...	24	18	15
,, 3	18	12	15	,, 15	...	27	10	15
,, 4	21	10	15	,, 16	...	27	12	15
,, 5	21	11	15	,, 17	...	27	14	15
,, 6	21	12	15	,, 18	...	30	12	21
,, 7	24	9	15	,, 19	...	30	15	21
,, 8	24	10	15	,, 20	...	30	18	24
,, 9	24	11	15	,, 21	...	30	20	24
,, 10	24	12	15	,, 22	...	36	12	21
,, 11	24	13	15	,, 23	...	36	15	21
,, 12	24	14	15	,, 24	...	36	18	24
				,, 25	...	36	20	24

Burn Anything, Cook Anything Anywhere, Maximum Heat, Minimum Fuel.
Neat, Simple, Strong. Satisfaction Guaranteed. Cheapest on the Market.

COCHRANE & SCOTT,

Ironfounders, 618, 620, 622, 624 Elizabeth Street, Melbourne

Cheapest & Best Assortment Ornamental Ironwork.

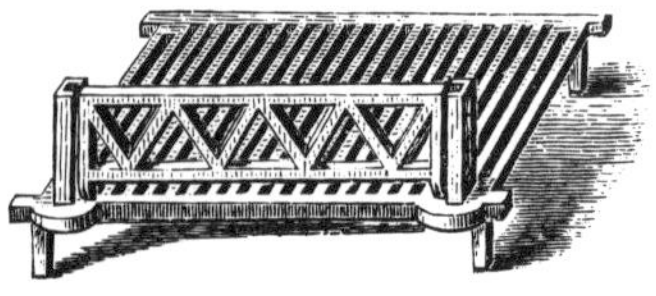

Colonial Grates, to stand on Colonial Ovens.
Will burn Coal, Coke or Wood.
No. C 809. 12 inches.   No. C 811. 15 inches.
No. C 810. 14 ,,   No. C 812. 18 ,,
With Front Extended Grate.
No. C 813. 12 inches.   No. C 815. 16 inches.
No. C 814. 14 ,,   No. C 816. 18 ,,

Fig. C 748.
Hill Top Co.'s Cast Iron Kettles, with Covers. Tinned.
4, 5, 6, 7, 8, 9, 10 Pints.

No. C 896. Stamped Steel Coal Shovels, Wood Handles. Size 10¼ by 8¼ inches.

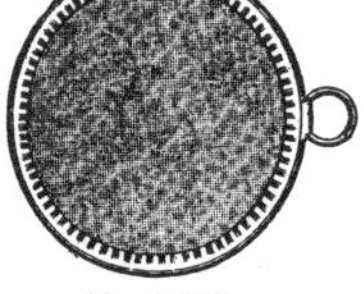

No. C 905.
Asbestos Stove Mats.

Fig. C 742.
T. & C. Clark's Improved Cast Iron Oval Boilers and Covers. Tinned.
2, 2¾, 3, 3¾, 4, 5, 6, 7 8, 9, 10, 12 and 14 Gallons.

Fig. C 756/1. Hill Top Co.'s Cast Iron Saucepans, Tinned. Tinned Covers.
Nos.   4   5   6   7   8   9   10   11   12
Pints   3   4   6   8   10   12   14   16   20

No. C 757. Hill Top Co.'s Cast Iron Lipped Saucepans. Tinned.
Nos.   2   3   4   5   6   7   8   9   10
Pints   1½   2   3   4   6   8   10   12   14

No. C 758. Hill Top Co.'s Enamelled Iron Saucepans. Tinned Covers.
Nos.   6   7   8   9   10   11   12
Pints   6   8   10   12   14   16   20

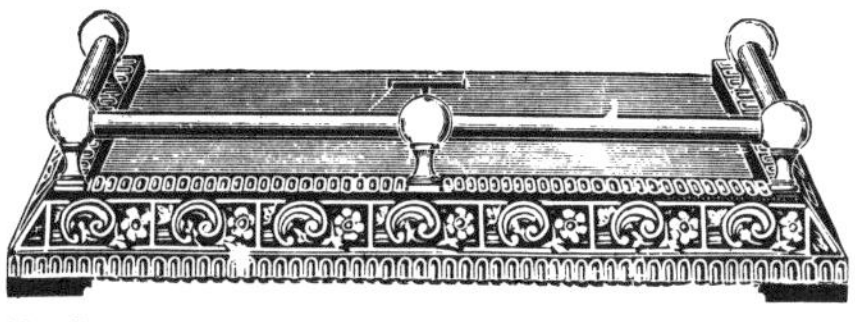

No. C 855. Berlin Black, Polished Steel Rails and Supports. 3 ft. 9 in.

Berlin Black, Bright Facings, Polished Steel Rails.
No. C 856. 3 ft. 9 in.   No. C 857. 4 ft.

Berlin Black, Polished Steel Rails and Supports.
No. C 858. 3 ft. 9 in.   No. C 859. 4 ft.

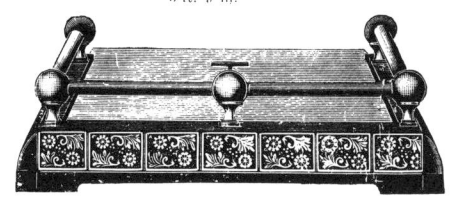

Berlin Black, Brass Rails and Supports.
No. C 860. 3 ft. 9 in.   No. C 861. 4 ft.   No. C 862. 4 ft. 3 in.

Berlin Black, Brass Rails.
No. C 863. 3 ft. 9 in.   No. C 864. 4 ft.

Berlin Black Kerbs, with Brass Rails and Supports.
No. C 865. 4 ft. inside.   No. C 866. 4 ft. 3 in. inside.   No. C 867. 4 ft. 6 in. inside.

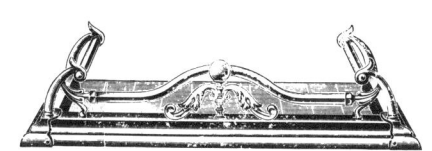

Brass Kerbs.
No. C 868. 4 ft. inside.   No. C 869. 4 ft. 3 in. inside.
No. C 870. 4 ft. 6 in. inside.

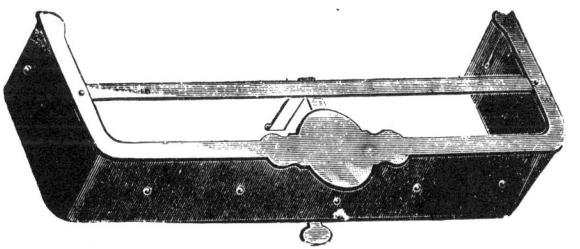

Kitchen Fenders, Berlin Black, Polished Tops.
No. C 871. 4 ft.   No. C 872. 4 ft. 6 in.   No. C 873. 5 ft.

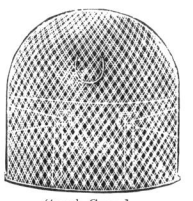

Spark Guards.
No. C 874. Galvanized Wire.
No. C 875. Japanned Wire.
No. C 876. Brass Wire.

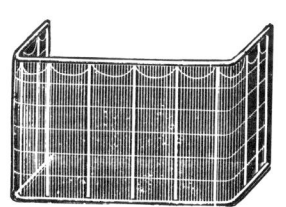

No. C 877.
Nursery Guards, painted Green, with Brass Top Rail.
Width 36, 39, 42, 45, 48 ins.

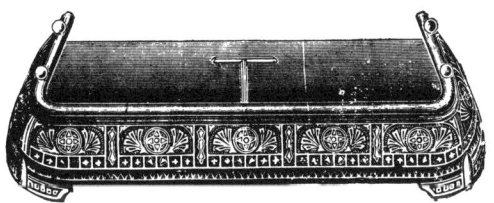

Berlin Black, Steel Bead and Knobs, Bright Facings.
No. C 851. 3 ft. 9 in.   No. C 852. 4 ft.

No. C 879.
Brass Fire Dogs.
Various patterns.

Coal Vases, with Linings.
Japanned, Various Colours,
Brass-mounted, with Assorted Floral
Decorations, and China Handle Scoops.
No. C 846. Small.
No. C 847. Large.

No. C 878. Iron Fire Dogs.
Various patterns.

No. C 893. Stove Pokers.
No. C 894. " Scrapers.
No. C 895. " Lifters.

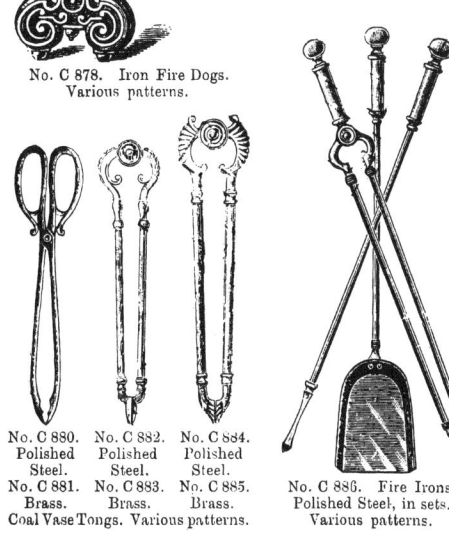

No. C 880. Polished Steel.	No. C 882. Polished Steel.	No. C 884. Polished Steel.						
No. C 881. Brass.	No. C 883. Brass.	No. C 885. Brass.	No. C 886. Fire Irons, Polished Steel, in sets. Various patterns.	Fire Companions. No. C 887. Brass. No. C 888. Polished Steel.	Various patterns.	No. C 889. Fire Brasses, in sets. Various patterns.	No. C 890. No. C 891. Kitchen Tongs. Various patterns.	No. C 892. Kitchen Pokers. Various patterns.
Coal Vase Tongs. Various patterns.								

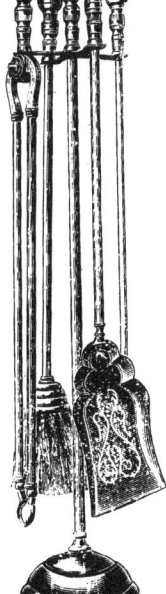

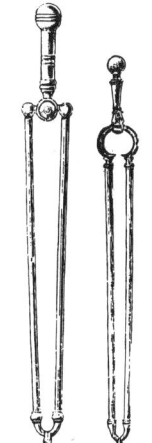

No. C 617.

No. C 618.
Decorated Glass Table Lamps, with Fancy Iron Stands.
A and B Collars. A very large variety always in stock.

No. C 619.

No. C 620. Coloured Glass Table Lamps, with Fancy Iron Stands.
A and B Collars.
Various patterns and colours.

No. C 621. White Glass Table Lamps, with Fancy Iron Stands.
A and B Collars. Various shapes.

No. C 622.

No. C 623.
Decorated Glass Table Lamps, with Fancy Iron Stands and Duplex Burners. Various patterns.

No. C 624. Decorated Glass Table Lamps, on Black Base.
Various shapes and sizes.

No. C 625. Coloured Glass Table Lamps, with Fancy Iron Stands and Duplex Burners. Assorted colours.

No. C 626. White Glass Table Lamps, with Fancy Iron Stands and Duplex Burners. Various shapes.

No. C 627. Coloured Glass Hand Lamps.
Assorted shapes and colours.

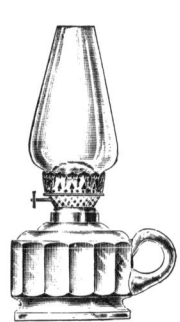

No. C 628. White Glass Hand Lamps.
Assorted shapes.

No. C 629. Decorated Glass Hand Lamps, with E Venus Burners. Assorted patterns.

No. C 630.
White Cut Glass Hand Lamps.
Assorted shapes.

No. C 631. Assorted Opal Colour Hand Lamps, with E Venus Burners.

We have a most complete assortment of **LAMPWARE** of every description.

No. C 632/1.

No. C 632/2.
Glass Hand Lamps, with Clinch Collars.
Various shapes and sizes.

No. C 633. "Home" Lamp, with No. 0 Miller Chimney and Wick.
Capacity, 1¾ pints. Burns 8 hours. Height, 6½ in.

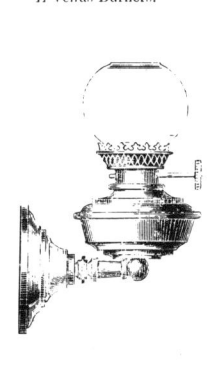

No. C 634. The "Diana" Lamp.
Can be used to stand or hang.
No. C 635. Extra Globes for the above.
No. C 636. ,, Wicks ,, ,,

No. C 637.
The "Stella" Hand Lamp.

Fig. 604.
No. 0 Miller Table Lamps.

Fig. 605.
No. 30 Juno Parlour Lamps.

Fig. 606.
No. 2 Miller Table Lamps, with Decorated Vases and Shades. Assorted Patterns.

Fig. 607.
"Miller" Pillar Table Lamps, a large variety.

No. C 608.   No. C 609.
American Table Lamps, with Decorated Vases and Globes.
An immense variety.

No. C 610.
"Bismarck" Table Lamps.

No. C 611.
Decorated "Bismarck" Table Lamps.

No. C 612.   No. C 613.
All Glass Table Lamps, fitted with A or B Venus Burners. A large variety of patterns.

No. C 614.
Floor Lamps. Various Patterns.

No. C 615.   No. C 616.
Decorated All-Glass Table Lamps, fitted with A or B Venus Burners.
Various Patterns.

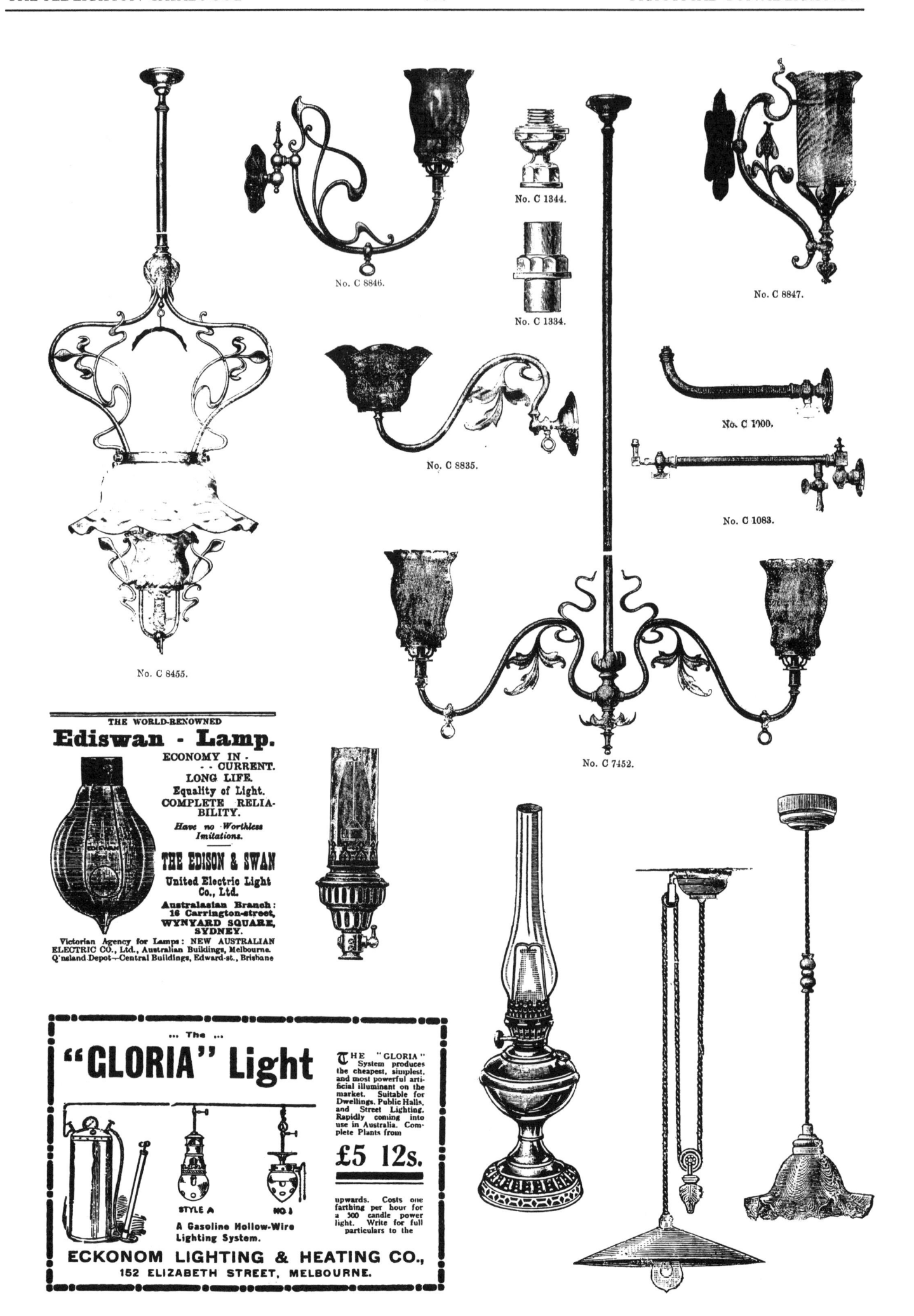

THE FEDERATION CATALOGUE 110 PRACTICAL CONSIDERATIONS

No. C 8846.

No. C 1344.

No. C 1334.

No. C 8847.

No. C 8835.

No. C 1900.

No. C 1083.

No. C 8455.

No. C 7452.

THE WORLD-RENOWNED
Ediswan - Lamp.
ECONOMY IN
— — CURRENT.
LONG LIFE.
Equality of Light.
COMPLETE RELIABILITY.

Have no Worthless Imitations.

THE EDISON & SWAN
United Electric Light Co., Ltd.
Australasian Branch:
16 Carrington-street,
**WYNYARD SQUARE,
SYDNEY.**

Victorian Agency for Lamps: NEW AUSTRALIAN ELECTRIC CO., Ltd., Australian Buildings, Melbourne.
Q'nsland Depot—Central Buildings, Edward-st., Brisbane.

... The ...
"GLORIA" Light

STYLE A   NO. 3

A Gasoline Hollow-Wire Lighting System.

THE "GLORIA" System produces the cheapest, simplest, and most powerful artificial illuminant on the market. Suitable for Dwellings, Public Halls, and Street Lighting. Rapidly coming into use in Australia. Complete Plants from

£5 12s.

upwards. Costs one farthing per hour for a 500 candle power light. Write for full particulars to the

ECKONOM LIGHTING & HEATING CO.,
152 ELIZABETH STREET, MELBOURNE.

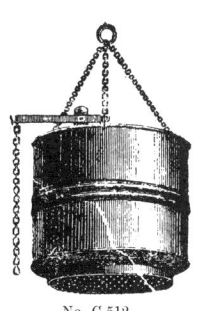

No. C 512.
Colonial-made Galvanized
Shower Bath to Hang.
10, 11, 12 and 14 inches.

No. C 513.
Colonial-made Galvanized
Shower Heads.
6, 8, 9, 10, 11, 12 inches.

No. C 514.
Colonial-made Cast Iron Baths.
White Silicate Enamelled Inside, Oak Grained Outside. 5 feet 6 inches.
Complete, with Plug and Washer.

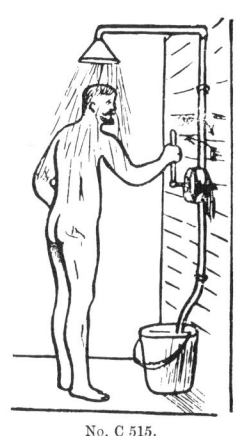

No. C 515.
Patent Shower Bath Apparatus.
Can be set up anywhere, even
where there is no bath room.

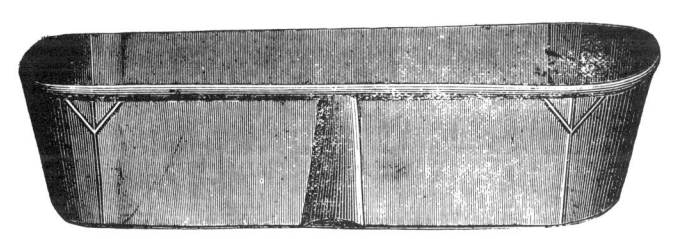

No. C 516.
Colonial-made Galvanized Plunge Baths.
26 or 24 gauge. 5 feet, 5 feet 6 inches, and 6 feet.
No. C 517. Can also be had with Flange.

Colonial-made Sponge Baths.
No. C 518. Japanned, Wired, 28, 30, 32, 34 and 36 inches.
No. C 519.   ,,   Beaded, 28, 30, 32, 34 and 36 ,,
No. C 520. Galvanized, 30, 33 and 36 inches.

Colonial-made Hip Baths.
No. C 521. Japanned, Best Tinned Steel, with Arm Rests.
Nos. 1, 2, 3 and 4.
No. C 522. Galvanized. Nos 1, 2, 3 and 4.

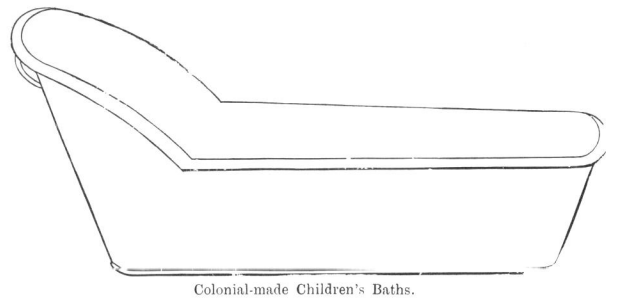

Colonial-made Children's Baths.
Equal End or Taper. With Raised Backs extra.
No. C 523. Japanned, Wired Edges, 20, 22, 24, 26, 28, 30, 32, 34 and 36 inches.
No. C 524.   ,,   Beaded ,, 20, 22, 24, 26, 28, 30, 32, 34 and 36 ,,
No. C 525. Galvanized, 24, 27, 30 inches.
No. C 526. Colonial-made Galvanized Child's Baths. No Hoop. 18 and 20 inches.

Colonial-made Japanned Sitz Baths.
No. C 527. Beaded. Nos. 1, 2, 3 and 4.
No. C 528. Galvanized Oak. Nos. 1, 2, 3 and 4.

Colonial-made Oval Foot Baths.
No. C 529. Japanned, Wired, 14, 16, 18, 20, 22, 24, 26 and 28 inches.
No. C 530. Japanned, Beaded, 14, 16, 18, 20, 22, 24, 26 and 28 inches.
Colonial-made Toilet Baths, with Cast Iron Handles.
No. C 531. Japanned, Wired, 14, 16 and 18 inches.
No. C 532.   ,,   Beaded, 14, 16 and 18 ,,
Colonial-made Tin Baths.
No. C 533. Oval, 16, 18, 20, 22 and 24 inches.

No. C 534.
Colonial-made Japanned Travelling Baths.
Wired Top, Hasp and Strap.
24, 26, 28, 30 and 33 inches.

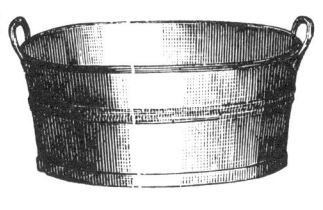

No. C 535. Colonial-made Round Galvanized Iron Tubs.
With Hoop Iron Bottoms. 16, 18, 20, 22, 24, 26, 28 ins.
535/1. In nests of 5 tubs, 16 inches to 24 inches.
535/2.   ,,   5 ,, 18 ,, 26 ,,
535/3.   ,,   6 ,, 18 ,, 28 ,,
535/4.   ,,   7 ,, 16 ,, 28 ,,
No. C 536. With Hoops and Double Straps across
Bottoms. 16, 18, 20, 22, 24, 26 and 28 inches.
536/1. In nests of 5 tubs, 16 inches to 24 inches.
536/2.   ,,   5 ,, 18 ,, 26 ,,
536/3.   ,,   6 ,, 18 ,, 28 ,,
536/4.   ,,   7 ,, 16 ,, 28 ,,

No. C 537.
Colonial-made Oval Galvanized
Iron Tubs, with Hoop Iron Bottoms.
16, 18, 20, 22, 24, 26 and 28 inches.
537/1. In nests of 4 tubs, 16 in. to 22 in.
537/2.   ,,   4 ,, 18 ,, 24 ,,
537/3.   ,,   5 ,, 18 ,, 26 ,,
537/4.   ,,   6 ,, 18 ,, 28 ,,

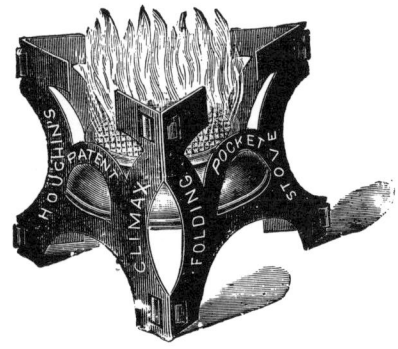

THE FEDERATION CATALOGUE 112 PRACTICAL CONSIDERATIONS

No. C 831.
"The Climax" Pocket Stove has a Folding Stand; it is light, durable, easily adjusted, and will not get out of order. Packed in Box 4¼ inches long, 3¼ inches wide, 1½ inches high; weighs 5 ounces.

No. C 832.
Folding Tripod Spirit Stoves, each in a Box, complete with Kettle.

No. C 833.
Clarke's Pyramid Nursery Lamp and Food Warmer.

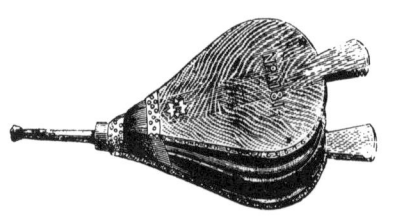

Fig. C 842.
House Bellows,
8, 9, 10, 11, 12, 14, 16, 18-inch.

No. C 836.
Curling Tong Lamps, in several qualities.

No. C 216.
Spong's "Bantam" Knife Cleaners, with Thick Buff Leather Cleaning Surfaces.

No. C 217.
"Alexander" Knife Cleaners. Knives cannot be damaged as in other machines, and the blades are cleaned right up to shoulders. The pressure of the rollers may be regulated, and the rollers are not liable to get damaged by the Knives.

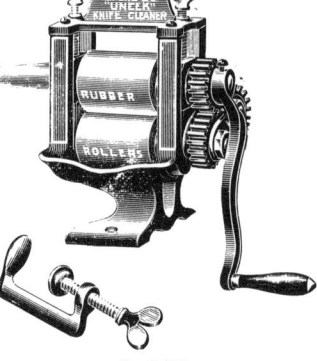

No. C 218.
"Uneek" Knife Cleaners.

No. C 839.
Pumps, for kerosene and other liquids. Handy, simple, clean. Prevents loss of kerosene and labour in lifting tin.

No. C 840.
Kerosene Pumps.

Fig. 205.
Spong's Coffee Mills.
No. C 0. Grinds 1 lb. in 12 minutes.
No. C 1.   ,,   9   ,,
No. C 2.   ,,   8   ,,

No. C 206.
Raisin and Grape Seeders. A simple and easily adjusted Machine, works rapidly and effectually, seeding Raisins wet or dry.
Will seed 1 lb. in 5 minutes.

No. C 207.
The "Crown" Raisin and Grape Seeders.

No. C 835.
Nos. C 834 and C 835. Cast Iron Gas Rings.

No. C 203.
The "Enterprise" Vegetable Slicers.

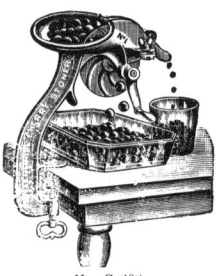

No. C 208.
"Enterprise" Cherry Stoners.

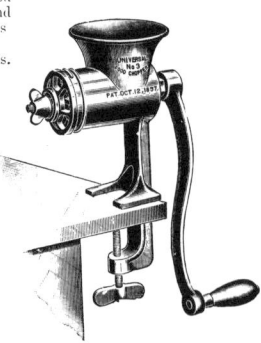

No. C 3.
The "Universal" Meat and Food Choppers, Tinned. Weight 8 lbs. Chops 3 lbs. of meat per minute.

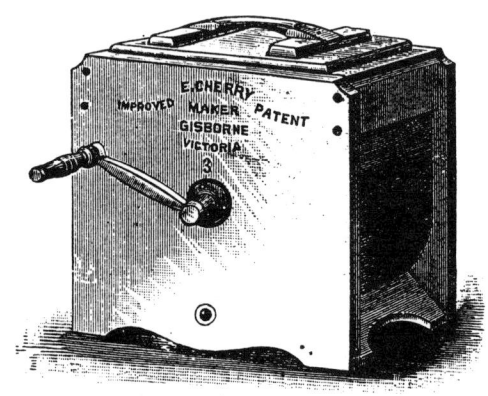

D807—Cherry's Churns.

Fig. C 202.
Spong's Household Mincing Machines, Enamelled.
Sizes, 1, 2 and 3.

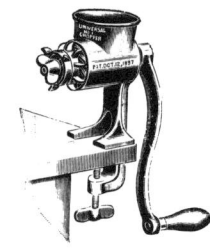

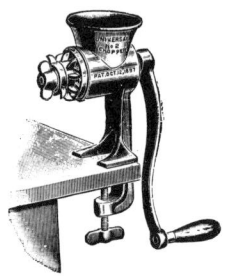

No. C 1.
The "Universal" Food and Meat Choppers, Tinned. Weight 4½ lbs. Chops 2 lbs. of meat per minute.

No. C 2.
The "Universal" Meat and Food Choppers, Tinned. Weight 5 lbs. Chops 2½ lbs. of meat per minute.

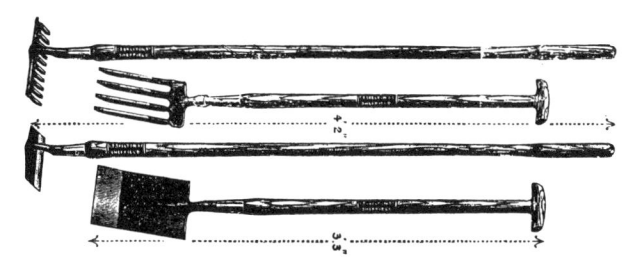

THE FEDERATION CATALOGUE — PRACTICAL CONSIDERATIONS

Fig. C 233. Ladies' Garden Sets. Several sizes and qualities.

Brass Garden Syringes, polished black handles.
No. C 1017. 12 × 1 inch.   No. C 1019. 16 × 1¼ inches.
No. C 1018. 14 × 1 "   No. C 1020. 18 × 1½ "

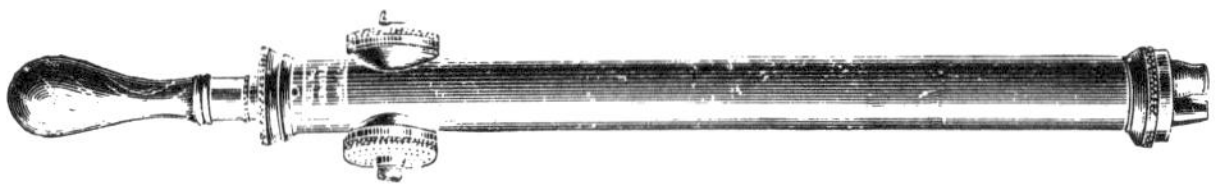

Brass Garden Syringes, with ball valves for easy filling.
No. C 1021. 16 × 1¼ inches.   No. C 1022. 18 × 1½ inches.

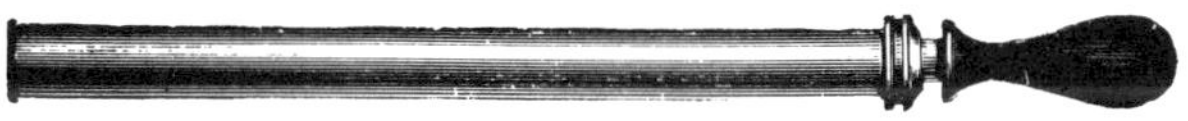

No. C 1023.
Zinc Garden Syringes.
18 × 1½ inches

No. C 1028.
Hose Bands.
A convenient device for securely binding garden hose to ordinary fittings.

No. C 1029.
Rose and Jet,
for Branch Pipe.

Galvanized Wheel Barrows.
No. C 1032. Wired Edge.   No. C 1033. Band Edge.

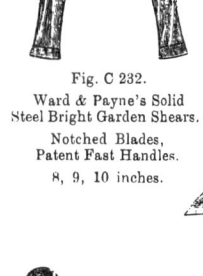

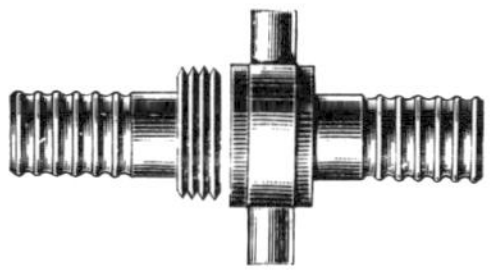

Hose Unions.
No. C 1030. ½ to 3 inches.
No. C 1030/1. Caps and Linings only,
½ to 3 inches.

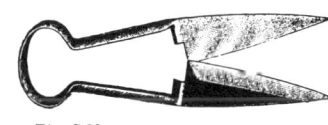

Fig. C 229.
Bleckmann's
Grass Shears.
10 and 11 inches.

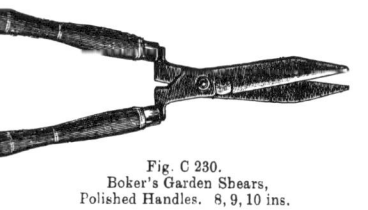

Fig. C 230.
Boker's Garden Shears,
Polished Handles. 8, 9, 10 ins.

Lawn Mowers, complete with grass boxes
No. C 1035. 10 inches.   No. C 1037. 14 inches.
No. C 1036. 12   "   No. C 1038. 16   "

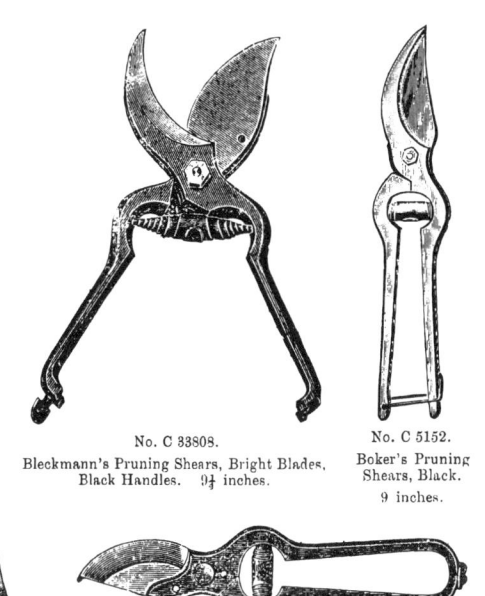

No. C 33808.
Bleckmann's Pruning Shears, Bright Blades,
Black Handles. 9¼ inches.

No. C 5152.
Boker's Pruning
Shears, Black.
9 inches.

Fig. C 232.
Ward & Payne's Solid
Steel Bright Garden Shears.
Notched Blades,
Patent Fast Handles.
8, 9, 10 inches.

No. C 38588.
Bleckmann's Pruning Shears, Bright Blades, Black Handles.
8, 8½ inches.

No. C 38035. Bleckmann's All Bright Seccateurs, extra Heavy
Double Brass Spring, Double Cut. 9, 9¼ inches.

Fig. C 235. Long Handle Weeding Forks, with 4 Bright and Blue Twisted
Prongs, Polished Handles.

Fig. C 236. Long Handle Weeding Forks, with 3 Black Flat
Prongs, Polished Handles.

Fig. C 234.
Garden Trowels
with Patent
Tanged Handles,
Bright or Blue.
5½, 6, 7 inches.

Fig. C 237. Weeding Forks, with 4
bright and blue twisted Prongs.
Polished Handles.

Fig. C 238. 3-Prong Weeding
Forks. Polished Handles, bright
and blue or black Prongs.

Fig. C 1039.
Wrought Barrow Wheels.
Complete, with mounts.
14, 15, 16, 18 inches.

No. C 1034.
Wood Wheel Barrows.

FEDERATION CATALOGUE

12. Federation Memorabilia

Achieving nationhood in January 1901 was the great formal step in a process which began with the first moves towards some degree of independence in the early settlements. It coincided with a growing sense of Australian identity felt by people in colonial times, whether they were born here or had embraced the country as their new homeland. Gradually, images and symbols evolved which captured this feeling of belonging. Painters, illustrators, writers, poets, reformers, politicians and citizens of every description created words and images which expressed nationalistic sentiments. Manufacturers and businesses of every size used Australian symbols, capturing the spirit of the times.

Pictorial symbols to represent Australia, the individual colonies and many groups, organisations and institutions began to proliferate in the second half of the nineteenth century. Australian flora and fauna, being so distinctive, were natural options. The kangaroo and emu were very early choices for unofficial coats of arms. Variations showing them supporting a shield with the words 'Advance Australia' on a scroll below can be traced back to the mid-nineteenth century. A much earlier example of their use is the flag designed by John Bowman and flown at his property at Richmond, New South Wales, in 1806 to celebrate Nelson's victory at Trafalgar.[1] Combinations of traditional British symbols and newer Australian ones were also favoured.

The Federation Era was a highpoint in the production of elaborate designs for decorated banners, posters, certificates and illuminated addresses. Apart from one-off pieces, superbly crafted with paint and pen, there were mass-produced items which were a tribute to both the printers and the artists who created them. The best process for colour work at that time was chromo-lithography which used blocks of finely polished stone imported from Germany. Rather than the standard four-colour process, the best works were given multiple runs to produce an extraordinary range and subtlety of colours.

The Melbourne firm of Troedel & Cooper were noted for their work in this field. Simpler works, such as local handbills and posters calling on residents to vote for or against Federation, were done on 'letterpress' with wood and metal type. Official guests at the Commonwealth of Australia Inaugural Celebrations held in Sydney on 1 January 1901 were sent an invitation showing a boatload of heroic maidens, one for each state, with the mast flying a Commonwealth flag and in the background the rising sun.

Ironically, lightly-clad females in classical poses appear on much Federation memorabilia and yet women had not been able to vote in the referendums. Men in Victoria who voted in the July 1899 constitutional elections were given a fully-illuminated souvenir certificate to display on their walls. Guests at the reception following the opening of the first Parliament of the Commonwealth of Australia, on 9 May 1901, received a stylish invitation with Arts and Crafts overtones. On one side of the invitation, we have a very trim and youthful Britannia with helmet and Union Jack shield and on the other a distinctly Pre-Raphaelite figure representing Australia, holding a Southern Cross shield.

The invitation to the main event earlier in the day suggested a medieval gathering with lots of shields and banners. While the Southern Cross graced one shield, it was hardly a vision of a bright new nation.

Decorations for the huge parades held in the major cities ranged from formal and very British affairs to boldly Australian or wonderfully exotic. Melbourne's Chinese citizens built an arch with pagoda-like towers and the whole creation was hung with beautifully worked banners and large ornamental lanterns. There was also an extremely long Chinese dragon in the Melbourne procession.

The German citizens used two giant Corinthian columns with Imperial eagles, banners and flags. When night came the wonders of electricity were able to sparkle in decorative illuminations way beyond any of the effects previously achieved using hundreds of gas jets. Flags were everywhere, including those of Britain and other nations. Australia had the Commonwealth flag and some of the new states also had official flags. There were also many unofficial flags made for the celebrations.

Everything from sheet-music to postcards had flags in their designs. Anthems and Federation songs graced many a music stand and again Australian and British symbols were liberally applied. Oak leaves with acorns or wattle blossom and foliage were both chosen for richly-coloured designs. Everyday reminders, which were around for decades after that heady time at the turn-of-the-century, were such items as boxes of Commonwealth Slate Pencils (see page 117) which show the Australian coat of arms, famous navy ships and, to one side, a map of Britain and the British Flag with Australia and the Australian flag on the other side. This is the official flag, with a white Southern Cross on a blue ground, which was first flown in September 1901, but did not gain publication of approval from His Majesty the King until February 1903.

Many of us well remember Commonwealth brand exercise books from our schooldays. The cover design seen on page 117 dates from the early 1900s but was current for many years. Manufacturers were keen to benefit from the Australian nationalism so much in evidence in the period under review. Brands such a Southern Cross, Federal, Federal Flag, Austral, Union and Commonwealth were typical examples. Then there were the other words and symbols such as Cooee, Dinkum, Bonza, Digger and all the animal names and images.

It was a time of complex loyalties, because a large proportion of the population considered themselves both British and Australian as well as citizens of the states which had previously been individual colonies. There were also many other loyalties to old homelands and to social classes. World War 1 refocused some of these divisions; Australians of German origin were suddenly affected by bigotry and propaganda campaigns and Irish Australians, who generally kept a sense of their own identity and could also be fiercely loyal to Australia, were on the opposing side of the conscription debate. The Chinese did their best to show their loyalty on special occasions, but were mostly treated as second-class citizens in a country with a new entrenched White Australia Policy. Savage wartime jingoism rather took the shine off innocent expressions of national pride, but ordinary Australians continued to travel toward a sense of individual nationhood with a lessening need to be 'British to the bootstraps'. In fact, many soldiers in the First World War had their Australian identity clearly confirmed as they mixed with other troops or were led by British officers. The lead-up to Federation and its subsequent celebration were memorable times, often looked back upon wistfully as the nation suffered two world wars and a second terrible depression. Now with the Bicentenary of European settlement also moving into history we have new challenges in the evolution of our society, including the possibility of a Republic of Australia to face the new millennium.

Notes
[1] Mimmo Cozzolino, *Symbols of Australia*, Penguin Books, Ringwood, Australia, 1980, p. 22.

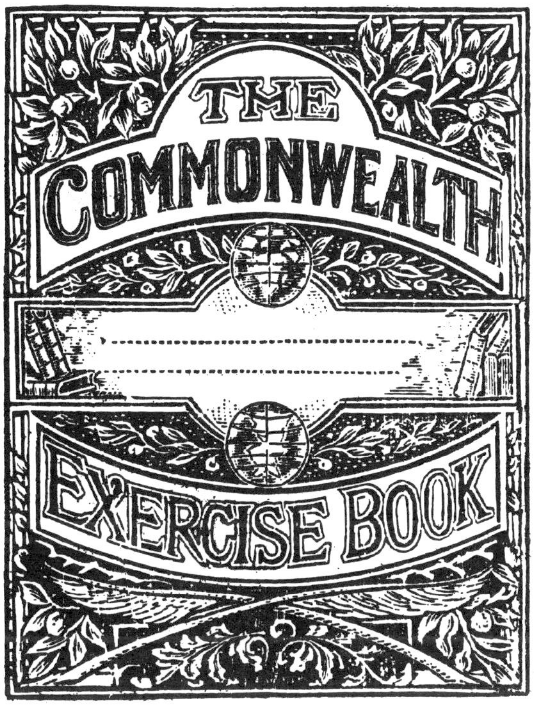
THE
COMMONWEALTH
EXERCISE BOOK

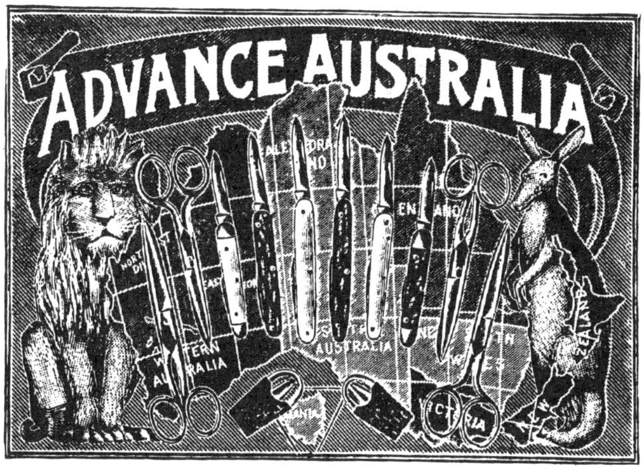
ADVANCE AUSTRALIA

The
COMMONWEALTH
CREAM
LAID
NOTE PAPER
Five Quires
Ruled Feints

FOSTER'S
AUSTRALIAN
LAGER

THE FEDERAL
DRAWING
BOOK

ADVANCE
AUSTRALIA

The New
COMMONWEALTH
Box
of
Stationery
SUPERIOR QUALITY

COMMONWEALTH
SLATE PENCILS

UNION

Decorations provided by Melbourne's Chinese citizens, who were keen to show their loyalty to the new Commonwealth on the occasion of the Duke of Cornwall and York's royal visit in 1901. As well as creating this pagoda-like arch, they provided a Chinese dragon to take part in the procession. *Courtesy:* La Trobe Picture Collection, State Library of Victoria.

FEDERATION CATALOGUE
Acknowledgements

Acknowledgements

Many people over many years have contributed directly or indirectly to this Federation Catalogue. My mother Catherine Cuffley has been telling stories of life in earlier times for as long as I can remember. A dear friend, Vivienne 'Babs' Mair continues to share wonderfully detailed memories which begin well before World War 1. My dear wife Barbara once again has typed the manuscript and provided moral support. For help with pictorial material, I would like to thank John Thompson, Garry Smith, Ashley Tracey, Julie Gittus and Ellie Goss.

Neil Lorimer took the delightful photograph on the cover, Dennis Russell copied prints and Ashley Tracey made four special prints from his collection of glass negatives.

Thanks also to Don and Zara Latimer; Anne Hadden; Sangeet Randhawa; Cutlack Antiques; La Trobe Picture Collection, State Library of Victoria; Mortlock Library, State Library of South Australia; the staff of Castlemaine Copy Centre; the staff at Bendigo Library and Castlemaine Library, and the Australian Electric Transport Museum (South Australia) Inc.

Catalogues' Key

McKell Speedie & Co. Melbourne, c.1904.
p 40, p 43, p 45, p 47, p 49, p 50, p 95.

Feldheim Gotthelf & Co. Sydney, 1905.
p 21, p 41, p 42, p 46, p 48, p 53, p 59, p 60, p 61, p 80, p 82, p 83, p 84, p 89, p 90, p 91, p 94, p 100, p 101, p 105, p 107, p 108, p 109, p 111, p 112, p 113.

Dimelow & Gaylard, Richmond, Victoria, 1906
p 20, p 44, p 52, p 66, p 67, p 68, p 69, p 70, p 71, p 73, p 78, p 79.

FEDERATION CATALOGUE
Bibliography

Books

Aronson, Zara B. (Mrs F.B.), *XXth Century Cooking ... and Home Decoration*. William Brooks & Co., Sydney 1900.

Clark, Manning, *Manning Clark's History of Australia*. Abridged Michael Cathcart. Melbourne University Press, Melbourne, 1993.

Cuffley, Peter, *Chandeliers and Billy Tea*. The Five Mile Press, Hawthorn, Victoria, 1984; reprinted 1989, 1994, 1996.

Cuffley, Peter, *Oil and Kerosene Lamps in Australia*. Pioneer Design Studio, Yarra Glen, Victoria, 1973; revised edn 1982.

Evans, Ian, *The Federation House*. The Flannel Flower Press, Glebe, NSW, 1986.

Evans, Ian, Lucas, Clive & Stapleton, Ian, *More Colour Schemes for Old Australian Houses*. The Flannel Flower Press, Yeronga, Queensland, 1992.

Horsphol, Leslie, *The Story of Australian Federation*. View Productions Pty Ltd, Sydney, 1985.

Irving, Robert et al, *The History and Design of the Australian House*. Oxford University Press, Melbourne, 1985.

McQueen, Humphrey, *Social Sketches of Australia 1881-1975*. Penguin Books, Ringwood, Victoria, 1978.

Wright, Elizabeth, *Soft Furnishings 1830-1930*. Historic Houses Trust of New South Wales, Glebe, NSW, 1995.

Catalogues

Australia in the Good Old Days. Facsimile pages from *Lassetter's Commercial Review*, no, 26, 1911, Ure Smith, Sydney, 1976.

Feldheim Gotthelf & Co., Merchants and General Importers, catalogue, Sydney, 1905.

McKell, Speedie & Co. Catalogue of Furniture, Melbourne, c. 1894.

Our Drummer for Autumn and Winter 1906. Dimelow & Gaylard, Richmond, Victoria, household catalogue.

The Grandest Display of Furniture in the Colony. The Catalogue of A. Hall & Company, Sydney, 1897; facsimile edn. with introduction by Garry Smith, Wongoolah Publishing, Taree, NSW, 1994.